Praise for *Comeback Cities*

"....(A)n optimistic book."

—*The New York Times*

"....Paul Grogan and Tony Proscio have released arguably the most important and insightful books on the American city in a generation."

—Ronald Brownstein, *Los Angeles Times*

"....(P)roclaims the work of grassroots organizations to revitalize urban neighbors. For that alone, this book is important and most welcome."

—Neighborhood Funder's Group

"[An] accessible and detailed chronicle of the nuts and bolts of urban revitalization...."

—*Business Week*

"....I have been reading a whole bunch of different books on urban and neighborhood revival. This one offers good reason for hope...."

—David Pepper, Appellate litigator and recently announced candidate for Cincinnati City Council

"From years of experience, Paul Grogan and Tony Proscio explain what impatient mayors and professional protesters are slow to learn. Urban decline can't be reversed in a single stroke. Here they analyze the forces behind new and encouraging progress in America's 'comeback cities.' And they size up the obstacles that remain in our way."

—Thomas M. Menino, Mayor of Boston

"Paul Grogan explains how cities are rebuilding themselves block by block and neighborhood by neighborhood through grassroots community effort and strong local leadership. Chicago has benefited from Grogan's leadership of the Local Initiatives Support Corporation, and policy makers around the country will benefit from the insights of this book."

—Richard M. Daley, Mayor of Chicago

"Paul Grogan has helped community-based organizations make miracles happen in America's toughest neighborhoods. For years I have waited—and waited!—for him to squeeze into a book some of his wealth of facts, wisdom and experiences. Here, at last, it is. Many have diagnosed the ills of high-crime, disinvested urban neighborhoods. *Comeback Cities* offers prescriptions that work!"

—Clarence Page, *Chicago Tribune*

"Paul Grogan is one of the heroes of the community development movement. *Comeback Cities* is a wonderfully optimistic book about a subject that Americans usually treat with self-fulfilling pessimism."

—Nicholas Lemann, author of *The Big Test* and *The Promised Land*

"At heart, this book is an inspiring story of human ingenuity and courage."
—David Gergen

COMEBACK CITIES

COMEBACK CITIES

A Blueprint for

Urban Neighborhood Revival

with a New Introduction

PAUL S. GROGAN
TONY PROSCIO

Westview Press
A Member of the Perseus Books Group

Copyright © 2000 by Westview Press,
A Member of the Perseus Books Group

Published in 2000 in the United States of America by Westview Press,
5500 Central Avenue, Boulder, Colorado 80301-2877,
and in the United Kingdom by Westview Press,
12 Hid's Copse Road, Cumnor Hill, Oxford OX2 9JJ

Visit us on the World Wide Web at www.westviewpress.com

Grogan, Paul S.
Comeback cities : a blueprint for urban neighborhood revival / Paul S. Grogan and
Tony Proscio
p.   cm.
Includes bibliographical references and index.
ISBN 0-8133-6813-8; 0-8133-3952-9(pbk)
1. Urban renewal—United States.   2. Inner cities—United States.   3. City
planning—United States.   4. Urban policy—United States.   5. Community
development—United States.   6. United States—Social conditions.   7. United
States—Environmental conditions.   I. Proscio, Tony.   II. Title.
HT175 .G76 2000
307.3'416'0973—dc21   00-040815

10   9   8   7   6   5   4   3   2   1

This book is dedicated to Mike Sviridoff,
who taught us all these things,
and much more.

The bustling retail strip of Chicago's predominantly Hispanic Little Village neighborhood, 1998. (Todd Buchanan ©1999)

CONTENTS

ACKNOWLEDGMENTS

This book could not have been written without the support—both financial and intellectual—of the Local Initiatives Support Corporation (LISC), its longtime chairman John P. Mascotte, its board of directors, its officers and staff (past and present), and its extensive contacts among America's community development corporations, several of whose stories appear in these pages. During much of the writing of this book, Paul Grogan was president of LISC, but the organization's support continued seamlessly under his successor, Michael Rubinger, and under Jake Mascotte's successor as chairman, Robert Rubin. We owe special, personal thanks to all three men.

Other LISC staff deserve particular gratitude for their contribution of ideas, helpful criticism, and encyclopedic information: Barbara Beck, Lisa Belsky, Tina Brooks, Paul Carney, Stephanie Forbes, Rick Gentry, Marc Jahr, Buzz Roberts, Sandy Rosenblith, Robert Schwarz, Mat Thall, Marshall Tyndall, and Bill Traylor provided information and analysis, as well as a few war stories from their many years in the trenches. Stephanie O'Keefe, Ed Lloyd, Mike Patterson, and Cathy Hogan made our work both better and easier, in ways too numerous to list.

Ideas and insight also came from other brilliant people who—even when they did not share our opinions—helped us refine and clarify our thinking: Elinor R. Bacon, Rick Cohen, Peter Goldmark, Ann Habibi, Caroline Hoxby, Bruce Katz, George Latimer, Anita Miller, Richard Moe, Richard Nathan, the late Kirk O'Donnell, Michael Porter, Fred Siegel, Jim Sleeper, Alexander Von Hoffman, and Louis Winnick are prominent among those.

Other sources who went far out of their way to be helpful included journalist Jack Shanahan, consultants Carol Glazer and Julie Sandorf, and a sampling of the country's finest community development leaders: Joel Bookman, Bishop Arthur Brazier, Genevieve Brooks, the Rev. Calvin Butts, Gail Cincotta, the Rev. Harvey Clemons, Bob Green, Mossik Hacobian, Perry Harenda, Richard Juarez, India Pierce Lee, Maurice Lim Miller, Bob Moore, Mary Nelson, the Rev. Michael Pfleger, Ralph Porter, Bobbi Reichtell, Sue Taoka, Juanita Tate, and the Rev. Preston Washington.

Andrew Pitcher supplied critical research, conducted many interviews, and helped in drafting several passages. Dawn Stockmo and Andrew's colleagues at North End Area Revitalization, Inc., patiently gave him time and flexibility to work with us over several months. Janet Moscinski painstakingly hunted down photographs and negotiated permission to reprint them. Marcia Novak and Helene Berlin went to great trouble to supply helpful photos. Andrew McCabe proofread drafts and corrected errors that had eluded many other eyes. And Jane Peno kept track of manuscripts, coordinated communications, and generally maintained order amid the chaos we went to such lengths to create.

Finally, Karen Sunnarborg and Peter Borrell helped with everything, and made many things possible that otherwise would not be.

We thank them all sincerely, though not nearly enough.

Paul S. Grogan
Tony Proscio

INTRODUCTION

The Argument In Brief

THE AMERICAN inner city rebounding—not just here and there, not just cosmetically, but fundamentally. It is the result of a fragile but palpable change in both the economics and the politics of poor urban neighborhoods. Though not yet visible everywhere, the shift is discernible in enough places to unsettle longstanding assumptions about the future of older urban communities. This book tells why that is happening, and where, and what can be done about it—either to accelerate the turnaround or, through carelessness or worse, to stop it dead in its tracks.

Admittedly, the argument is neither easy to make nor incontrovertible. Some fragile evidence supports it: The first glimpse of data from the 2000 Census (most of which is still emerging as this edition goes to press) shows surprising growth in some cities that had suffered population losses or stagnation for years—most strikingly in Chicago, reversing a 50-year trend, but also in New York, Atlanta, and Denver. Even cities that lost population, like Cleveland or Philadelphia, saw an unexpected uptick in in-migration from the suburbs and immigration from abroad that could be an early sign of better news to come. Median incomes in central cities rose in the 1990s, with nearly 1.8 million inner-city households rising above the poverty line.

Still, most of the available statistics argue against a pronounced urban rebound. Volumes of data, and the many books and articles based on them, paint a persuasive picture of unrelieved and deepening misery: concentrated poverty and pathology, racial isolation, a widening gap between suburban haves and urban have-nots.

That bleak picture is not wrong but misleading. It takes a fair measure of the intense residue of 40 years of urban decline, but it sees no bend in the path we are on, namely, toward more of the same. In the toughest urban neighborhoods, despair has an almost automatically intuitive appeal: At least in our lifetimes, major cities have gone mostly downhill, burdened by industrial obsolescence, physical rot, riots, crime, poverty and the serial failure of big Federal rescue missions. The losses have been so

1

great for so long—and so carefully chronicled by decades of statistics—
that it's hard to conceive how any of it would ever be different.

But something different *is* happening. It's not yet potent enough to
leaven (at least statistically) the legacy of abandonment and decay, but it
is unmistakable nonetheless. The evidence demands a close inspection.
Some of it is anecdotal, and most of it is still too early to prove anything
like an irreversible momentum. But it's visible, and it's mounting.

After so steady and profound a decline, the first stirrings of recovery
naturally won't be obvious to the casual eye. Nor will numbers capture it
all. In a world where the best data can lag reality by as much as 10 years,
statistics alone aren't very helpful during periods of rapid change. The
1990s were, we will argue, such a period.

Further, as the decade closed, there was no sign that the remarkable
improvements in inner-city America were slowing or faltering. Some of
them have no doubt been the fruit of a sustained, national economic expansion that (unlike past expansions, it must be said) produced some
benefits for older city neighborhoods. But much of it has also been the
slow harvest of decades of patient rebuilding, and some is a return on
more recent public and private investments that have applied the lessons
of past failure, to productive effect.

To be sure, these improvements don't reach the (unreasonable and
largely irrelevant) goal of most 20th Century urban policy: eliminating
poverty. The national "antipoverty" obsession has not merely resulted in
a costly and demoralizing string of ambitious failures, it has tended by its
sheer mass to overshadow other, far more immediate and achievable
goals. Until we find a way to make everyone middle-class, one might ask,
aren't there ways of helping poorer communities remain stable and pleasant to live in, rather than spiraling into physical blight, disorder, political
isolation, and ingrained cynicism?

The failure of the antipoverty agenda has not been absolute—some
antipoverty programs have reduced suffering and disadvantage without
spinning off intolerable side effects. But it has been so great, and come in
for such persistent ridicule, that it has led many people to conclude that
the only cost-effective thing to do about poor inner-city communities is
ignore them (or, in the nastier political camps, berate them for their feck-
lessness). Even people who otherwise claim to be friends of cities—"metropolitanists" like David Rusk or Myron Orfield, for example—seem to
feel that the only hope for an urban turnaround lies in changing municipal boundaries to capture the wealthier tax base of the suburbs, or redis-
tributing poor city residents into less-than-enthusiastic hinterlands. Attracting better-heeled people back into existing city neighborhoods, they

seem to feel, is a lost cause. Making the city pleasant and livable with its current base of residents they consider just as hopeless.

There is a strange double standard to this point of view. On one hand, some metropolitanists—notably Rusk—have explicitly dismissed the idea of reviving existing urban neighborhoods because, they feel, the obstacles are too great. The poverty of these areas is irreversible, weighed down by factors far outside neighborhoods' or cities' control (technological change, global markets and what-have-you). And poor neighborhoods, they feel, are inherently unsalvageable. Yet as an alternative way of saving cities, this school of thought embraces an even more complex and ambitious vision: harmonizing the politics and economics of whole, fractious metropolitan regions—without apparent worry over the far greater improbabilities on which that would depend. They are willing to posit the happy premise that suburban majorities will someday be persuaded to subordinate their needs to those of long-neglected cities and poor families. Yet they are unwilling to imagine that urban neighborhoods might build, on their own, a sufficiently inviting environment so that working people will be more likely to remain or return.

Now, we have no doubt that cities would be happier and easier to govern if they could simply collect the taxes of their wealthier neighbors, disperse their poorest families to remote jurisdictions, and halt suburban expansion by fiat. But in the politics of most urban areas, the idea of elastic city boundaries and "smart growth" is only slightly less whimsical than that of eliminating poverty. The dream of metropolitanism, like that of the antipoverty utopia, insists on an elusive perfection to the neglect of the achievable good. Cities can be—and increasingly *are being*—made more livable, more attractive to businesses and investors, and more inviting to people of various levels of income. That isn't short-term work and it's had a late start in many places. But there is more and more evidence that it's happening, and building steam.

This evidence consists of four trends, quite different from one another but nevertheless linked. Together, they constitute a "surprising convergence of positives" that seem to presage a broad inner-city recovery.

The first is the maturing of a huge, rapidly expanding grassroots revitalization movement in America. Ordinary residents of the inner city have formed thousands of neighborhood-based nonprofit organizations in the past 20 years. They have used these organizations to invest in their assets rather than nurse old wounds, and to build productive partnerships rather than wage ideological warfare. From the wreckage of 1960s-style "community action" and the War on Poverty, the vast majority of these groups have learned to steer clear of the race-baiting and us-versus-them ideology that mired grassroots groups for decades. Some motivated by faith, others by frustration, they have executed strings of small miracles in once-desperate slums. They have built and renovated thousands of houses and apartments, recruited businesses into their neighborhoods, organized child-care centers and charter schools, formed block watches and civic clubs. As individual groups, their achievements are sometimes laughably modest. In aggregate, they are becoming monumental.

Political, business, and academic support for these groups, though far from universal, is strengthening. In the past decade, a coalition of corporations, foundations, and the Federal government has pooled more than a quarter of a billion dollars for a concerted capital infusion into resident-led development projects, called the National Community Development Initiative. In the months since the first edition of this book, the Initiative's 17 members renewed their commitment for another three years, pledging $120 million more, along with a more aggressive effort to get the word out on the possibilities for this kind of investment.

A second, related trend is the rebirth of functioning private markets in former wastelands where, until recently, the only vigorous market activity had been the drug trade. Now, fed by the work of the revitalization groups and gathering steam from the long economic boom of the 1990s, jobs and commerce are returning to cities. Retailers, facing less and less opportunity in suburbs, have finally discovered the untapped markets at their backs—in the very neighborhoods they fled 10 or 20 years ago. More and more, private sector prophets and planners are hailing the inner city as the undiscovered emerging market of our times.

The reappearance of functioning inner-city markets is not just a matter of big retailers suddenly re-discovering urban customers. Small businesses—both ordinary mom-and-pop stores and more entrepreneurial start-up companies—are finding inner-city business strips attractive and profitable again. In 1999, *Inc.* magazine's "Inner City 100" told a story of small, new businesses deliberately seeking out older, central neighborhoods for their low costs, available labor, easy commutes, and in some cases, architectural interest.

Meanwhile, thanks to regulatory pressure and structural changes in the financial markets, credit is reaching inner cities for property renovation and small businesses at levels not seen in decades. The first effects have been in housing, where community groups and individual homeowners have been able to re-create a stable, decently maintained residential base, from which businesses can then draw customers and employees.

At the same time, relatively liberal immigration policies have brought new blood to many inner cities in recent years, restoring vitality to neighborhoods and their markets. Not only have immigrants spurred growth in cities with once-sinking populations, but they have often concentrated in the very neighborhoods those cities had once written off as lost. By now, the consequences are so unmistakable that a few cities, like Pittsburgh and Philadelphia, now have deliberate policies or programs aimed at attracting immigrants. Thanks in large part to Russians in Coney Island and Brazilians in Newark, Mexicans in Chicago and Houston, and Asians in Oakland, rundown neighborhoods are suddenly seeing a burst of new activity—not just in numbers of residents, but in small-business investment, street life, and an asset that hardly anyone associated with these places 20 years ago: cultural élan.

In all these ways, the advance guard of market formation has been the creation of stable, occupied housing, followed by retail, followed by broad reconnection of formerly isolated communities to the economic mainstream.

The third propellant of inner city revival is dropping crime. Talk about unlikely! Until recently nearly everyone accepted rampant crime and attendant fear as an as an article of faith, a permanent, immovable fact of city life. But cities like New York and Boston have turned that conventional wisdom on its head, witnessing historic drops in crime and—perhaps better still—in the perception and the fear of crime. Nationwide, the National Crime Victimization Survey found an astonishing 15 percent drop in violent crime in just 1999 alone. The property crimes that most plague inner-city neighborhoods—robbery, car theft, burglary—were down markedly. Experts disagree, often fiercely, about the cause of all this, and who should get the credit for it. Some cite ephemeral factors like demographic fluctuations, or the vagaries of the drug market— things that no doubt explain some part of the recent improvements (though they don't explain why some places have succeeded more than others).

We believe that a growing revolution in police practices, in league with unfolding revitalization, has played a key role and can play an even greater role in the years ahead. Viewing revitalization as both a cause and an effect of falling crime rates isn't exactly conventional wisdom—at least not yet. But neither are we are alone in making the connection. Several cities have started to concentrate on blighted and abandoned properties, not for aesthetic reasons, and not just to alleviate housing shortages, but specifically to thwart gangs, drug trafficking, and other crime. Even where cities didn't make that precise calculation at first, they soon discovered that their best success in dampening crime rates was in neighborhoods where houses and stores were being fixed up and occupied. If this two-pronged attack lasts long enough, the dynamic may prove self-reinforcing: Holding crime to tolerable levels would have an incalculable effect on rebuilding confidence and commerce; the resulting investment could contribute to further drops in crime.

In the meantime, more and more urban police departments have embraced the main tenets of the policing revolution that started in New York and Boston, under the twin influences of criminologist George Kelling and reform cop William Bratton. Cities that hadn't shared much in the national crime-rate plunge—Baltimore, Philadelphia, and New Orleans, for example—have belatedly but dramatically seen the light. Since we started surveying urban law enforcement for this book a few years ago, Baltimore and Philadelphia have both picked former Bratton associates to head their police departments, and New Orleans recruited an architect of New York City's most far reaching police management reform, the data-driven accountability system called Compstat. (The political consequences of all this are remarkable. In New York's 2001 mayoral contest, Democrat Mark Green — surely among the most liberal candidates on the ballot — proudly claimed the endorsement of Republican Rudolph Giuliani's first police commissioner: Bill Bratton.)

Fourth, and finally, has been the unshackling of inner-city life from the giant bureaucracies that once dictated everything that happened there—in particular the welfare system, public housing authorities, and public schools. These massive, immovable systems were all formed with the noblest intentions, and even succeeded at many of those intentions for a time. But in recent decades, each has proven to be a bureaucratic albatross and a social disaster—concentrating poverty, insulating failure, limiting upward mobility, and stifling initiative.

By the end of the 1990s, by an astonishing bipartisan consensus, each of these behemoths has begun to disintegrate. Most surprising, perhaps, was the 1996 compromise in which President Clinton led his still-uneasy party into a historic bargain with the Republican Congress to end "welfare as we know it." The uneasiness was understandable: A verdict on the wisdom and humanity of this change will await years of experience, including a recession. But in its first few years, at least, welfare reform has largely been a success, with public assistance rolls falling radically, and most cities participating proportionally in that reduction. The timing, certainly, could not have been more propitious—nudging people off the welfare rolls in the late 1990s, into the strongest American economy in thirty years. But as a result, something more durable may be building, something that could sustain the good news through leaner times. It's a subjective assessment, to be sure, but early reports suggest that a culture of work seems to be taking hold in many inner city neighborhoods where examples of success and self-sufficiency had been absent for decades.

As welfare reform was taking shape, Republican reformers and a newly-savvy HUD leadership began to open the once-impregnable fortress of public housing—a nucleus of blight where decades of government rules had, in *The Washington Post*'s phrase, "stacked poor people in human filing cabinets." At the start of the 21st Century, 100,000 public housing apartments are being razed and replaced with mixed-income communities where the architecture suits the surrounding neighborhood. The first completed projects already show a wholesale transformation of the physical appearance and social dynamics of these communities—places once so isolated that, in some cities, they had achieved the status of economic leper colonies. Meanwhile, the vast tracts that the old "filing cabinets" used to occupy now offer enormous potential for new development—on land that had been off limits to the private market forces that were gathering strength in adjacent areas.

Finally, though not as far along, a tide of reform and competition is beginning to engulf urban public schools—perhaps the institutions most impervious to change for the longest time. What began as an ideological assault mainly from the political Right is gradually changing into a parents' movement, increasingly backed by elected officials (particularly mayors) of both parties. In some ways, the new battle over schools is the final frontier of inner-city revitalization. All the other incipient positive trends will fall short of their potential if city schools continue to push huge numbers of working and middle class families out of the city—which has been, unfortunately, their principal contribution to the urban cause in the past 20 years. If that dreadful "push factor" can be neutralized in time by some combination of charter schools and privatization—a force sufficient to drive genuine reform within public schools as well—the ultimate victory might be in the cities' grasp.

The first, indispensable step is being taken in more and more places: wresting control of the schools from inept and patronage-ridden School Boards, and vesting it in mayors who can't duck the implacable reckoning of Election Day. The wisdom of that course may not yet be entirely beyond debate, but more and more it's uniting the partisan camps that have warred over school reform for decades. Significantly, the one issue on which New York Mayor Rudolph Giuliani and Senator Hilary Rodham Clinton now completely agree is giving the mayor control of New York City Schools.

Reviving markets, dropping crime rates, and deregulating public systems open vistas for the inner city not seen in nearly 50 years, before the great postwar exodus and decline. These new trends combine powerfully with the now-extensive grassroots revival efforts. Together these four trends could engineer a far reaching change in the social, economic, and physical environment—indeed, the whole *idea*—of the American inner city.

Since the first edition of this book went to press in mid–2000, Congress has moved further along the course these trends chart. Two measures seem specifically designed to advance the cause of bringing capital to inner city neighborhoods, attracting retailers and other businesses to their streets and storefronts, and widening the potential of community development groups. The first is an expansion of the Low-Income Housing Tax Credit, a federal lever that encourages private investors to shoulder much of the risk — and front a big percentage of the money — to produce affordable housing. The second is a similar device, though smaller and more tentative, to lure private investment into neighborhood commercial property. The latter effort, called the "New Markets Tax Credit," became law with the joint sponsorship of a Democratic president and a handful of Republican members of Congress, including the Speaker of the House. It is hard to escape the conclusion that a political middle ground is forming here—something almost unheard of in most areas of domestic policy, and entirely uneard-of in urban affairs for nearly half a century.

The good news, though palpable, is still subtle. It is entirely reversible, if treated with indifference or with the heavy-handedness of past Federal programs. And to be sure, in most cases, it has not produced anything like the urban sentimentalists' dream: primly restored historic dwellings above savory shops decked out in Parisian awnings. Even the fastest-recovering inner cities are still hardscrabble places occupied largely by poor families and struggling businesses. The point is not that poverty has been abolished, or will be, nor is it that inner cities can or should return to the full glory of their wealthier pasts. The point is that they are becoming places where people want to live, shop, run businesses, and go to school. Joel Bookman, whose northwest Chicago community organization has led one of the more successful inner-city revitalization programs anywhere, says of his rapidly rebounding neighborhood, "It's not pretty. It's still not clean. We've got problems. But economically, it works, and people like it here."

The modesty of that statement makes it easy to disregard. *People like it here.* Were Bookman talking about a middle-class community of trimmed lawns and above-average schools, the statement would be unexceptional. But as a description of a neighborhood from which the middle class once fled, where poverty remains high, shops are thinly capitalized, and investment had disappeared for decades, it is a perfectly remarkable accomplishment, on which a great deal can now be built.

To put this accomplishment in perspective, we turn in Chapter One to the place once singled out as the capital of urban hopelessness: the South Bronx. Admittedly, the South Bronx story has lately become a mainstay of feel-good news reports, and we re-visit it here with some trepidation. It is often told in unduly poetic tones, with the unwarranted implication that New York City and its plucky residents somehow conjured a suburban utopia out of 40 years of social and economic implosion. The fact is that the South Bronx is still poor. Much of it remains unsightly. Crime is higher there, and academic achievement lower, than in many other New York neighborhoods. The war has not been won, but it is now clearly winnable. In much of the South Bronx today, something that was once altogether unthinkable has happened: *People like it here.*

The next chapter views that achievement both from the vantage point of the Bronx's nadir in 1977, and from that of today's still-unfinished rebuilding. Thereafter, the remainder of this book dissects the four trends that are making such transformations possible all over the United States. We argue throughout, and particularly in a concluding reflection, that there is plenty that the public and private sector can do to enlarge and accelerate those trends: to make the community development movement an even more potent force; to speed the recovery of inner city economies; to sustain the recent drops in crime; and to ensure that the deregulation of the inner city is successful.

For all this to reach its potential, some national policies still need to change. Deep anti-urban biases infect much of the behavior of the federal government in both its regulatory regimes and its programs and investments. That historic bias contributed hugely to the decline of the cities in the first place, and it remains a significant barrier to their full recovery.

In all this we find things to praise—and many defects—in the traditional approaches of the two political parties. But the emerging turnaround has followed a path that neither party envisioned, and that does not fit any of their ideological paradigms. The cities' stubborn refusal to march to the prevailing politics has meant that national leaders have been tardy in recognizing the changes afoot, and frequently off the mark in connecting those changes to policy. Forging a healthy connection between what is working locally and what needs to be done nationally is one overarching ambition of this book.

But first, a new look at the notorious South Bronx.

President Jimmy Carter on Charlotte Street, the South Bronx, October 5, 1977.
(Theresa Zabala/NYT Pictures)

PART ONE

The Case for a Turnaround

T HE REBIRTH of the South Bronx has become one of those national legends that lots of Americans are fairly sure they've heard
before, at least in broad strokes. And it has, from time to time, enjoyed a brief spell in the headlines, especially when the TV networks
or prominent politicians pay a celebratory visit. But like most legends,
the South Bronx turnaround has tended to mutate in the telling, with
different heroes and morals for different occasions. In several versions,
it has been distilled (often for political or ideological reasons) into almost pure myth.

Among people who are not particularly attuned to cities and their
fate, on the other hand, the story may not be well known at all. So famous was the horror of the old South Bronx—immortalized in novels
and films, even for a time a fixture of late-night comedy—that some
people probably believe the whole area long since burned to oblivion.

The recovery of the South Bronx is not total. There remain some
rough and dangerous enclaves, to be sure. But to anyone with a clear
image of the area from, say, the early 1980s, the change is awe-inspiring.
Most of the once-decimated neighborhoods are now inviting and pop-
ulous; the sidewalks are safe enough to be crowded with baby strollers
and elderly people and kids on roller-blades. The plywood is off the

President Bill Clinton on Charlotte Street, December 10, 1997, with Ralph Porter, executive director of MBD Development Corporation. (Stephen Crowley/NYT Pictures)

storefronts, and commercial traffic is back on the main streets. Property values are fantastically higher.

How all this happened—both the bleak "before" and the heroic "after"—is a tale so often distorted, and its complex meaning so often missed, that it warrants a detailed retelling. Among other things, the South Bronx was not saved the way decades of reformers insisted it would have to be saved: by eliminating poverty. Poverty levels in the South Bronx at the end of the 1990s were little changed from those of the 1980s (though significantly, the rate of employment was higher). What changed the South Bronx from Fort Apache to a functioning community was not a sudden influx of wealth, but a careful restoration of order—in the built environment, in public spaces, and in people's lives.

That's not to say money wasn't involved—in fact, the whole twenty-year exercise cost billions of public and private dollars. But the South Bronx repaid that investment with an achievement that was unthinkable in its day, and remains unorthodox in many circles even now: the reclamation of a ruined neighborhood without removing or suddenly enriching its poor and working-class residents.

After parsing the sunny lessons of the Bronx, we turn next to the shadows—to the volumes of learned arguments about why cities can't, or probably won't, ever recover, and why America is doomed to become a scatter-plot of secluded suburbs, their backs uniformly turned to the obsolescence of a ruined urban core. However much we find these arguments distasteful—and, more to the point, contrary to some firsthand observation—we do not refute most of the evidence on which they're based. Cities are not becoming significantly wealthier, and many have grown steadily poorer in the last half of the twentieth century. Conceded. Most Americans still prefer the bigger lots and quieter climes of suburbia over the greater density of urban neighborhoods. Conceded. City infrastructure is aging and often unsightly, burdened by decades of mismanagement and deferred maintenance. All conceded.

Yet it's significant that most of these bleak arguments are now aimed at cities' residential areas, not their downtowns. Why? Because the story no longer fits a huge, coast-to-coast regeneration in downtowns of every kind, from Boston to Cleveland to Milwaukee and even to sprawling Los Angeles. It's important to remember, though, that the same clouds of doom once hung over American downtowns that now hover over the neighborhoods. It's possible—more than that, it's lately observable—that the neighborhoods are the next to recover.

That recovery is not yet accepted in the conventional scholarship, mainly for two reasons: First, it's still in progress, and most socio-economic data are very slow to capture such changes until they're far along (the ten-year Census, for example, is practically the only consistent set of data for comparing many trends from year to year and city to city). Second, as the South Bronx story illustrates, urban neighborhoods are not recovering the way everyone expected them to: by getting wealthier. They are becoming healthy and desirable *without imitating the suburbs,* economically or socially. They seem to be achieving viability, in a sense, by the back door, while the scholars are busy debating in the parlor. Chapter 3 sketches out the array of positive forces lately converging on urban neighborhoods, a convergence that seems to suggest a future more like the South Bronx than the fate decreed by the bleaker academics.

Yet at this stage, the story of the South Bronx may be more important as a cautionary tale than as an inspirational one. Seen in the dim light of the late 1970s, the area's assets looked merely pitiful, and its liabilities seemed insurmountable. The long struggle to defeat those odds could have derailed at any moment (and came perilously close several times), in part because the whole thing, by the lights of conventional wisdom, was a fool's errand. But what few people outside the Bronx saw in those days—and what certainly showed up in no official statistics or formal scholarship—is that people who are determined to save their homes and their neighborhood will do so, given the political and financial resources and the regulatory latitude to proceed. It helps to see how that happened in one place, before examining the similar rumblings elsewhere.

Chapter 1

THE SOUTH BRONX:
FROM THE BOTTOM UP

NEW YORK, October 5, 1977—Around 9:30 on a bright early-autumn morning in the worst neighborhood in America, two men teetered on a rotting curbside, mouths agape. Along a ruined street of dilapidated housing and charred hulks of commercial buildings, in a place where the smart set never strayed and no one ever slowed down, a column of sparkling limousines twelve cars long, escorted by six police motorcycles with sirens blaring, eased past at a regal (some might have said funereal) pace.

One of the men, slightly older, cradled a bottle in a brown paper bag. From a window seat in the motorcade press car, Associated Press reporter John Shanahan heard the man tell his companion, with a shake of his head, "Damn. Imagine the president of the United States on Brook Avenue."

Several cars ahead, behind tinted layers of bullet-proof glass, the president of the United States was hearing the short, miserable tale of the obliteration of the South Bronx, as told by New York Mayor Abraham D. Beame and Patricia Roberts Harris, secretary of Housing and Urban Development. Through every reinforced window, the end of the story unfolded around them: a Gothic landscape of destruction and concealed menace, the burned-out remains of 40,000 arson fires in just the past four years, blocks of abandoned tenement buildings punctuated now and then by the odd survivor—the not-quite-empty ruins where apparently, against all odds, thousands of people still slept and ate and raised children.

Jimmy Carter had landed in New York less than twenty-four hours before, to deliver an internationally telecast speech on the Middle East before the UN General Assembly. The Middle East must have seemed safe territory compared to New York City politics, in which Carter found himself knee-deep within minutes of stepping out of his helicopter. On the Wall Street helipad, at what was supposed to have been a cordial welcoming ceremony, Democratic mayoral candidate Edward I. Koch had greeted the president with a letter accusing him of, among other things, abandoning Israel. It was a classic New York political moment (and a typical Koch ploy), but it startled and infuriated the president.

Before he knew it, Koch was off the list of people who would accompany the president on his various New York stops. Thus it was that lame-duck Mayor Beame, whom Koch had defeated in a primary two months before, found himself rousted the next morning for a surprise trip in the presidential limousine, creeping along Brook Avenue in the Bronx's notorious Melrose neighborhood (soon to be made grotesquely famous in Tom Wolfe's novel *Bonfire of the Vanities*) and extemporaneously trying to explain how his city had permitted the South Bronx to turn into a char pit.

❏

Nearly half a million people had lived in the South Bronx in its heyday—a city-within-a-city, larger than St. Louis, Seattle, or Miami. Just fifteen years before Carter's visit, the Grand Concourse, the area's signature boulevard, was still a showplace of elegant residential buildings with spacious apartments, more than a few of them boasting dumbwaiters, servants' quarters, and uniformed concierges. It was a place of comfort and style, with a European graciousness to suit an overwhelmingly European-American population.

The South Bronx started as an area of refuge for upwardly mobile families, many of them first- and second-generation immigrants who wanted to escape from raucous, overcrowded Manhattan. ("Those who wish to secure a quiet home," proclaimed an 1860s advertisement, "sufficiently remote from the city to be out of its turbulence and yet within a convenient business distance, had better seek out North New York"—an early name for the South Bronx.)

But just over a century later, the neighborhood stumbled off a cliff. Legendary planning czar Robert Moses had carved up the area with new expressways, and welfare bureaucrats then crammed the remaining fragments of neighborhood with destitute and rootless families who had nowhere else to live. The fires began in 1967 and continued throughout the next decade. Arsonists descended in every shape and color: vandals scavenging for metal and marketable debris, young delinquents after a thrill, landlords fabricating insurance claims, and welfare recipients betting the government would find them a new address.

In those years, more than 300,000 people fled the neighborhood, never to return. Behind them smoldered a wasteland of cynicism and anarchy.

Soon unemployment rates were running as high as 85 percent. In a 1969 study of death records on three streets in the South Bronx's Hunts Point section, the *New York Times* reported that residents had only a one-in-twenty chance of dying a natural death. Most died in homicides or from drug overdoses. In just one block of Fox Street, thirty-four people had been murdered in a single year.

"Many city services taken for granted elsewhere in New York," the *Times* reported later, "such as police protection, garbage collection, some semblance of civil order, could not be predicted with certainty in Hunts Point."

Now, as the presidential caravan inched up Third Avenue to Claremont Parkway, turned right onto Boston Road, and headed toward the infamous hypodermic heaven of Crotona Park, Mayor Beame and Secretary Harris were explaining how the city had become the South Bronx's biggest landlord. The owners of more than 8,000 South Bronx houses and apartments had stopped paying taxes. The uncollected bills had reached $40 million and were rising. The city consequently owned thousands of empty or abandoned parcels whose owners had thrown up their hands and walked away. (Sometimes, it was said, the hands thus thrown up still reeked of gasoline and matchsticks.)

The president surely knew parts of this story already. So many of its images had traveled around the world that, six years earlier, Mother Theresa had established a South Bronx outpost of her Missionaries of Charity, an organization founded in the bowels of the Calcutta slums to care for the most hopeless of the poor. So famous had the arson become that Howard Cosell, broadcasting the 1977 World Series from Yankee Stadium one month earlier, had periodically cut to an aerial shot of a massive blaze several blocks from the stadium and intoned, "There it is again, ladies and gentlemen. The Bronx is burning."

More than 40 percent of the South Bronx housing stock was destroyed in those years. When the city got around to demolishing the torched buildings, the result was simply vast tracts of rubble, with piles of bulldozed bricks and debris sometimes rising two stories, the masonry mesas of the new urban desert.

❑

Finally, just before ten A.M., the motorcade reached its destination. As the president's car eased into place, Secret Service agents hustled along its sides, and reporters and technicians scrambled for front-line position, cameras and boom mikes steadied amid bricks and shards of glass along the roadside.

Somberly, head lowered, Carter eased out of his cream-colored limousine onto what had become a kind of consecrated ground, the graveyard of the American city. Empty buildings like tombstones surrounded blocks of nothing but basements, filled in with the derelict masonry and bricks of buildings that once had stood five to seven stories high. On a corner two blocks away, a bent green sign bore the road's dainty name, almost childlike, reminiscent of a favorite storybook title: Charlotte Street.

Mayor Beame followed, less steadily. Failing to watch his step as he spoke to a reporter, the mayor stumbled on a stray piece of concrete, saved only by the reporter's quick reflexes. A Washington commentator later saw a metaphor in this, but New Yorkers apparently thought nothing of it.

After a slow 360-degree scan of the devastation, Carter turned to his Housing secretary and asked, "Most of this occurred in the last five years after Nixon cut off the Urban Renewal funds?" She dutifully answered "Yes."

Not true. The Bronx's problems had started well before Nixon took office. Under three earlier presidents, the Urban Renewal and Model Cities programs, with their massive slum-clearance apparatus, had done more to empty the Bronx than Nixon could have had time to conceive. Conversely, the housing subsidy program known as Section 8, a Nixon invention, had done more to produce affordable housing in other parts of the United States, including other parts of New York, than all the ambitions of the Great Society combined. Pinning the blame on the disgraced Nixon administration may have been politically irresistible, but it was far off the mark.

Still, it must have helped ease the horror of the moment, and the palpable embarrassment of a dejected Mayor Beame. AP newsman John Shanahan, the only New York–based reporter with the president that morning, later recalled the stunned look on Carter's face as he surveyed the desolation around him:

"The President seemed appalled by the extent of the destruction. It struck me that he must be thinking 'How could you have let this happen to your city?' From the expression on his face, you could see that he was devastated."

"See which areas can still be salvaged," the president told Secretary Harris. "We can create around the edge. Maybe we can create a recreation area and turn it around. Get a map of the whole area and show me what could be done." With that, Carter spoke briefly to reporters and returned to his car.

The motorcade sped off, headed south on Southern Boulevard and eventually across the Willis Avenue Bridge to Manhattan, but not before passing two men standing along a crumbling curbstone by the collapsed warehouses of Brook Avenue, where no one would ever have imagined seeing the president of the United States.

❏

The next morning's *New York Times* immortalized the scene along Charlotte Street—a grave-looking Jimmy Carter huddled with his Ministers of Devastation, the determined Harris and a dispirited Beame, all of them encircled by distant fire-gutted ruins like a malignant Stonehenge. A reporter years later compared the image to the hoisting of the flag at Iwo Jima: the icon of a turning point in history.

But the turning point that Jimmy Carter saw in progress in the South Bronx was not at Charlotte Street (that came later). It was at a stop that his motorcade had made a few minutes before, on the 1100 block of Washington Avenue, between 167th and 168th Streets. The president had left his limousine there, too—this time to visit a place that Patricia Harris and other staffers at HUD regarded as a small but significant sign of hope.

The six-story building had been renovated—an event so unheard-of in the South Bronx of the mid-1970s that for months, many of the building's neighbors still thought the construction crews were there for a demolition, even as new flooring, drywall, and windows were incredibly marching indoors. By that October morning, the building sported twenty-eight shining new apartments with oak floors and modern kitchens, and solar heat collectors on the roof.

More remarkable still, the renovation was not the work of an opportunistic investor or some missionary of charity, but of forty seemingly bedraggled residents, who lived in the vicinity and inexplicably preferred not to leave. They had organized a nonprofit group for the task, called People's Development Corporation. By the time President Carter appeared at their doorstep, they were already planning the reclamation of five more buildings nearby. The second-phase renovation was backed by $3 million in federal financing and grants from the Comprehensive Employment and Training Act, or CETA, to train and pay construction workers.

As the president strode onto the worksite, Claude Briley, one of the tenant/construction workers, greeted him with a cheery "Hi, Jimmy, glad to see you in the Bronx." Carter, unfazed, returned the greeting and asked, "How do you think you're making out?"

"Fine," Briley answered. "We hope to make more progress on a wider level."

Turning to the head of People's Development, a local radical in his twenties named Ramon Rueda, the president said he was proud of what the group had accomplished. How could they do more?

"We need more money, Carter," Rueda answered, friendly if abrupt. "We could use more CETA [Comprehensive Employment and Training Act, a 1970s-era wage subsidy]."

The president never promised any money, though in later years he was widely reported to have done so. Nonetheless, when he told Harris that "we can create around the edge," he seemed to be referring to the kind of work he saw in progress on Washington Avenue. That was, in fact, exactly the kind of work in which the Carter administration tried to invest in the Bronx. But only a few hundred thousand dollars actually arrived there by the time Jimmy Carter returned home to Plains, Georgia, in defeat.

❑

In the next two decades, Brook Avenue and Washington Avenue and Charlotte Street and the rest of the South Bronx saw no more presidents of the United States. They did, briefly, see candidate Ronald Reagan, who appeared in the midst of the 1980 presidential campaign at the same spot on Charlotte, near Boston Road, where Jimmy Carter had stood less than three years before. Nothing had changed. Reagan took a few moments to talk to reporters about tax incentives, ridiculed the Carter administration's "failed activism," lost a shouting match with a group of hecklers, and sped away.

"From that time on," a Senate staffer said later, "the place was politically toxic. No President would go near there, for fear of appearing to make a promise, or of being identified with the blight. Jimmy Carter had taken that cross on his shoulders, got nothing for it, and ended up with most of the blame. Who wants to repeat that?"

Where presidents feared to tread, candidates rushed in. In 1988 alone Gary Hart and Walter Mondale dropped by for a photo-op, and Jesse Jackson famously shared a home-cooked chicken dinner with a South Bronx family and then stayed the night. But in those visits, residents were quick to point out, the message was always promises or criticisms, a string of "if-I'm-electeds" and "what-I-would-dos." For two decades, no one who held Washington's purse—or the responsibility for what it could buy—dared retrace Jimmy Carter's steps.

Until December 1997—almost exactly twenty years after Carter's visit. In a political image that landed on the top-center of the *New York Times* page one, exactly where Carter's photo on Charlotte Street had appeared twenty years before, President Bill Clinton brought the motorcade, the cameras, his HUD secretary and other presidential entourage, and the same winded Washington press corps, back to the South Bronx for another look at the urban wasteland.

What they saw could well be the most important story of urban America at the dawn of the twenty-first century. At worst, it is the story of how things *could have been* in every run-down neighborhood, had only neighbors and governments paid attention. It is not the story of the federal government creating "a recreation area" in the midst of the squalor. Nor is it the story of solitary heroism by the likes of the People's Development Corporation, which faded from public view sometime in the 1980s.

It is something far better and more profound than either of those stories, yet it combines something of both. What Clinton and his entourage saw in December 1997 was a prim neighborhood of shady trees and manicured lawns, lace curtains, sprinklers and gardens, neighbors walking their dogs and baby strollers coursing along smooth sidewalks, past an upright green sign still bearing the dainty name Charlotte Street.

It had been done by community organizations and New York City, with a considerable helping of federal money. No one has sole credit for saving the South Bronx. But those who have the credit have a lot of it. The results, Clinton noted, were nothing short of astonishing.

Crime and drug abuse had plummeted—in the worst areas, shootings were down by more than two-thirds, and robberies and assaults by more than half. School attendance was dramatically improved. Vandalism was no more common than in any New York neighborhood—and by some measures a good deal less. Property values on Charlotte Street had risen so high that many residents of tonier neighborhoods in Manhattan, Staten Island, and Queens could scarcely afford to live there. Yet many of the residents were once the tenants of bombed-out South Bronx hulks where the only reliable heat had come from two blankets and a cat.

Although frequently dubbed "miraculous," the transformation of the South Bronx was nothing of the sort. It was simply work and money—the work often performed by thoroughly ordinary people, and the money typically parceled out boldly but strategically by surprisingly cash-strapped governments.

Most of the elements of the transformation of Charlotte Street were present on October 5, 1977: community organizations willing to stay and build, a federal government willing to finance their efforts, and a local government that had learned clear but bitter lessons from decades of massive, top-down "renewal."

These elements in combination took twenty years to finish the job (with more wisdom and less complicated politics, they could probably have done it in fifteen, but not much less). It was massively expensive—though it eventually proved a sound long-term investment. It took the political will and persistence of a mayor and a Bronx borough president far outside the city's political norm. In short, it was not a story built on government-as-usual. But government was, throughout, an indispensable part of the solution.

Still, it's also worth noting what Clinton and his crew did *not* see. Most of the lost population of 300,000 people from the 1970s had not returned to the South Bronx. Though the population has risen through the 1980s and '90s, the gains are small compared to the earlier loss. Poverty is still significantly higher than in most other parts of New York. The South Bronx has not regained its former grandeur, nor is it likely to do so. It has instead become something more necessary and more lasting: It has become pleasant and livable.

❑

The work set in motion by Jimmy Carter's visit to the South Bronx was initially slow and stumbling. Ed Koch was elected mayor a month after Carter left town (his much-predicted landslide spoiled by a stubborn third-party contender named Mario M. Cuomo), and in little more than a year he had established what governments always seem to establish when they want to accomplish something big: a giant new agency.

Koch entrusted the newly formed South Bronx Development Organization (SBDO) to Edward J. Logue, the quintessential Urban Renewalist and a master development planner from Boston. It might have been just another massive government project, with the dismal results that such things repeatedly wrought in other cities, but for a crucial insight early in its development. Under heavy persuasion from the Ford Foundation (from whose orbit Koch had drawn several of his top officials), Logue enlisted resident groups and their nonprofit organizations in the planning and redevelopment of his first target blocks. And the first among these was Charlotte Street.

Besides the cost of operating SBDO, New York City turned over sizable tracts of land that had come into its possession during the waves of abandonment and tax delinquency in the 1970s. Through the Comprehensive Employment and Training Act (CETA), Section 8, Community Development Block Grants, and other HUD programs, the federal government contributed mightily to the early effort in the South Bronx, though the Reagan administration soon pruned back most of these programs and eliminated a few, most notably CETA.

By 1983—more than five years after Jimmy Carter's impromptu tour—two new single-family ranch-style houses stood on Charlotte Street, manufactured in a factory in Berwick, Pennsylvania, and set on lots and foundations prepared by SBDO. The two houses served as models for a planned project of ninety such homes, to be known as Charlotte Gardens. The houses were being marketed, at $47,800 apiece, by a community-based nonprofit group with the hardly reassuring name of Mid-Bronx Desperadoes.

Their name aside, the Desperadoes were in fact becoming a hardheaded development organization. The group had arisen three years before President Carter's visit, cobbled together by people who had channeled their frustration with government failure and empty promises into a burning determination to rebuild the neighborhood themselves if need be. With little experience and no money of their own, they already had grown, like People's Development Corporation, into a modestly sophisticated housing renovation company gleaning government grants, loans, and contracts for small-scale projects, mostly one building at a time.

But unlike the more radical People's Development, the Desperadoes showed a talent for working diplomatically with the city to raise money and finish projects. They saw their partnership with Logue and SBDO as a test of the city's willingness finally to tackle the South Bronx as a solvable problem, rather than wringing its hands and dispensing condolence money. With the beginning of Charlotte Gardens, their bet seemed to be paying off.

In no time, however, New York City politics intervened. Under the city's nineteenth-century charter (later scrapped by a federal court) federal grants to New York City first had to be "accepted" by the city's de facto governing board, called the Board of Estimate. It consisted of the mayor, the comptroller, the president of the city council, and the heads of each of the city's five boroughs. All the boroughs, though hugely disparate in size, had an equal vote (hence the eventual displeasure of the federal courts). Not surprisingly, the other four boroughs soon grew irritable over the bales of federal money being pitched into the Bronx. They were looking for their cut. Finding little or none, they marshaled a majority to reject the federal dollars outright. Charlotte Gardens screeched to a halt.

It took nearly a year, and some deft intracity diplomacy by Koch, to reconnect the Bronx's federal life supports. By the time all eighty-nine of Charlotte Gardens' new houses were completed, Jimmy Carter's visit was a nine-year-old memory.

But in the meantime, something remarkable was happening—something that had little to do with the city's centralized planning or its new blue-ribbon development agency. Nonprofit community organizations like the Desperadoes were continuing to form, build, and prosper—a church-based group called the South East Bronx Community Organization, a block-club-turned-builder named the Banana Kelly Community Improvement Association (because of a distinctive bend in Kelly Street), and half a dozen others, all renovating and managing apartment buildings that once had seemed scarcely worth the cost of demolition. Their combined output of new housing vastly exceeded whatever support they received from SBDO, and their production speed was double or triple what was possible for any city agency, with its complex procurement rules and labor politics.

Late in 1986, just as the finishing touches were going up in Charlotte Gardens, Koch changed course. At that point, the mayor was confronting three seemingly hopeless challenges that, if tackled together, might actually make for a common solution.

First, a crusading state judge had ordered him to move homeless families more quickly out of shelters into permanent apartments, just as New York was suffering through one of its periodic bursts of sky-high housing costs.

Second, the city's mammoth supply of abandoned, tax-foreclosed real estate was draining municipal coffers and casting the city as the biggest and most inept of slumlords.

And finally, the interborough rivalries that had erupted over federal money for Charlotte Gardens had not disappeared. The attention and funds lavished on the South Bronx, particularly through Logue and the SBDO, made the efforts of other blighted neighborhoods, especially in Brooklyn and Manhattan, seem neglected by contrast. New York's fractious political structure (especially under the old Board of Estimate system) could not long tolerate those kinds of resentments.

All three forces pointed in one direction: The city had to find a way to unleash the resources of the private sector—including the city's widening battalion of nonprofit development groups—on its foreclosed housing stock, to get the property back on the tax rolls, move formerly homeless families into some or most of the apartments, and spread the benefits (and the responsibility for combating homelessness) to boroughs outside the Bronx. No city agency could develop all that real estate in the short time available. The age of the big-government local development agency was about to end.

By the time SBDO closed its doors in the late 1980s, it had taken part in building or renovating hundreds of units of housing, and channeled millions into the South Bronx's long-starved real estate market. It was, in many ways, a remarkable achievement in a city where labyrinthine work rules and stifling bureaucracy can make a multiyear ordeal out of even the most routine construction project.

Still, in roughly the same amount of time, the Desperadoes, Banana-Kelly, the South East Bronx church group, and their cohort had renovated thousands of units with a total investment several times the size of SBDO's. To his lasting credit, Koch recognized the difference, and switched his bet to the faster horse.

❑

It helped mightily that New York City had emerged, by this time, from the capital drought brought on by its decade-old fiscal crisis. With renewed access to the bond market and the prospect of restoring thousands of properties to the city's tax rolls, Koch was able to marshal sums that dwarfed even the federal government's fondest promises. By 1988, committing some $3.6 billion of mostly city-raised capital, Koch had launched what would become the largest municipal housing construction program in American history (the sum eventually rose above $5 billion). For partners, he relied not only on community organizations, but on private landlords and developers of every size, often brought to the table with extensive technical help from the New York City Housing Partnership, a group that grew out of the corporate response to the city's near-bankruptcy a decade earlier, and the Community Preservation Corporation, a specialized development bank for small landowners and poor neighborhoods.

In six years, the city enabled the construction or renovation of nearly 100,000 units of housing. At its peak, the Koch administration was pouring half a billion dollars a year into the effort—more investment in housing than in the other fifty largest U.S. cities combined. City financing for the nonprofit developers flowed through two nonprofit national development institutions, the Enterprise Foundation and the Local Initiatives Support Corporation. It was a mobilization of private-sector forces, including both nonprofit and for-profit, on an epic scale. The city was planner, financier, supplier of vacant or run-down property, and sometimes strategic planner—but only rarely developer.

Of this explosion in residential development, a sizable share—certainly more than one-fifth—went to the South Bronx, partly because that area still contained the largest and ugliest swaths of vacant property, decaying buildings, dilapidated infrastructure, and sweeping brown prairies of empty, buildable land. At the end of the 1980s, more than one-third of the tax lots in the South Bronx were vacant.

But what sealed the South Bronx's advantage in the competition for city investment dollars was its record of success against long odds. By the time of Koch's massive housing initiative, the South Bronx already contained the city's richest concentration of grassroots development groups, tried and proven in the hard years before any Washington entourage ever set foot there.

New York City invested more than $1 billion in South Bronx housing between 1988 and 1997. Private investment—including investors' equity and bank financing—came to some $365 million. More than 10,000 new houses and apartments went up, blending city, state, and federal subsidies with private capital. At its peak, in 1992, the production machinery was cranking out 2,700 units a year in the South Bronx alone.

Remarkable as that achievement is, the most significant consequences are those that extend beyond housing. The nonprofit Citizens Housing and Planning Council, in an exhaustive 1997 study of South Bronx redevelopment, reported that the widespread construction and renovation seemed to have created a "greater sense of community order."

Policing methods in the Bronx also improved, as they had citywide, building alliances with community organizations and other city services that targeted low-level crimes that undermine the local quality of life, and often incubate more serious criminality. The combined effects of these changes included a plunge in South Bronx crime rates considerably steeper than in the rest of the city—despite a jump in the number of teenagers and young adults living in the South Bronx, a usual catalyst for rising crime. Elsewhere in the city, these age groups declined 12 percent, compared to a 15 percent *increase* in the South Bronx.

In the notorious 40th Precinct—subject of the 1980s Paul Newman film *Fort Apache: The Bronx*—total felonies dropped by more than 61 percent between 1990 and 1996, a decline 23 percent greater than in the comparably run-down East New York section of Brooklyn, and at least 5 percent greater than in Manhattan's central Harlem neighborhood, where middle-class occupancy was rising. Grand larceny had dropped more than 57 percent—37 percent better than East New York and 26 percent better than central Harlem. Car thefts had declined an amazing 74 percent, even as the number of car owners in the South Bronx was rising.

In the same period, real estate tax collections in the South Bronx roughly doubled. Residents' opinion of the neighborhood jumped markedly, with a near doubling of the percentage of residents rating the area "excellent or good." Roughly one quarter of the residents reported living near boarded-up buildings in 1996, compared to nearly two-thirds in 1987.

And perhaps most significantly, the Housing and Planning Council found "an upsurge in civic participation as measured by voting trends and other community activities." From having lived as virtual captives in a neighborhood that everyone fled when they could, residents of the South Bronx had become citizens again, participants in the forces that had restored their community to a livable place.

That is significant not only in itself, but even more in light of what was *not* achieved in the Bronx, and in some places was never even attempted: The poverty rate did not decline. Employment, though considerably higher than in the 1970s, did not rise more rapidly than anywhere else in New York, and lagged behind some comparable neighborhoods. Participation in the labor force is mostly unchanged. Adolescent pregnancies did not decline significantly (although it is arguable that the next generation, not yet in adolescence, will be the one most affected by the Bronx's physical and social turnaround).

The South Bronx has not become a middle-class neighborhood. No surprise there. But it has become something that, in the midst of New York's stratospheric rents and high-skills job market, is more needed and more valuable: It is a place where lower-income people can live affordably, in tranquillity and safety.

To weigh the enormity of that accomplishment, it helps to view the landscape from the windows of the presidential limousine on October 5, 1977. In a barren terrain, where the best thing the president of the United States could imagine was maybe a recreational field, there now stands a prim, middle-class housing development. In the rubble-strewn field that furnished the opening murder scene in *Fort Apache: The Bronx,* there is now a sprightly development of white duplexes, complete with gardens, shutters, and awnings. The renovation of the South Bronx is far from over, but it has become manageable, even profitable.

In fact, the process has given rise to an entirely new (and frankly more welcome) generation of problems. In some parts of the South Bronx, like the once-dismal Mott Haven section, there is now a housing shortage. On one of the few remaining city-owned lots there, at Crimmins Avenue and East 141st Street, a group of neighbors had years ago planted a community garden. But in 1998 the gardeners were massing their political forces against another group of neighbors who, with the city's help, were determined to build three new duplex homes on the site. Neither the city nor the prospective home builders have anything against gardening. Their problem, according to the nonprofit group that wants to build the houses, is that there are only six vacancies among the neighborhood's 900-plus dwelling units. Mott Haven can no longer keep up with the demand.

"If you can do it," President Clinton told residents of the South Bronx twenty years after Carter's visit, "everyone can do it." In fact, more than 2,500 other communities have come to a similar conclusion, forming development organizations and strategic revitalization programs similar to (and in some ways more inventive than) the one that changed the Bronx. Are they right? Can every poor neighborhood and blighted inner city achieve what the South Bronx achieved, given enough time and resources?

A substantial body of scholarly opinion says No.

Viewed from the streets of the South Bronx, that answer seems illogical in the extreme, yet it is both too widely believed and too carefully argued to be dismissed out of hand. Before looking to the Bronx and other such success stories for a model of urban reclamation, it would be wise to consider the negatives carefully, and see whether, and how, they undermine the unmistakable optimism in the lawns and window boxes of Charlotte Street.

Chapter 2

MASS EXIT: A VISION
OF URBAN DOOM

NAVIGATING A SEA of tumbledown neighborhoods in 1997, officers of the Ford Foundation took a team of reporters through an archipelago of bold renovation projects in Washington, D.C.— mostly the work of residents like those who had rebuilt the South Bronx. The projects, individually impressive, were nonetheless dispersed—scattered beachheads in a huge unconquered terrain of blight. At a debriefing later, an unimpressed writer for the *New Republic* lobbed a deflating if reasonable question: "Why even bother with these places? Why not just help the residents move out?"

This wasn't a new idea. Twenty years earlier, seminars at elite public policy schools were zeroing in on essentially the same solution. It traveled in those days under a variety of technical-sounding aliases, of which the most popular were "dispersion incentives" and the more upbeat "migration subsidies." (Participants at one such discussion at Princeton in the late 1970s—mostly advanced-degree candidates planning careers in the top ranks of national urban policy—coined the commendably blunt phrase "evacuation bonuses." It never caught on.) Just point people toward the exits, the proposition went, and hand them a check on their way out. In academic circles, at least, any opposition to the idea usually had more to do with cost than principle.

In the intervening years, it seemed, the concept had lost some of its academic cachet but otherwise hadn't changed all that much. It still apparently held a certain fascination for those, including the *New Republic* reporter, who could somehow overlook the quicksand of racial politics into which it inevitably leads (one guaranteed headline: "City to Minority Neighborhoods: Get Lost"). Nor would the quicksand end with race: Imagine the political and legal response of landlords whose real-estate holdings would thus be made worthless.

One thing in its favor, though: Concerns about the cost of this idea were fading slightly over time. As inner-city populations dwindled in the 1970s and '80s, paying the remnant population to leave was starting to seem, at least in a few places, a little less prohibitive.

"Dwindle," in fact, was hardly the word. In the preceding decade, the population of just one neighborhood on the Ford Foundation's tour, the Marshall Heights section of southeast Washington, had plunged by 48,000 residents. The same death rattle seemed to be sounding at once from central cities all over the country. More than half the nation's 100 largest cities shrank in the 1980s: Gary, Indiana, lost nearly one quarter of its population, Philadelphia lost 100,000 people, Detroit lost 175,000, and Chicago nearly a quarter of a million.

Nor was this bolt for the suburbs just a spasm of 1980s materialism. Its roots, paradoxically, stretched back to the 1950s, when southern African Americans and rural whites were still moving into northeastern and midwestern industrial cities by the tens of thousands, and the baby boom further swelled their numbers. Yet despite these huge inflows of population and the natural increase they generated over the next four decades, twenty-nine of the nation's largest cities had fewer people in 1990 than they did in 1950. St. Louis lost an incredible 53 percent of its population over this period. Cleveland, Buffalo, and Pittsburgh each dropped more than 40 percent. Philadelphia lost nearly half a million people; Chicago and Detroit lost more than 800,000 each. In almost every case, the cities' metropolitan regions were growing rapidly. Americans (at least the ones who needed no "dispersion incentives") were voting with their feet, and central cities were losing in a landslide.

Poorer households, however, mostly stayed put. The result was a concentration of poverty in central cities so malignant that it established oncology as the seemingly permanent metaphor of American urban policy debate. (By this route, "dispersion incentives" soon earned their medical degree and donned the high-tech mantle of "surgical removal.")

By the end of the twentieth century, this population shift away from cities has achieved its natural political effect: Cities have lost their place on most Washington cue cards. The century's final round of congressional redistricting finished the slow calculus begun in the Eisenhower era: A majority of the House of Representatives today can ignore cities without worrying about Election Day.

In these years, the scholarly dream of "dispersion" seemed to have found its way to a well-earned oblivion. Yet not much has come along to take its place. Even in many of the circles where urban affairs (lately renamed "metropolitan affairs") still claim attention, the "dispersion" idea has not given way to some smart new approach with its own distinctive metaphors and policy playbooks. Instead, the discussion about inner cities and their fate has simply fallen silent, or at best into a murmur about tax breaks. In the tenacious language of the cancer ward, the inoperable inner city has quietly been transferred to hospice care, where it can await its sad but inevitable end in peace.

❑

The starkest, most eloquent, and surely most incredible example of this shrugging fatalism came in 1997 from the least likely man in America: Philadelphia Mayor Edward G. Rendell, who in his first term brought the city back from the brink of fiscal disaster and later staked his reputation on its physical and economic rebirth. Despite inheriting a deficit that would have reached $1.25 billion by 1997, within two years Rendell had stanched the red ink and the flight of businesses from the city, was riding a 76 percent approval rating, and found himself proclaimed "America's Mayor" by Vice President Al Gore. Yet after barely six years in city hall, Rendell seemed ready to write off his city's future, along with those of New York, Chicago, and other capitals of the industrial age.

Just as a political biography of Rendell, the best-selling *A Prayer for the City,* was hitting the bookstores, the mayor curiously turned up in newspapers around the country, throwing in the towel. "No matter what we did to cure the bullet wound," Rendell told the *Washington Post,* "this doctor didn't have anywhere near the resources to cure the cancer."

His reasoning closely tracks that of the most pessimistic observers and scholars—a list that also includes some of the most distinguished names in the field. Middle-class flight, they argue, combined with the concentration of poor families in inner cities, has amounted to a knockout combination for the inner cities—or worse, has prompted a process of metastasis that will consume not only the cities but their inner suburbs as well.

So firm and unyielding has this grim view become that its proponents have come to speak of it in absolutes and universals, as if all wisdom on the matter were by now long settled. In his 1993 book *Cities Without Suburbs,* for example, David Rusk proclaims it a "law of urban dynamics" that *"ghettos can only become bigger ghettos"* (italics his). Rusk goes so far as to label twelve cities "Past the Point of No Return" (capital letters also his), based on continued population loss, high and increasing minority populations, and a widening chasm between city and suburban per-capita income.

Similarly, in his book *Metropolitics,* Myron Orfield flatly proclaimed that "the lack of social mortar to hold neighborhoods together and build communities makes economic development in extreme-poverty tracts or ghetto areas all but impossible." Fatalism of this degree from someone like Orfield is especially striking. As a member of the Minnesota House of Representatives, he had deftly shown how a coalition of cities, inner-ring suburbs, and cash-strapped outlying suburbs could wrest power over public development dollars from the wealthiest suburbs. It seemed a hopeful lesson in power politics for the economically disenfranchised. But even so, optimism for Orfield evidently can't reach the poorest neighborhoods of the inner city.

Even when the arguments are stated more modestly, their conclusions are no more hopeful. William Julius Wilson, Anthony Downs, and John D. Kasarda, to name only some of the best known, all have described the future of inner cities in carefully modulated terms that nonetheless spell doom on a near-biblical scale. So sobering are these views, and so precisely argued, that it is unwise at a minimum, and very nearly impossible, to advance any contrary approach to the inner cities without taking account of them—and without acknowledging, however much regretfully, that a good deal of what they say is true.

❑

As described in the bleaker literature, the final agonies of the American city come in four waves, all of which were to some degree already well under way at the core of the older industrial cities as the American century drew to a close.

The first of these is middle-class flight. In this view, the aging infrastructure of old cities and the newer, lower-cost amenities of the suburbs propel the middle classes farther and farther toward the suburban horizon. A middle-class consumer taste for detached houses, larger lots, and (at least among whites) homogeneous racial and ethnic environments accelerates the flight.

Kenneth Jackson summed up the process succinctly in his book *Crabgrass Frontier:*

> The move to the suburbs was almost self-generating. As larger numbers of affluent citizens moved out, jobs followed. In turn, this attracted more families, more roads, and more industries. ... High quality municipal services, and especially well-funded public schools that offered racial homogeneity and harmony, attracted still more residents, which in turn made select suburbs even wealthier and more attractive. As early as the 1950s, suburban real-estate advertisements were harping on the themes of race, crime, drugs, congestion, and filth.

The result was the great urban population hemorrhage of the last half of the twentieth century. Rising real incomes during much of this period enabled hundreds of thousands of families to buy larger and more modern homes in rapidly expanding suburbs.

For the American middle class, the lure of suburban living has been tightly bound up with a desire to be surrounded by people of comparable means, hence the growing concentration of wealth in suburbs. In 1990 the typical affluent household, defined as earning at least four times the poverty line, lived in an area where more than half of the neighborhood is also affluent. Yet in 1970 slightly less than 40 percent of the neighbors of such a household were affluent. Either the preference for economic homogeneity had increased in those two decades, or the means of achieving it had expanded. Or, of course, both.

It's worth pointing out that under this mostly familiar story of market preferences, rising incomes, and centrifugal wealth lies a less well-known subplot. Suburban flight, and even some of the "preferences" that underlay it, were frequently a by-product of government subsidies—a "dispersion incentive," to borrow a phrase—tailored for the white middle class.

Urban taxpayers helped subsidize new highways, sewer systems, and other public works in the suburbs while their own deteriorated beneath them. The exact cost of these subsidies is hard to pinpoint, but one estimate puts the total for highways alone in the tens of billions. The home-mortgage deduction became a disproportionately suburban subsidy, thanks in part to mortgage redlining in central cities—an inequity that's abating rapidly, but has not ended. In 1995 alone, the home mortgage interest deduction cost the federal government some $60 billion.

Regulations in the telecommunications industry have also artificially deflated the cost of relocating homes and businesses to suburbs. AT&T, for example, won from the Federal Communications Commission the right to charge flat rates for local telephone service across an entire metropolitan area even though the cost of serving outlying areas was significantly higher.

Though suburbanization certainly would have occurred without subsidies, they radically altered its pace and character. Forced to bear the real cost of development, suburbs could not have grown as quickly or offered such low property tax rates or other inducements to prospective residents. Given time to adjust to changing tastes, cities might have adapted more competitively and kept a greater portion of the middle class. They certainly could then have avoided the impression of impending collapse, which created real-estate panics in many cities in the 1970s.

All of this takes little away from those who argue that the depletion of urban populations was overwhelming and devastating. But it weakens, perhaps, the argument that these movements either were inevitable or are unalterable.

Alongside market forces and government subsidies, race played a formidable role in launching the caravans of fleeing middle- and upper-income white families. White neighborhoods closest to majority black neighborhoods emptied of whites more rapidly than neighborhoods far from concentrations of minorities. In a 1976 survey, researcher Reynolds Farley found that only 25 percent of white respondents would live in a neighborhood that was one-third black. Similar studies in 1992 by Farley and William H. Frey found that 41 percent of whites would live in such a neighborhood, an apparent improvement. But if the neighborhood's balance rose to 60 percent black, only 27 percent in the later survey said they would be willing to live there.

John D. Kasarda, an authority on the demographics of metropolitan America, concludes that no reversal in the flow of middle-class families from city to suburb has occurred, and is not likely to occur any time soon. In a 1997 article Kasarda and colleagues investigated migration patterns in twelve major metropolitan areas across the country, and found that not one central city could boast even a stabilization of the number of above-average income households, let alone any net growth. For example, between 1985 and 1990 Chicago lured more than 7,000 higher-income families from the suburbs into the city, but it lost more than 40,000 in the other direction. In Detroit, six high-income families headed for the suburbs for every one that moved back inward. Even Sunbelt cities like Houston, Dallas, and Los Angeles lost substantially more above-average income households than they gained.

The second of the urban death throes is the evaporation of inner-city jobs and businesses. The argument goes more or less like this: As industry becomes more and more mobile, the jobs follow the most desirable (i.e., highest skilled) workforce, and likewise flee to the hinterlands. This leaves the largely minority poor not only stranded in crumbling inner cities, but more and more isolated from the employment that might help them rebuild or move.

In other eras and under other circumstances, American workers had a long history of picking up and moving to where the jobs were (often finding themselves decidedly unwelcome when they arrived). But in the postwar suburban boom, the old Unwelcome Mat took on the spiked armor of zoning law. Limits on lot sizes and the construction of new housing put the clamp on in-migration, leaving many poor job seekers pressed against the outside of a legal and economic fence that neatly encircled suburban America.

Nor was public transportation much of a help. Suburban planning that overwhelmingly favored the automobile—effectively creating an entirely new urban design built around the unsightly institution of the parking lot—left people without cars stranded at the commuter-rail station, with little option beyond taxis for getting to far-flung job sites.

Meanwhile, as suburbs grew fertile, the cities' economic well was drying up. Dependent on manufacturing, inner cities suffered as the American economy traded blue collars for white. Manufacturers fled to less unionized, lower-wage environments, first in the American Sunbelt and, more recently, abroad. As proximity, face-to-face communication, and the cost of transportation became less important, the manufacturing universe expanded far beyond cities' once-convenient boundaries. From 1967 to 1987, New York, Chicago, Philadelphia, and Detroit each lost *more than half* their manufacturing jobs. New York lost more than half a million; Chicago, 326,000; Philadelphia, 160,000; and Detroit 108,000.

And even if city residents could find service-sector work to replace their disappearing factory jobs, advancement in that sector depended more and more on skills and education that were becoming inaccessible in ossified urban school systems. As city school systems deteriorated, unemployment rose in lockstep. Using select three-year periods from 1968 to 1992, the table on the following page, borrowed from John Kasarda's research in the early 1990s, tells the whole story.

William Julius Wilson, in *When Work Disappears,* illustrates the consequences: "For the first time in the 20th Century most adults in many inner-city ghetto neighborhoods are not working in a typical week." The intensifying poverty, together with the discouraging physical and social environment it breeds, drives away not just businesses that employ residents, but those that provide essential goods and services. Myron Orfield summarized the resulting damage in Chicago this way:

During the 1960s, Chicago lost 500,000 white residents, 211,000 jobs, and 140,000 private housing units. As the West Side of Chicago was

TABLE 2.1   Percentage Not at Work of Out-of-School Central City African-American and White Male Residents, Ages 16–64, by Region and Education: 1968–70 to 1990–92

Education	1990–92	1980–82	1968–70
	Northeast		
African-American			
Less than high school	57.1	44.4	18.8
High school graduate	31.1	27.2	10.8
Some college	19.9	17.2	11.2
College graduate	7.3	4.3	8.6
White			
Less than high school	36.7	33.6	15.1
High school graduate	23.9	17.1	6.6
Some college	14.4	10.7	7.4
College graduate	11.9	6.0	5.6
	Midwest		
African-American			
Less than high school	63.3	51.6	23.5
High school graduate	40.5	29.6	9.8
Some college	29.8	15.0	6.9
College graduate	11.5	10.0	N.A.
White			
Less than high school	34.4	29.1	11.5
High school graduate	18.3	15.8	5.1
Some college	11.5	15.7	3.8
College graduate	5.2	6.2	2.6

NOTE: *Northeast* cities are: Boston, Newark, New York, Philadelphia, and Pittsburgh. *Midwest* cities are: Chicago, Cleveland, Detroit, Milwaukee, and St. Louis.

SOURCE: Bureau of the Census, *Current Population Survey:* March File: 1968, 1969, 1970, 1980, 1981, 1982, 1990, 1991, and 1992, as presented in John D. Kasarda, "Cities As Places Where People Live and Work: Urban Change and Neighborhood Distress," in *Interwoven Destines: Cities and the Nation,* ed. Henry G. Cisneros. New York: W. W. Norton and Company, 1993.

enveloped in an expanding core of poverty during the 1960s, 75 percent of its businesses disappeared. By 1980, the West Side's ghetto North Lawndale neighborhood included 48 state lottery agents, 50 currency exchanges, and 99 licensed bars and liquor stores, but only one bank and one supermarket for a population of some 50,000.

Soon the community becomes a place only to eat and sleep. Every other necessity demands traveling somewhere else. In many such places, the local motto might as well be that of the famous Los Angeles barrio where Cesar Chavez grew up: *Sal si puede.* Get out if you can.

In the next wave of urban decline, the blight creeps outward. Study after study, through only slightly different lenses, presents the same grim picture: Marginal communities between the slums and the suburbs gradually succumb to the creeping decay, victims of the centrifugal pull of skills and money toward the suburbs, and the slow gnaw of poor households spreading out from the core.

Those who remain in that core are increasingly likely to be the most desperate and immobile, stuck in irredeemable places for which even scholarly literature has no euphemisms. In 1997, 3.7 million people lived in these "ghetto-poverty neighborhoods," defined as places where more than 40 percent of the residents are poor. That designation fits, wrote Jargowsky and Mary Jo Bane in 1991, because the 40 percent threshold "comes very close to identifying areas that looked like ghettos in terms of their housing conditions" and "corresponded closely with the neighborhoods that city officials and local Census Bureau officials considered ghettos." The stark reality, summed up by Jargowsky: If all the ghettos so defined were laid side by side, they would constitute the largest city in the United States, at 8.4 million.

When the threshold for "poverty neighborhoods" is set at 20 percent living below the poverty line, instead of 40 percent, the population of such neighborhoods has risen steadily in recent decades. In 1970 less than half the urban poor lived in places that meet this description, but by 1990 the proportion had risen to two-thirds.

Marching outward from this core is the visible advance guard of poverty and expanding blight. Defined at the 20 percent threshold, there were 63 percent more poverty tracts in the 1990 Census than there had been two decades before. The number of "ghetto" or extreme-poverty neighborhoods, based on the 40 percent threshold, grew at an even more alarming rate: more than 160 percent.

The expansion of Milwaukee's ghetto over these years provides a dramatic illustration. The shading on the following map, drawn from a 1993 study by Douglas Massey and Nancy Denton, corresponds to the year in which the Census first counted more than 40 percent poverty in a given tract. The "borderline" tracts, it seems, are the ones most likely to become ghettos in the 2000 Census.

FIGURE 2.1   MILWAUKEE METROPOLITAN AREA GHETTO EXPANSION, 1970–90

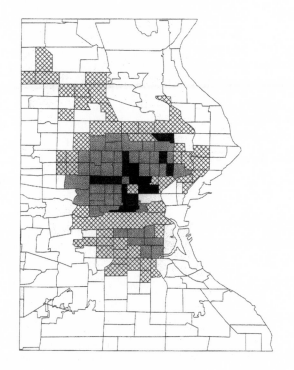

Year Census tracts first exceeded 40 percent poverty

☐ Never	▨ 1990	▨ 1980
■ 1970	▨ Borderline in 1990	

SOURCE: Census tract data for 1970–90. Paul A. Jargowsky, *Poverty and Place: Ghettos, Barrios, and the American City.* New York: Russell Sage Foundation, 1996, p. 53.

Nor have the city limits provided anything like the *cordon sanitaire* that the earliest suburbanites might have wished. A clear indicator that blight has escaped its urban quarantine is the sinking suburban property tax base, arguably the main vital sign of any locale. A mid-1990s study of the Chicago metro area found that no less than fifty-nine suburbs had a lower property tax base per household than the city itself.

As suburbs lose tax base, they face a difficult decision between lowering services or raising taxes, both of which create an incentive for families and businesses to move out. Thomas Bier, who has studied demographic changes like this in the Cleveland metro area for more than fifteen years, concludes that if nothing is done for inner-ring suburbs on the wane, "they're on their way to becoming the next slums. Urban problems will continue taking down suburb after suburb in a domino fashion."

The last and deadliest stroke is social implosion. The unrelieved isolation of the poorest communities leads, in this view, to social disintegration and deepening demands on public services (particularly health, social services, public safety, and sanitation)—from a city that no longer has the tax base to provide any of these services effectively. The resulting squalor further undermines social structures already unsettled by abandonment and unemployment.

Once again, Jackson captures the dynamic in a few sentences:

The cities were often caught in a reverse cycle. As businesses and taxpayers left, the demand for middle- to upper-income dwelling units in older neighborhoods declined. At the same time, population increases among low-income minorities, coupled with the demolition of inner-city housing for new expressways, produced an increase in demand for low-income housing. The new residents required more health care and social-welfare services from the city government than the old, but they were less able to pay for them. To increase expenditures, municipal authorities levied higher property taxes, thus encouraging middle-class homeowners to leave, causing the cycle to repeat. In contrast, suburbs were often able to keep their tax burdens low by having private trash collection, volunteer fire departments, and unpaid ambulance services. In particular, they benefited from having a small percentage of the population living at the poverty level and so requiring government assistance.

Based on extensive interviews with poor families, recounted in *When Work Disappears,* William Julius Wilson describes how the growth and persistence of unemployment in inner cities destabilized families, undermined marriage and child rearing, and deprived children of the necessary models of stability and work.

Earlier, in his 1987 book *The Truly Disadvantaged,* Wilson had already shown the effect of middle-class abandonment on inner-city communities. In that widely influential book, Wilson introduced the notion of middle-class residents as a "social buffer," cushioning the effects of economic downturns by sustaining local businesses, churches, and other mainstream institutions. As middle- and upper-income residents moved out of inner cities in large numbers, the lower-income households that remained had to contend with the business cycle and growing social problems with much more limited financial resources and social capital. The combination of high unemployment, an ever-weakening family structure, and a dearth of mainstream institutions meant that inner-city communities were ill equipped to combat the triple plague of crack cocaine, AIDS, and homelessness that exploded during the 1980s.

Nor, of course, were financially strapped city governments in any position to respond adequately where communities were flailing. The best that most of them could do was to apply a tourniquet of welfare and social services to hemorrhaging neighborhoods. And as state and federal social-service funding declined, first relatively and later absolutely, most cities gave up even on the tourniquet. In more and more places, the social unraveling proceeded freely all the way to the city limits, and then kept going.

❑

Anthony Downs of the Brookings Institution, an authority on urban issues for more than three decades, offers only faint hope to cities suffering these four agonies. Downs listed their consequences in a 1997 article, using terms that vary only minimally from those we have cited elsewhere: "high rates of crime and insecurity, poor-quality public schools, white resistance to living in racially mixed neighborhoods, and ineffective public bureaucracies." Of those, he believes, only the bureaucracies seem even remotely remediable. The rest, it seems, are past curing.

"Declining cities," Downs wrote, "cannot realistically count on any significant near-future increases in their middle-class populations (of any ethnic group) as a major means of improving their situations." And middle-class populations, Downs and virtually all the discouraged scholars agree, are the sine qua non of healthy neighborhoods.

One apparent hope—if not for the lost neighborhoods, then at least for their besieged cities—is regional consolidation, meaning in effect the annexation of the wealthier suburbs. David Rusk, in *Cities Without Suburbs*, reserves his optimism for "elastic" cities that manage to expand their boundaries into wealthier and less densely populated areas. But the slim political odds of such expansion seem more obvious to Downs. Since it would require a consensus among legislators and voters who are well served by the current system (at least in the short run), he regards annexation on any significant scale as a political dead letter. It's hard to disagree.

Nor do these writers leave much hope for community development—the kind of resident enterprise that transformed the South Bronx. Here, too, the most striking words of discouragement come from the least likely source: the head of a community-based financial institution in Philadelphia, Jeremy Nowak. Borrowing Rusk's premise that the only hope lies in harnessing the city's future to the wealth of its suburbs, Nowak in a 1997 article wrote that neighborhood-focused organizations are ill equipped to take advantage of the burgeoning regional economy. He even feels that the traditional approach to community development, which begins by renewing a neighborhood's housing stock, "can reinforce the segregation of the poor by building housing in the worst employment markets."

❑

The whole of these discouraging arguments is considerably more disquieting than the sum of the parts. It is grim enough—and no doubt as depressing to the scholars as it is to the reader—to argue that one tactic or another won't help, and that enterprising mayors and community leaders are wasting their time on this program or that strategy.

But taken together, these analyses make it hard to escape the conclusion that *no* strategy is effective, that the very existence of city survival plans is a dismal waste of paper, ink, and binding. It is hard to imagine any civilization—particularly one so intrepid as that of twentieth-century America—accepting such a fate for its economic and cultural capitals without demanding at least an honest fight.

Yet at least in academic circles, and not infrequently in the legal sausage-shops where federal and state policy are made, that is exactly what has happened. Hunched at the bedside of ailing cities, an incredible number of suburban and exurban politicians—along with an assortment of constituents and advisers—seem to have concluded with a shrug that the whole cause is miserably lost. More incredibly still, they apparently are persuaded that the urban demise *poses no danger or cost to those lucky masses who managed to escape.*

Impressive as all the scholarly augury is, it thus arrives at a conclusion that both offends the national character and defies observable evidence and common logic. It is compelling but wrong. For example: If a return of the middle classes is so indispensable to creating livable neighborhoods, then how is it that the South Bronx, with no appreciable increase in its median income, has managed to become livable again? Surely it's possible that poverty is not equivalent to blight, and that neighborhoods can improve without first becoming wealthier.

Beyond individual neighborhoods—for cities as a whole—are the population flows truly irreversible? Even if cities have lost more middle-income residents than they've gained, why are they gaining any? Is it possible that some households are coming back to cities for a reason other than mere folly? And if so, does it really matter that these residents don't constitute a majority? Something is drawing them back, and that something may have more potential than has yet been realized. Surely cities do not have to reclaim all their lost glory—all the population, density, economic mass, and social and political hegemony of the first half of this century—to remain livable and adapt to a new economy. If that's the standard of success, then everything's a failure.

This isn't the first time some scholarly stickum has been used to paste a collection of dark snapshots into a lifeless montage. Consider the death sentence pronounced on American downtowns in the 1960s, when suburban shopping centers started siphoning business from central commercial districts, leaving acres of vacant retail space behind. For nearly twenty years, a somber column of urban economists paid last respects to downtown Philadelphia, Cleveland, Indianapolis, Boston, and Chicago, writing off as lost the places that once had been the cultural and economic centers of giant metropolitan areas.

Now fast-forward three decades or so, and thread your way among the new skyscrapers of downtown Cleveland, to get to the trendy restaurants lining the once-flammable Cuyahoga River. In downtown Boston, where parking is at a premium, the city's "Big Dig" is burying a whole interstate highway to create more room for development and public amenities. Even in central Philadelphia—which, like the others, is hardly without its problems—new office towers, renovated historic homes, museums, theaters, and strips of outdoor cafés attract people from all over the region and beyond.

These downtowns no longer stand alone as the center of all significant commercial and cultural activity in their regions. Nor is the real estate in all these areas yet fully put to its highest and best use (in fact, the accelerating conversion of downtown office space to apartments shows that a new "best use" is still emerging—and drawing robust demand). There are vacancies and patches of blight. But whatever their challenges, these places are neither dead nor dying. They are, in some cases, shrinking to more sustainable densities and a higher ratio of residential to commercial uses. But those are signs of adaptability, not decline. These downtowns survived and prospered not by remaining what they were, but—like all successful enterprises—by adapting to new circumstances and markets.

The renaissance isn't universal, of course. The point is not that downtowns or urban neighborhoods are indestructible—obviously. The point is that they are not necessarily foredoomed either, and plenty of downtowns have proved their crêpe-hangers dead wrong. Like the Bronx, many of these places needed a couple of decades to regain their stability and discover new markets. Cleveland, perhaps the most remarkable of the success stories, took between ten and fifteen years to create a visible, self-sustaining recovery.

In time, places and local economies are adaptable, with the right governance and timely investment. A dead place is not a historic inevitability, it is someone's failure. A living place is someone's success. These are matters of choice and skill, not laws of physics.

❑

None of the conclusions presented here, neither bullish nor bearish, has yet been proven. The evidence is by no means obvious, widely known, or beyond debate. The signs of urban vitality don't answer every objection conclusively, nor do they impress every observer (as the Ford Foundation discovered to its chagrin when it invited the *New Republic* on its tour). But there is more than a decent chance that these signs contain the elements of a solution to urban decline—a decline that, left undeterred, will ultimately spare almost no one. Before reaching the radical conclusion that American cities are beyond saving, it would be worthwhile to look again at the places that seem to be, if not saved, at least durable enough to survive the hard decades just past, and to build communities that will survive those ahead.

Chapter 3

A SURPRISING CONVERGENCE OF POSITIVES

IN LIGHT of all the dark forces pressing on American cities, it's certainly possible, and in some circles almost mandatory, to shrug off the most dramatic urban success stories as somehow beside the point. The conventional response is to salute these communities for their pluck in the face of disaster, but then essentially to enclose them in brackets as weird exceptions that somehow prove a grimmer rule—aberrations of government profligacy, perhaps, or the irrelevant quirks of a few exceptional markets.

A typical response to the transformation of the South Bronx, for example—or for that matter, to any of New York City's dozens of neighborhood recoveries—is that it's all an artifact of Mayor Ed Koch's massive, and partially court-induced, investment in housing in the 1980s. That is an extravagance of which, supposedly, few other cities would be capable. (There is a curious revisionism in this image of 1980s New York as a kind of municipal Daddy Warbucks, given that New York City in those years was still rebounding from a spell of near-bankruptcy. But leave that aside.)

The temptation to treat recovering neighborhoods as just an asterisk in a great urban Decline and Fall is hard to resist. There's no denying the intellectual integrity of the grimmer diagnoses. As a purely descriptive matter—leaving aside, for a moment, the question of prognosis—the academics probably have it about right. Things are not bright on the inner-city horizon, any more than they were on the downtown landscape of twenty years ago. So how *do* we reconcile the story of the South Bronx with the encyclopedia of urban gloom that the last chapter summarized?

Although the grassroots commandos of the Bronx and its counterparts apparently weren't deterred by the daunting odds they faced as they tried to rebuild, maybe they should have been. Everything they achieved was in the teeth of disappearing jobs and markets, the scourge of drugs and drug-related crime, and the corrosive effects of monolithic systems of welfare, public housing, and public schools. And although their work made these problems more visible, and therefore focused more critical attention on them, neighborhood groups could not "build" their way around these forces, or leverage some market dynamic that would magically make them disappear.

Consequently, since the 1960s, the conventional wisdom has held that cities would continue to empty out, hemorrhaging both people and jobs to the suburbs and beyond, specifically to avoid these blights. These generation-old movements have only drawn new impetus from the computer and communications revolution, which in the view of people like Microsoft founder Bill Gates will continue to erode the historic economic rationale for cities.

Yet without minimizing any of those sober realities, it is more than possible to conclude that an inner-city renaissance in America is eminently achievable, with incalculable benefits to the nation. In fact, the outlines of this turnaround are already visible in what once was an unrelieved wasteland of desolate neighborhoods and rotting downtowns. Growing populations, block after block of new and refurbished housing, and the awakening of long-dormant markets describe the strongest of these emerging areas. If they are asterisks, there are enough of them by now to qualify as a constellation.

Among these, the South Bronx is unique only in a couple of respects: It was among the worst, and surely the most famous, of the allegedly irredeemable slums of the 1970s; and it was among the earliest to get the kind of attention and public imagination that a lasting recovery demands. So it's distinctive for long odds and a historic head start, but otherwise it's just one story among hundreds.

Much of this revitalization, as in the South Bronx, is the work of an army of self-help renewal efforts that grew up in the 1970s and '80s and by now are reaching critical mass in many cities. By themselves, these indigenous attempts at renewal have some beneficial social consequences, but they probably wouldn't stand a chance of changing the complete economic landscape of their neighborhoods, much less those of the city as a whole.

Indeed, for much of the recent past, the results of local community development were hemmed in by extreme countervailing forces, some of which were described in the last chapter—forces well beyond the reach of even the most effective local rejuvenation programs. Though most or even all of these negative forces are still at play and working their ill effects in many places, startling changes are unmistakably afoot. After a long decline, markets are reviving in many neighborhoods far from—and far different from—the South Bronx. And most important, they'll continue to do so, if aided by sound public policy and strategic public and private investment. It's a big *if*, granted. But it's also a far cry from the inevitable collapse that the conventional wisdom seems to expect.

❑

Take just one of these forces, one that seemed not long ago among the most inexorable signs not just of urban collapse, but of social failure on a national scale. Until very recently, orthodox opinion was that little could be done about crime, particularly the drug-related variety, in city neighborhoods. If anything, the growing percentage of American children living in poverty and reared in single-parent households, more and more often with parents too young and unprepared for child-rearing, seemed to portend unending escalation of an already desperate situation.

Yet contrary to all expectations, crime—particularly violent crime— is dropping spectacularly in many cities—including places that were supposedly among the graveyards of urban civilization. But the cities experiencing the most dramatic declines did so by more than merely participating in some national demographic or cultural zeitgeist. They are, in fact, the same cities that pioneered revolutionary community policing and criminal justice strategies that could be studied, evaluated, and widely emulated. And sure enough, as these tactics are replicated elsewhere, crime rates have steepened their decline. In New York and Boston, cities that devised some of the most innovative policing strategies, the results have been truly breathtaking. Overall, crime was down 44 percent in New York between 1993 and 1997, with murder down 56 percent and robberies cut in half. Violent crime has plunged a stunning 80 percent in Boston since 1990.

The components of the new policing strategy in these cities are strong community cooperation, relentless tracking of crime patterns, and less tolerance of the so-called "quality of life" crimes that fray the social fabric. They are painstakingly local, responsive to neighborhood patterns and needs, and accountable for outcomes on a level of detail practically unheard-of in public management.

Ironically, in its belief that little things lead to big things and that even modest positive results build morale and momentum for the future, the new orthodoxy of law enforcement is unwittingly reflective of the best grassroots community developers. In that sense, the new policing could converge powerfully with grassroots revitalization— and in a few places is already doing so—to create communities that, even if still poor, display the attributes of safety and order that are indispensable to social stability and commerce.

Progress against crime has brought a hitherto unimaginable tranquillity and civil order to residential communities that were in utter chaos only a brief time ago. There is no more important factor in a neighborhood's long-term viability than that. And there, in a great many places once written off for lost, the trend is positive.

❑

City governments that can fight crime and preserve order have gone a long way toward fulfilling their most important (or at least most visible) responsibility. But the recent successes, happily, are part of a much broader improvement in municipal government in many major cities. Indeed, an extraordinary group of mayors are receiving deserved national acclaim for pragmatism and break-the-mold policies in the privatization of city services, education, and economic development, as well as public safety.

Similarly, until just a few years ago, the big public-sector systems virtually identified with inner-city life were changing glacially if at all. Until a patchwork version of welfare reform took effect in 1996, the vast, grinding system of intergenerational entitlement, with its presumption that "clients" would be forever dependent on its subsistence handouts, seemed able to withstand an almost boundless public opposition.

But in what constitutes nothing less than the deregulation of the American inner city, these hidebound systems in the 1990s have finally started coming unglued. Welfare "as we knew it" has been ended by legislation and will be ended by events within a few years, as residents and their local governments develop new ways of dealing with poverty outside the rigid template of a federal entitlement. Next, the federal government, in rare bipartisan consensus, launched a process that will reengineer virtually all inner-city high-rise public housing into attractive, architecturally appropriate, mixed-income communities. This reengineering will be, in some ways, even more complicated than welfare reform, and will surely take at least as long. But its effect on recovering neighborhoods will be every bit as great.

Like traditional welfare programs, public housing for decades had isolated the poorest of the poor in a gulag of ghettos-within-ghettos, cut off from work and any other meaningful participation in mainstream life. Public housing is actually a success story in most of small-town and rural America. Only in the high-rise "vertical slums" of most major cities had government-owned homes and apartments been an unmixed disaster for a generation. But beginning in 1997, more than 100,000 units of blighted public housing were finally being replaced in what actually amounts to a kind of "Marshall Plan" for cities that the Great Society never was. If the change is followed through, the result will be not an abandonment of federal investment in housing (the solution normally advanced in the 1980s and early '90s), but an end to the heavy-handed, cookie-cutter federal control that turned housing into a blight on the very communities it was meant to help.

This undertaking, massive though it is, will still not ease the very serious shortage of affordable housing for the poor. But it will open the possibility of incorporating public housing residents into the broader community instead of isolating them from it. Further, it will open public housing's "turf" for the first time to the beneficial influences of surrounding revitalization.

But of all these public behemoths, the schools have always been the most awesome and the most awful. Protected by the impregnable alliance of teachers' unions, elected officials, and the American civic faith in government-run education, urban public schools have been the system that was both the most necessary to change and the most resistant to change.

Despite many remarkable individual schools sprinkled in cities across America, the big-city school systems as a whole are ossified, unresponsive, and indifferent. Because of them, upwardly mobile working families—immigrants and indigenous minorities alike—continue to depart city neighborhoods. In recent years, many immigrants have even come to leapfrog urban neighborhoods altogether, with large numbers settling directly in suburbs for the first time in American history.

Until very recently the immune systems of public education monopolies were intact. But reforms are gathering speed. A few mayors—notably Thomas Menino of Boston, Richard Daley of Chicago, and Michael White of Cleveland—realizing that the failure of the schools is propelling their working and middle classes out, are moving to take over the schools to demand accountability and performance.

From within the public schools, the charter school movement, though still small, is rapidly growing. More than thirty states have passed enabling legislation for charter schools—essentially self-governing institutions within the public school system, accountable for results but free of most of the bureaucratic restrictions that bind other schools. Many more such laws are pending. As of this writing more than 1,700 charter schools are in operation, offering new choices to restless parents within the public school framework. And from without, a relentless pressure is mounting from a host of privatization schemes. It seems, even at this early moment, that we will look back on the turn of this century as the time when the urban public school monopoly came undone.

These cracks in the public monopolies—in welfare, in public housing, and in education—are critical because the combined effects of these systems worked powerfully to concentrate poverty and related social turmoil in the inner city. But if they can in fact be dismantled, or even shaken into some kind of internal reform, the opportunities that would open up for reengineering and rebuilding cities are practically immeasurable. Beginning with those cities' most troubled neighborhoods.

❑

Moribund markets, drugs, crime, and public institutional monopolies have been the great "fixed negatives" of inner cities for more than a generation. That neighborhood development groups have been able to achieve so much without being able to alter these fundamentally adverse conditions does make their accomplishments seem miraculous. Plenty of other observers had concluded that neighborhood revitalization efforts, however praiseworthy, would forever be fatally limited by the overwhelming force of these negatives. Loyola University of Chicago Professor Robert Halpern, for example, writes in his book *Rebuilding the Inner City* that "even the most sensible policies, practices, and investments, if limited to local reform or community renewal, will have only marginal impact without attention to societal context."

Sure enough, the continuing negative context for inner-city revival efforts did lead to a kind of "oasis" strategy, in which community development corporations and others managed to carve out areas of revitalization and relative stability while the forces that would undo their fragile improvements crouched just outside the door. But the limits of that strategy are all too obvious. More far-reaching and sustainable change would depend on these fixed negatives becoming not so fixed, and that is an order too tall for any neighborhood group to fill.

Fortunately, though, in ways almost wholly unforeseen, inner-city markets are stirring, crime is plunging, and the public systems of welfare, housing, and schools are in fact undergoing wrenching change. We will look more closely at the causes and consequences of these changes in later chapters. But even a quick survey at the outset suggests that what strikes some observers as an inexorable decline in urban life is actually anything but. The very factors that seemed to form impregnable barriers to recovery are slowly but visibly beginning to crack.

❑

If we affirm, for the moment, the still-unproven hypothesis that the renaissance of the South Bronx can now be repeated and expanded beyond what once seemed immovable limits, what kind of renaissance are we talking about?

Here is what we are not talking about: This is not a story about the end of poverty and social tensions in America. Even after the revitalization of poor and blighted neighborhoods, very wide income disparities between city and suburbs will probably persist indefinitely, and substantial racial segregation and isolation will continue. To some, no doubt, that fact alone makes the renaissance we are describing one not worth pursuing. To that, our answer takes the form of a question: Which South Bronx would we rather have? The 1977 version or the 1997 version?

Today, replacing bombed-out landscapes are communities where people may still be poorer than their suburban neighbors, but where they are well housed, where functioning private markets are restored, public services and public investment have reappeared, crime has gone down and stayed at tolerable levels, and a lively civic realm has reemerged. And less tangibly but no less crucially, hope begins to compete with despair.

"A sense of possibility," Randall Kennedy of the Harvard Law School wrote in the late 1990s, "is essential nourishment for any political endeavor." In neighborhoods that have had a few years' experience in rebuilding and solving local problems, that sense of possibility is reappearing, and it is making possible a much wider transformation than seemed even remotely possible when the prevailing attitudes were resignation and cynicism.

What changed the attitudes, and therefore the odds, was neighbors' firsthand experience of rebuilding. This is only part of the story of how these communities came back from the brink, but it is too often overlooked, discounted, or forgotten. The instigators of the Bronx miracle were the residents themselves, who formed grassroots groups out of block clubs and churches. Most of these groups, typically called community development corporations, or CDCs, began forming in the mid- to late 1970s—at the lowest point, when the advanced processes of depopulation, disinvestment, and city neglect had put their neighborhoods in extremis.

The idea was admittedly implausible: Could a ragtag band of neighborhood groups make headway against the implacable forces then at work in the cities? Even sympathetic observers termed their first, scattered successes anecdotal or cosmetic. But the groups persevered, scrounging seed capital from a few foundations, and began executing a string of house-by-house, block-by-block victories: renovating homes and commercial strips, rousting drug dealers, and haranguing city officials into restoring some level of public services.

Fifteen years later community development corporations—because of their tenacity, resolve, and results—have won for themselves an armada of support from philanthropy, the private sector, and government at all levels. The unambiguous good news for America is that the community development phenomenon has spread like wildfire. More than 2,500 CDCs are now at work, producing a dizzying variety of redevelopment activity. Since 1994, grassroots organizations have built or renovated between 40,000 and 50,000 homes and apartments per year, virtually all in the most damaged inner-city neighborhoods.

As a result, the new life has spread from the Bronx to Harlem, where a huge residential and commercial revival is under way, and to more than a dozen of New York's most beleaguered neighborhoods. Similar metamorphoses have taken place in many of the nation's former "riot corridors," including Linwood-Prospect in Kansas City, the Hough section of Cleveland, and the Central Ward of Newark, among many others.

Like the South Bronx, these were not "marginal" areas that simply needed a little investment, a few years of generalized economic growth, and some political TLC to make a comeback. In the early 1980s the producers of a made-for-TV movie, *The Day After,* were looking for a location that most resembled the aftermath of a nuclear bombing. They found it at the intersection of Linwood and Prospect

Boulevards in Kansas City, in the African-American heart of that segregated city. Now, after more than fifteen years of steady effort, the CDC of Kansas City has produced two major shopping centers there, built more than 300 homes, a library, and a senior center, and in all created a bustling, thriving, urban crossroad, remarkable only to those who remember the wasteland that came before.

Seven days of rioting in 1966 left the Hough neighborhood, on the east side of Cleveland, a physical, economic, and social ruin. Although the ravages of that time certainly have not vanished, CDCs and private developers have built 2,400 homes in Hough just since 1990, many on vacant lots obtained from the city for a token price. Block after block has come back, and now even some luxury homes are starting to appear—selling briskly at prices well above the median home-sale price for Cleveland as a whole.

Newark's Central Ward, likewise gutted by riots in 1967, has been the site of an amazing turnaround led by the New Community Corporation. Founded a year after the riots by a Catholic priest, Father Bill Linder, this CDC has developed and financed more than 3,000 homes and apartments and a supermarket-anchored shopping center. The programs and services its 1,500 employees provide touch 25,000 people per day. It operates several day care centers, a job training and placement center, an elementary school, a nursing home, a newspaper, a restaurant, and a credit union with more than $2.7 million in assets.

Most telling of all, New Community is no longer carrying the load alone. Private developers are now building market-rate housing on adjoining blocks. What the community organization created was not just a string of successful "projects" for its residents to take pride in. It created a market, in which other enterprises found ways of adding value, making money, and widening the recovery in ways that needed little or no civic or philanthropic prodding.

These community organizations and their achievements are just part of the far broader and more complicated machinery of urban recovery. But they are emblematic of a national revitalization movement where prodigious housing production is attracting (mostly minority) returnees from the suburbs, as well as new immigrants.

Census and housing data show newly robust home ownership markets arising in formerly abandoned sections of cities like Houston,

Philadelphia, and Detroit, where cleared land can sometimes accommodate whole new suburban-style subdivisions at once. In nearly every case, the advance guard of this activity was the neighborhood-based community development corporation.

Still, for these scattered accomplishments to reach the scale necessary to turn whole neighborhoods and cities around, there eventually must follow a significant level of new public and private investment. To catalyze that kind of investment, federal tax credits and flexible "block grants" to cities are working far more effectively than the old top-down government programs. These credits and grants, along with federal regulations that prod banks to lend, have triggered a flood of private capital for both neighborhood-based projects and the for-profit, market-driven developments that tend to follow.

❑

In 1996 alone commercial banks made $18 billion in inner-city loans for a range of affordable housing, small business, and commercial loans. The speed of bank commitments to cities is clearly on the rise. In 1998, President Clinton and Treasury Secretary Robert Rubin pointed out that, in the previous four years, bank pledges to inner cities under the Community Reinvestment Act had amounted to a staggering $355 billion, more than 89 percent of all loan pledges made under the CRA over its twenty-year life.

Importantly, the major banks decided somewhere along the way that lending in redeveloping neighborhoods made economic sense. Don Mullane, then an executive vice president at Bank of America, spoke for many by saying in 1998 that "the CRA is both profitable and smart business." The national home ownership rate reached an all-time high of 66 percent in 1997, with minorities accounting for fully one-third of new home owners. Since 1993 home mortgage lending for blacks was up 67.2 percent and for Hispanics 48.5 percent in an overall market where home lending rose only 18 percent.

Not all these loans were in disadvantaged neighborhoods, obviously. But what's significant about them is that they show a sudden, dramatic expansion of private lending and investment into markets that for decades had been starved for capital. The potential of this new activity to fuel investment in all sorts of neighborhoods—including the toughest ones—is just now becoming clear. The effect on redeveloping neighborhoods is already dramatic, and it's still nowhere near its limit.

All of this capital was surely playing a role in enticing people of means either to stay in or return to some inner-city neighborhoods. *USA Today,* after analyzing unpublished Census data through 1996, disclosed that fully half of the growing number of black families earning more than $75,000 per year were choosing to live in the cities. "In a trend that is defying predictions made in the 1980s," the newspaper reported, "professional and middle-class blacks are snubbing the suburbs and leading a new gentrification movement in cities across the nation."

❑

All of this is good news, especially for individual neighborhoods that no longer see the future as a slow march to extinction. But is it enough to describe a broad-based urban recovery? Not nearly. Good housing is crucial to stable families and viable neighborhoods, but it won't take the incipient inner-city recovery to completion. Creating jobs, reducing crime, and reforming moribund public systems will.

On the other hand, the unfolding inner-city housing resurgence is highly relevant to the most important task, that of restoring markets and jobs. A 1997 study of New York City's massive ten-year housing program showed that residential investment has a huge economic multiplier, whose most visible payoff has been a rising demand for retail services. Major supermarkets and other retail stores departed the inner city fifteen to twenty years ago. Today, they are starting to return, driven by slow growth and hyper-competition in the suburbs and the lure of an immense underserved population.

Michael Porter of Harvard Business School estimates that inner-city households, despite lower average incomes, still possess between $85 billion and $100 billion of annual retail spending power, larger than Mexico's entire retail economy. Fully one-third of this demand is unmet because of the paucity of supermarkets, department stores, and pharmacies in the areas where poor families live. Yet the density of these neighborhoods means that the total disposable income there is considerable, even if each separate income is individually low. The arithmetic of this is fairly obvious. But until recently, the economic implications apparently weren't.

The lightbulb is going on for some in the private sector. The Food Marketing Institute, the leading food industry trade association, identifies the inner city as the growth opportunity of the future. Some major supermarket chains like Finast in Ohio and Pathmark in the Northeast have already committed themselves to major multistore urban expansions, and they are being joined by pharmacy chains like Walgreen's and Rite Aid. When stores open in these neighborhoods, they turn out to be wildly profitable, not just because of population density, but because at this point, at least, they face little competition. Fifty thousand people per month shop at the Pathmark supermarket in Newark's Central Ward. That makes it one of the chain's highest grossing stores.

New stores are, in and of themselves, hugely beneficial to these neighborhoods. They make shopping easier, and they demonstrate to residents and other potential investors that someone has confidence in the neighborhood's economic potential. But apart from its effect on the neighborhood's image and quality of life, successful retail is also a potent and accessible job generator. A big supermarket creates 150 to 200 permanent jobs with benefits and opportunities for advancement, and these jobs can be captured by people who live nearby. In addition, supermarkets and other retail clusters attract traffic and therefore opportunity for franchises and other local business to sprout and multiply.

Clearly, retail expansion isn't enough by itself to fuel a recovery, but it is a ready, untapped opportunity for cities, and it builds naturally on the platform of housing. It also creates important connections between the mainstream economy and isolated communities. For neighborhoods that have had no business investment for years, it's essential to start somewhere, and that start needs to be quickly, visibly successful. More and more, retail is proving that it fits that immediate need, and can lead to business investments of other kinds.

❑

Reviving markets, falling crime rates, and deregulating public systems open vistas for the inner city not seen in nearly fifty years, before the great postwar exodus and decline. These new trends can converge powerfully with the now extensive grassroots revival efforts to engineer far-reaching change in our inner-city environments. We use the word "engineer" advisedly, because the newly favorable prospects have largely been produced by human endeavor rather than some economic or political deus ex machina.

We turn now to a more detailed examination of the elements that are coming together to unlock the potential of the inner city. We will conclude with a more speculative rumination on what further changes in policies and practices could accelerate this revival.

Major retailers vie for prime locations on Harlem's booming commercial strips. (Eli Reed/Magnum Photos, Inc. ©1999)

PART TWO

The Grassroots Revival

B Y THE MID-1990s, evidence was mounting that the rebirth of the South Bronx was anything but sui generis. The instances of grassroots revival had become so plentiful in so many regions and types of cities, that even the mainstream media paused briefly in their obsession with partisan politics in Washington to take some notice.

David Broder, acclaimed syndicated columnist for the *Washington Post*, wrote in April 1997:

> It appears that the several thousand reporters who descended on last summer's Democratic National Convention [in Chicago]—me among them—missed a big story that was under our noses. ... All around the United Center are signs of revival in a once-blighted neighborhood— freshly painted houses, a new park and library, start-up small businesses. And similar locally led neighborhood revival efforts are beginning to halt the downward cycle in many cities and offer a brighter future for their residents.

Earlier that year, under the headline "Good News," a long article in the *Atlantic Monthly* by historian Alexander Von Hoffman proclaimed that "from Boston to San Francisco the community-based housing movement is transforming bad neighborhoods. ... There is new life at the ground zeroes of urban America." *Business Week* chimed in: "These days, something remarkable is happening in Washington Park [Chicago], as it is in small corners of Los Angeles, Cleveland, Boston, and other cities. ... Think of the power of a thousand Washington Parks ... each renewing a neighborhood block by block. ... Block by block, cities could become places people want to live in once more." The *Boston Globe* in a 1998 editorial accorded community development corporations a special place in the largely disappointing array of post–World War II antipoverty efforts: "Many initiatives of the 1960s, like community control of schools, rated high in rhetoric and low on results. Community development corporations, however, exceeded their promise."

More and more in the mainstream press, the stories of remarkable urban comebacks were being associated with these obscure little outfits with the wonky-sounding name: Community development corporations, said story after story, are behind the stunning turnaround of places long ago written off and forgotten.

This section describes how that happened, drawing from a wide sampling of cities and neighborhoods. It pieces together a picture of physical and social turnaround engineered by no central authority, foreseen by no master plan, but created piecemeal by the independent effort of tens of thousands of people who had a hunch they could do something that decades of credentialed experts could not.

Chapter 4

"WE CAN SURE AS HELL DO BETTER THAN *THIS*"

THE FIRST community development corporations had begun to appear in the late 1960s, springing from organizing efforts and from church and block-level activism in depressed urban and rural areas. Among the first, and certainly the most celebrated, was Brooklyn's Bedford-Stuyvesant Restoration Corporation, though that prototype had loftier beginnings than any of the ones that followed. It was the brainchild of then-Senator Robert F. Kennedy, and was piloted in its formative years by an elite board of *Fortune* 500 CEOs. Its founding executive director, Franklin A. Thomas, had been a top aide to then-Mayor John Lindsay. Just over a decade later, Thomas's next career move was to the president's suite at the Ford Foundation.

Most CDCs have nowhere near that kind of marquee sponsorship. Most, in fact, had to stumble through early years of inexpert planning and amateur leadership—which for many of them meant that they were beholden to no established way of thinking about problems, and hidebound by none of the rigidities of the established bureaucracy. After ten or twenty years of "professional" urban renewal, most neighborhoods were ready for a creative dose of inexpert leadership. And the results—as we shall see momentarily—frequently defied the received wisdom about what was possible in poor neighborhoods.

In some cases, it must be said, the haphazard origins of some grassroots groups led in the 1960s and '70s to widely publicized problems: bungled politics, ideological excesses, fiscal and legal mismanagement, political patronage, and now and then, outright criminality. This was particularly true in the late, sputtering years of the War on Poverty, when some proto-CDCs (really just community advocacy and social service groups, at that point) found themselves inundated with federal dollars they had neither the skill nor the organizational strength to use wisely. In the run-up to that period, in the 1950s and '60s, radical community organizers like Chicagoan Saul Alinsky had trained many of these groups to spend their energies antagonizing and demonizing City Hall. Radical black nationalists and other militants took the confrontation a step further, organizing communities more to threaten the local "power structure" with violence or political upheaval than to negotiate practical solutions.

The community organizing and planning of that period was soon squandered on divisive or extremist political tactics, including the in-your-face style of protest that Tom Wolfe famously dubbed "mau-mauing." Flush with money and new political cachet, inexperienced community groups became ripe fruit for enterprising racial demagogues, who deftly hijacked many of the more prominent community action programs for their own ends. With federal imprimatur from the Johnson administration's Poverty Warriors, many of these groups found themselves demanding "control" over local government agencies and expenditures, and threatening violence if they didn't get their way. The aftertaste of this form of "community action"—utterly alien to most of today's community *development* groups—nonetheless lingers for some politicians and business leaders who would otherwise make enthusiastic allies. To be sure, every so often community groups still turn up with all the earmarks of what Fred Siegel, in *The Future Once Happened Here,* calls the "riot ideology": racial demagoguery, demands for patronage, hints of unrest if demands aren't met, a preference for confrontation over visible results. And some politicians remain oddly susceptible to this sort of saber-rattling. But today, fortunately, the old-style "mau-mau" operations normally stand out in bright contrast to the productive mainstream of community developers. And as we describe later in this chapter, CDCs are becoming more and more effective at driving out these exploitive imitators.

Yet even these missteps of the "community action" years gave many poor neighborhoods their first taste of common effort and political assertiveness. When true CDCs emerged in force, after the War on Poverty's gravy train had stalled, that early sense of organized strength was still alive. Many veterans of the "community action" programs of the 1960s and '70s, exhausted by the antagonisms and fruitless turmoil, were more than ready to turn their newfound community-organizing talents to some practical redevelopment *projects*. From that rethinking and regrouping—which started with the likes of Robert Kennedy and Frank Thomas, but soon engulfed a whole generation of ordinary city dwellers—the idea of the modern community development corporation was born.

Most of today's actual CDCs were formed long after the whole tumultuous "community action" episode was over, and many of them can scarcely imagine what all the fuss was about. They now make up a wide variety of citizen-formed self-help groups trying to revitalize their own neighborhoods or towns, in close league with local governments, businesses, churches, and other branches of the "establishment" their predecessors had so reviled. But that's not to say that they don't continue to emerge from a spirit of protest or dissatisfaction. Quite the contrary—most CDCs start precisely because residents become fed up with the failure of "normal channels" to address their problems, and begin looking for a way to change things on their own. The difference is that, nowadays, "changing things" means seeking investment, developing or renovating property, building on assets, and generally drawing power and capital *in* to the community, rather than scaring it away.

Sometimes a particular crisis ignites one of these groups—an upsurge in housing abandonment or drug traffic, say—or people may be mobilized by an act of government, like a plan to place an undesirable facility next door. That's what galvanized Juanita Tate in South Central Los Angeles in 1985: the city's intent to build a large trash incinerator at 41st Street and Long Beach Avenue. Tate, a fiftyish retired Pacific Bell clerk, and neighbors she recruited to the cause managed to stop the city cold. But then, surveying the economic and social catastrophe of South Central (now spared the incinerator), Tate said to her cohorts: "Well, we stopped something. Now can we build something?"

She and others subsequently answered the question by forming Concerned Citizens of South Central, a CDC that in turn organized and maintains more than fifty block clubs, built 139 units of housing, is embarking on a new supermarket-anchored shopping center, and has a deal with the DreamWorks SKG studio for a comprehensive job training and placement program focused on getting Los Angeles kids into the film industry.

Juanita Tate's story is vitally important in South Central LA's slow but measurable return to social and economic health. But the story is not important in the obvious way. The national explosion in the number and accomplishments of CDCs—and the friendly media attention they are lately attracting—may be an inspiring example of American pluck and communitarianism, as most commentators warmly point out. But that is not what's most important about them. The quirky sentimental details about "little people" fighting City Hall and neighbors finding common interests all make good feature stories, but they obscure a more fundamental fact that makes these institutions hugely significant for the next generation of American urban policy. CDCs in effect answer the question, "if government on its own has repeatedly failed to save inner cities, who can save them?"

Long dismissed as merely amateur beautification schemes, the best CDCs are actually a way for ordinary people to change, create, and make use of market forces to alter the fundamental economics of their neighborhoods. They are to urban development what start-up companies and new technologies are to the business world: a channel through which individual energies and ingenuity tap and transform the wider market. CDCs are, as a result, far more ambitious, versatile, and responsive to market changes than government on its own can ever be. Yet like government, they pursue common, not individual, wealth, and they leverage common assets (like vacant land, underused streets and parks, and the labor and leadership of their members). With government support, and a minimum of regulation, they are among the most effective vehicles for public investment in the inner city. And in many places they are the only vehicles.

Admittedly, they don't usually start with talk about assets and markets. Many inner-city residents are moved to start CDCs just by a general sense that things are going downhill. Describing the birth of the Mid-Bronx Desperadoes (which today is a sizable real-estate empire with an appropriately pinstripe name: MBD Development Corp.), current CEO Ralph Porter said "CDCs come from people sitting around on the stoops, saying, 'man, we got to do something about this. ... '" Many begin simply with an outraged assessment of what other people—principally governments—have done in their community, and a reasonable conclusion that, as one volunteer put it, "whoever we are and whatever we got, we can sure as hell do better than *this*."

Yet however broad the discontent that gives rise to them, CDCs generally grow in response to highly specific, concrete, and local conditions. Their focus is most often on physical structures and tangible assets that are either derelict or misused. Because they are not prone, like governments, to unveiling master plans that purport to solve vast problems in a stroke, they start more often as businesses do, with one product or service that solves one problem. As successes build credibility, experience, and revenue, their efforts expand and begin to influence the behavior of other market players. Only then are they beginning to swing whole markets.

That process may take five or ten years, maybe more (in the South Bronx, it took close to fifteen). Because their projects are designed for public benefit and not fast profits, they require sustained support from government and philanthropy. For large and ambitious CDCs, the total of these grants over the years can be large (though the bill is tiny compared to what it would cost government to do the same work, and to fail in the process).

In short, conditions have to be right for CDCs to grow—including sustained public investment and patient, persistent neighborhood leadership. But after three decades of organizing, growing, and multiplying, many CDCs have found or created those conditions, and now are at the advanced stage. In some cities, including Boston, New York, and Chicago, large, livable sections of the city would today still be in ruins without them. Yet even now, they are more often noticed for their humble origins and folksy style than for their strength as economic and social forces, or for their mounting collective importance as a distinctive industry.

Nevertheless, an industry they are—numbering more than 3,600 groups. Although more numerous in the large cities of the Northeast and Midwest where the first CDCs began, the groups now cover the nation. Ninety-five percent of the 133 largest cities in the United States now have at least one active CDC.

It took some community organizations a while to discover how effective they could be, and the power of the market forces open to their influence. In the first generation, in the 1960s and '70s, many CDCs spent years trying to be bulwarks *against* local housing and retail markets—organizing residents to oppose private investment, and seeking to preserve local concentrations of poverty (in the name of maintaining affordability) rather than developing integrated communities where profit and subsidies could coexist.

But in the past twenty years or so, those ideological impulses have worn thin in most places, and communities have learned to use markets to their advantage—by buying and developing property themselves, encouraging compatible private investment, and forming mutually beneficial alliances with businesses and government. In the process, CDCs have become prodigious producers of housing: By 1988 they were turning out more than 20,000 affordable houses and apartments every year, and by 1994 that number had risen above 40,000—a number that eclipses the federal government's total output at the apex of the public housing program. A further surge of production erupted between 1994 and 1997, as CDCs generated 247,000 new and rehabilitated houses.

This rapid evolution of CDCs from market foes to market players soon began turning heads even in top financial circles. In a speech in Chicago in October 1997, Federal Reserve Governor Laurence H. Meyer said, "There has been an explosive growth in the diversity and sophistication of community development organizations. ...Today, there is a quite identifiable community development industry, complete with a diverse set of production companies, financial intermediaries, and other support mechanisms."

It's worth noting that CDCs reached these production levels in spite of the constricted federal budget climate of the last fifteen years. How do they do it? They offer, it turns out, an instructive counterpoint to the disappointing results of Washington's large-scale housing development programs of the 1960s and early 1970s.

To begin with, CDCs aren't creatures of any single federal program, and thus aren't easily whipped about by Washington's annual bureaucratic intrigues and fiscal storms. They draw from many sources of money to accomplish multiple ends: Their purpose is not just to produce housing, but to produce housing as a catalytic and integrated element of overall community renewal. They start with housing because houses are *there,* often abandoned, usually cheap, and nearly always contributing to an overall physical blight. But unlike typical housing developers and most federal housing programs, CDCs integrate their development of affordable housing with any number of other public services and improvements beyond bricks and mortar.

They succeed at this blending-and-diversifying strategy for four primary reasons. First, they are true public-private hybrids, responsible both for the productive husbanding of resources and for pursuing a social mission that keeps them going. They use bank loans and corporate equity investment to feed inner-city development with private capital alongside public grants. Private investors increasingly rely on CDCs to channel and monitor their investments—especially when those investments trigger complex and tightly regulated federal tax credits—and to handle the sometimes distasteful work of brokering deals with government. Meanwhile, community residents, who govern the CDCs, hold the groups accountable for the resources leveraged on their behalf.

The bruising experience of the Community Action Program in the 1960s also taught neighborhood organizations that waging war against local government is a dead end. Just as grassroots organizations discovered that investors are not the enemy, they have learned, little by little, to make common cause with city hall. Reckoning that local government is indispensable to fighting poverty and improving neighborhoods, CDCs have replaced confrontation with cooperation. As a consequence, municipal governments and their mayors are increasingly recognizing their value as the delivery system of choice for restoring neighborhoods, and are providing support for CDC developments and operations.

The second reason that CDCs can combine multiple programs and sources of revenue is that they become recognized anchors in their neighborhoods. Once a CDC has proven its competence in housing, it soon becomes an experienced, legitimate vehicle for addressing other neighborhood and community needs. Unlike antipoverty groups of the past, they don't claim entitlement to a piece of every government program as a matter of right (and in any case, that trick long since stopped working in most cities, as we discuss in a later chapter). Successful CDCs attract dollars from public officials who need to get things done, and are looking for partners who deliver. Successful housing initiatives serve as concrete evidence that the community group is an actor to be nurtured, bargained with, and consulted.

For the CDC's purposes, becoming involved in a wide range of public and private activities affecting the community is a good way to protect assets and promote development. Dealing with unemployment and gang crime, building day care centers, and promoting and improving the retail strip are all ways to ensure that housing efforts won't be undermined by other developments. A 1998 survey found that CDCs have developed more than 70 million square feet of commercial and community facilities, and supported 5,900 businesses, quite apart from their work in housing.

The third reason for CDCs' ability to diversify and adapt over time is that they have to live amid the consequences of their work. That gives them a long-term investor's approach to development: They have only one enterprise—their neighborhood—and they will stand or fall with it. Unlike past government programs, which tended to "adopt" one neighborhood today, another tomorrow, these groups have a business investor's relationship with their environment. From that position, they can leverage both the self-interest and the social motives of other players, weaving whatever resources might come along into a persistent strategy of strategic improvement.

Rather than just fixing some houses and cleaning a park, for example, CDCs will fix houses *along* the park, and negotiate with other landlords there to do the same. Having established a beachhead of investment there, they will look for the next such cluster of assets and potential partners. And so on.

Joel Bookman, the longtime head of Chicago's North River Commission, tells this story from the early years of his organization, by way of illustration:

> We created the first neighborhood streetscape program in Chicago in the late '70s. The city didn't want to plant trees, because they said trees don't survive in the city environment. So we found a horticulturist who was an expert in this, who identified three species of trees that thrive on

city air and light. Fine. So when we finally convinced the city that these trees were a good idea, they then wanted to scatter them here and there along the shopfronts, where they'd break up the scenery, all very nice.

We said, "No way!" We concentrated those trees at the major intersections and entry-points of the community. We needed to make a statement that would *change the market,* not just provide a little shade here and there. In the same vein, we developed a new park at the corner of Lawrence Avenue and the river—not just because we wanted a nice park, though of course we did, but because we wanted people driving across the river to see something dramatic and inviting. We wanted them to say, "Gee, things are really happening there."

Finally, CDCs succeed in so many diverse places with so many diverse sources of support and investment because they embrace American values that transcend political ideology: self-help, entrepreneurship, community building, local control, and public/private partnership. These are, of course, among the elements that make them so popular with editors looking for a light, upbeat story. But it is these essentially nonideological values that constitute CDCs' greatest comparative advantage in the market for public and private dollars in the inner city: They have been able to generate broad participation, lasting accountability, and a wide mix of sources of capital because they have mostly stayed out of the ideological camps.

Governments of every ideological stripe will work with CDCs because doing so brings decisionmaking down to the neighborhood level, where it's closest to the people it affects. And they recognize that no single organization can revive a neighborhood alone, so they collaborate actively with city and state officials as well as with other local agencies. Most importantly, CDCs get results. Their tangible successes in communities all over the country offer more than mere promises to a nation that is increasingly demanding measurable returns on its public investments.

❏

Because CDCs grew up in the declining neighborhoods of the old northern and midwestern cities, for a time it was thought their relevance was confined to those environments. CDCs were slow to develop in the Sunbelt, where cities had been growing, not shrinking, and where the attitude until recently had been, "we don't have these problems here." But in reality, poverty is every bit as concentrated and virulent, housing conditions as poor, and the races as isolated in the Fifth Ward of Houston as they ever were in the South Side of Chicago. Now that CDCs have proven their usefulness in cities whose problems are older and more entrenched, they are sprouting in the South and Southwest as well.

Throughout the 1970s and '80s, Houston's Fifth Ward was the kind of place that caused ambulance drivers chronic fatigue. In 1979 a *Texas Monthly* reporter found that the emergency medical technicians at the Fifth Ward's Fire Station No. 19 made 3,237 ambulance runs the previous year, making the Fifth the city's leader in shootings, stabbings, beatings, and dead-on-arrivals. One of the main intersections in the neighborhood, Lyons and Jensen, was nicknamed "Pearl Harbor" for the blood that flowed there. *Texas Monthly* described the community as the "toughest, proudest, baddest ghetto in Texas."

That kind of reputation is hard to shake, but the Fifth Ward is shaking it. According to the Rev. Harvey Clemons of the historic Pleasant Hill Baptist Church, no one much refers to his neighborhood as the "Bloody Fifth" anymore. Reverend Clemons was a central figure in the founding of two CDCs in the area: the Fifth Ward Community Redevelopment Corporation and the Pleasant Hill CDC, organizations that have given the neighborhood a new look and new hope. Together, the two groups have built or rehabilitated 234 single-family homes, 314 apartments, 24 four-bedroom townhomes, a 165-unit senior living complex, a child-development center, a police storefront, and a home health clinic that employs 100 people—all in a neighborhood with a median income of $7,600 per year. A successful Chase Bank branch and a thriving Walgreen's sit on Lyons Avenue, in the heart of a commercial strip formerly plagued by drugs and related violence.

More than twenty years earlier, when the neighborhood was steadily earning its grisly reputation, Harvey Clemons was on a path that easily could have been his ticket out of the Fifth Ward. With a background in architectural engineering from the University of Houston, he joined the Air Force Reserves, and shortly thereafter began a string of assignments at big-name corporations in the Houston area. But all that would change as the ministry called in his late twenties. From that point, Clemons and the Fifth Ward had a bond that transcended mere opportunity.

In 1988, his fourth year as pastor of Pleasant Hill Baptist Church, Clemons got a call from Carl Umland, leader of the local chapter of Habitat for Humanity, the volunteer home-building group. Umland's all-white group of volunteers hoped to build their first home in Houston in the Fifth Ward, but some neighbors greeted their efforts with suspicion, hostility, and even vandalism. Discussing the matter with Umland, Clemons expressed his own concerns about the Habitat program: "I did not want the Fifth Ward to become an incubator and a lure for only low-income individuals."

He described a different vision for his neighborhood, an economically diverse one where "individuals who have matriculated to the top of their profession, who want to spend two to three to four hundred thousand dollars for a house would also want to live here and not be embarrassed by the community." When Umland agreed that the Fifth Ward should have decent housing for people of all incomes, Clemons recalls, "I thought: Well, if you agree with me, then let's start off on how to make this happen."

Umland put Clemons in touch with contacts in city government. Houston's former housing director told them about "this new movement called community development corporations," and suggested they form one. And he referred them to the Local Initiatives Support Corporation, a national support institution for the CDC industry. With help from LISC, Clemons founded the Fifth Ward Community Redevelopment Corporation and hired Habitat volunteer Stephan Fairfield, at the time a city employee, as executive director. Ten years later, Fairfield is still running the Redevelopment Corporation; in the meantime, Fairfield and his wife built their first home in the Fifth Ward.

Just as in other cities, rebuilding the Fifth Ward was not solely the work of CDCs, nor could it have been. But they provided the vision, a market stimulus, and eventually some technical help to other players. The Redevelopment Corporation, for example, has helped three local entrepreneurs break into the for-profit home-building business in the neighborhood, and they now are producing and renovating houses alongside the CDC's own projects. Furthermore, Fairfield estimates that for every new house his CDC builds, another three home owners in the area fix up their properties.

Clemons is justly proud of what he and his colleagues have accomplished in little more than a decade, especially since their work didn't immediately begin with construction. Their earliest efforts, in fact, involved improving police-community relations, especially between officers and teenagers. Only later did they move to building homes and "changing the face of the main thoroughfares." All of this, says Clemons, "resulted in a newfound sense of civic pride."

Even so, Clemons readily acknowledges that they are still short of their ultimate goal, "where individuals who live outside the community, whether Anglo, Hispanic, Asian, or African American, will say 'I want to live five minutes from downtown Houston,' and somebody will recommend to them, 'Well, have you looked in the Fifth Ward? Man, that is really a nice neighborhood.'"

❑

An equally remarkable group is transforming Barrio Logan, the historic center of San Diego's Hispanic population. Throughout the 1940s and '50s, this heavily industrial area about two miles southeast of downtown provided work and housing for thousands of people, mostly Mexican Americans, in its canneries and shipyards. "Many of us in San Diego whose families have been here awhile have some family connection to Barrio Logan," says Richard Juarez, vice president for community development for a local nonprofit called Metropolitan Area Advisory Committee (MAAC). "That's where all the jobs were."

The community that industry and ethnic solidarity formed did not disperse easily when the jobs began to disappear and the neighborhood deteriorated to become one of San Diego's poorest. In the early 1960s, the construction of Interstate 5 tore out a sizable portion of the area's housing and decimated its retail district. The late 1960s brought the construction of the San Diego–Coronado Bridge, which destroyed more housing and compensated the neighborhood with nothing more than a looming mass of concrete. Besides the freeway and the bridge, nothing of consequence was built in Barrio Logan from the 1950s to the early '90s. Juarez believes city planners hoped that, since they rezoned the whole neighborhood industrial, "the people would just leave."

But the residents hung on. In 1970, when the state decided to build a highway patrol station where a park had been promised for years, what Juarez describes as a "major, spiritual, community uprising" occurred. For two weeks, Barrio Logan residents occupied the land, holding protests and ultimately staring down bulldozers to preserve the land for the community. On April 22, still a local holiday today, Chicano Park was born. The community completed their victory by painting murals on the concrete walls of the Coronado Bridge that have since gained international acclaim.

Rich Juarez was a young man working for the City of San Diego when the Chicano Park uprising took place. In 1965, he had spent the summer in Washington, D.C., with a godmother who worked for the U.S. State Department's Agency for International Development. She and other colleagues allowed him to sit in on nightly meetings on Latin American development policy, an opportunity that set Juarez's professional life on a new course. Throughout the 1970s and '80s, as planning director of San Diego's Model Cities program, as chief of staff to southeast San Diego's city councilman, and in a variety of other posts, Juarez had steadily "built his toolbelt," as he says, searching for a way to bring the principles of international development to the stubbornly depressed neighborhood where he lived as a child, and where his grandparents still lived. In 1990, he became vice president for the newly formed community development department at MAAC.

Unlike the great majority of community developers, who often start by rehabbing a single home or a few apartments, Juarez and his colleagues attacked the problem differently. They wanted to tackle the community's broad range of needs, and they wanted to do it on a large enough scale that the whole city would notice that something positive was happening in Barrio Logan.

That started to happen in 1994, when the Mercado Apartments opened with a rousing community celebration. After years of planning and negotiations to secure land and financing, MAAC built a gorgeous adobe and tile-roofed complex of 144 apartments in twenty-six two-story buildings on 4.4 acres, a block from Chicano Park and four blocks from the San Diego Bay. It houses an on-site childcare center, and provides a wide array of educational and job training services for the 320 young participants, partly through the efforts of seniors who live there. All the tenants earn less than 60 percent of the area's median income, but they were selected by the same careful process that any responsible landlord would use.

Any new, attractive development can improve a community's self-image for a time. But the impact of the Mercado Apartments on Barrio Logan is difficult to overstate. Prior to Mercado, no significant residential development had been built in the neighborhood in fifty years. And it's a relatively small community, with no more that 5,000 residents in an area of six blocks by three miles. Twenty-six buildings, in that context, change the feel of the landscape—especially given a design that incorporates the style of the urban townhouses of 1930s and '40s Mexico, set alongside the community park and with the murals as a backdrop. As the apartments were opening, neighbors were already asking for the color codes of the paint MAAC used, and the color scheme soon began spreading across the neighborhood.

After the housing development, Juarez and his colleagues turned next to the commercial market. Like most real estate development in poor urban neighborhoods, the process is long and full of pitfalls. But in 1998, the group brought in a private developer to help build a $14 million shopping center near Chicano Park, which will bring retail choices to the community not seen since Interstate 5 sliced through the community in the '60s.

"There is this strong energy about the healing of the community," says Rich Juarez. "Something magical has happened here."

❑

Thirty years ago, no American city needed a miracle more than Cleveland, a city whose catalog of horrors had become a staple of late-night standup: riots, white flight, escalating poverty, runaway crime, financial ruin, farcical politics, and to crown the scene, a river so filthy it caught fire. Yet by the mid-1990s, the old jokes had become passé, replaced by a wave of stories on a daring Cleveland comeback—a gleaming downtown boasting the Rock and Roll Hall of Fame and Museum, blocks of office towers converted to housing, a winning baseball team in a spectacular new stadium, a renovated central theater district, and a trendy enclave of restaurants and nightclubs almost exactly where the Cuyahoga River once ignited.

Yet crucial to the remaking of Cleveland has been the lesser-known story of what some thirty CDCs have accomplished in the city's poor residential neighborhoods. What began as a trickle of activity in the aftermath of the 1968 and '69 riots picked up considerable speed in the 1980s and grew into a full-fledged citywide industry in the 1990s. Since 1990 alone, the Cleveland Housing Network reports that its forty-two members have restored more than 2,100 homes; created more than 700 units of rental housing; and built 1,400 new houses.

By itself, adding 4,500 units to Cleveland's housing stock would be significant, though hardly history-making. What makes these numbers remarkable is that the construction is concentrated in neighborhoods that, before CDCs began their work, had not seen any significant building since the 1950s. They were considered the city's problem zones, its eyesores and social powder-kegs. CDC projects reopened these neighborhoods to investment and construction—not just by marketing new or renovated homes, but even more fundamentally, by showing that home repair and construction paid off, and that private investors could feel comfortable returning.

The classic example is Hough. Nearly three-quarters of the people in this historically African-American community near the shores of Lake Erie fled the area after the riots of the late 1960s. A decade later, local nonprofits began rehabbing houses and apartments, in very small increments at first, and one of them built the first new homes in Hough since the 1950s. Today, twenty years of steady work by nonprofits and foundations has attracted private developers and a new growth market: African Americans dissatisfied with the suburbs. Since 1992, private developers have built and sold nearly 120 custom homes that range from $150,000 to $700,000 each. At a time when "gated communities" are on the rise, longtime Cleveland community activist India Pierce Lee points out that in Hough, "you have $400,000 homes next to $14,000 ones ... with no fence between them."

Not all of Cleveland's poor neighborhoods have been as successful as Hough in attracting private developers, but nearly all have benefited enormously from a strong philanthropic base, an innovative and flexible city government, and years of dedication from community-based nonprofits. Broadway, Union Miles, Ohio City, and more than a dozen other Cleveland neighborhoods boast CDCs that have produced and sold more than 1,500 new or rehabilitated homes over the last decade.

One of the more dynamic of these nonprofits is the Broadway Area Housing Coalition (BAHC), which, like many of the city's CDCs, traces its roots to the Commission on Catholic Community Action in the late 1970s. As with many groups born from that church-based organizing movement, BAHC started by rallying and organizing members around political action, confrontation, and advocacy. The organizing work continues, but today, Project Manager Bobbi Reichtell credits the group's success to a style more entrepreneurial than confrontational. Says Reichtell, BAHC is continually "figuring out how to get the money to provide the services that we need, and empower residents to change their lives." At the end of the 1990s, that means rehabbing and selling 40 to 50 homes a year to low-income families on a lease-to-own basis; building a cluster of 210 new single-family houses; creating 60 units of senior housing in an abandoned school; turning an old Board of Education warehouse into 13 loft condos; fixing up and maintaining local parks; operating a summer recreation program for local kids; and continued organizing and advocacy work to confront racial tensions in the neighborhood.

"The thing that I absolutely love about this CDC in particular," says Reichtell, "is that there is no limit on what people can do within their program. We do the things that need to be done."

❑

San Francisco's urban headaches never approached those of Cleveland. But even amid the astronomic property values and dainty facades, San Francisco contains a more hidden base of acute poverty—and a desperate shortage of decent, affordable housing. In poorer communities across the bay, the poverty is more visible and more widespread. Partly as a result, nearly every year since 1968 has seen the formation of at least one CDC in the Bay Area, and sometimes as many as four, that remain active at the end of the century. Even through a recession, these organizations built more than 12,000 houses and apartments in just the half-dozen years between 1988 and 1994, amounting to total development of more than $1 billion. As of 1996, seventy-four non-

aggressive marketing, in the next six years home ownership more than tripled, to 59.8 percent. In 1993 the area had had thirty abandoned, boarded-up houses; by 1998 just two remained. Sure enough, local crime dropped by more than half in those same years.

Yet Green is the first to point out that his group couldn't have accomplished what it has on its own: "It's good planning. It's having technical support from the various sources," he explains, "and it's knowing how to get to [that support]." Among other things, the "technical support" came from police, other branches of city government, and other CDCs. One result: With help from all these sources, the Residents Association turned 92 properties owned by a notorious slumlord into owner-occupied, single-family, or duplex homes.

With home ownership skyrocketing, the association started making plans to lure a full-size grocery store to the area. That's when Green came across the story of Frank Crivello, a local developer, who had just been sentenced in federal court to 400 hours of community service for making false statements to a bank.

> Well, I'm reading the Op-Ed page and here's this developer, at one time he owned nine grocery stores in Milwaukee. He had developments all over the country. Arguably his gross worth was $500 million ... went into bankruptcy eventually. So I called the local district attorney, who put me in touch with the federal probation officer in Milwaukee. We all sat down and had a talk. [Normally] you couldn't hope to afford his time, let alone would he have any interest. Now he's our consultant on this supermarket deal.

The Residents Association is now courting several supermarket chains, and the city has created a special financing district around the site of the new store.

The Near West Side, it turns out, has been a kind of breeding ground for neighborhood-development talent. Not far from where the Merrill Park Residents Association and RAP have prospered, builder Perry Harenda was likewise working, in one way or another, with housing improvements all across the Near West Side. Harenda learned the construction trade as he grew up, working in his father's business. In the late 1970s, when interest rates skyrocketed, business dried up and Harenda had to strike out on his own. He started by rehabbing apartments and houses for an organization called the West Side Conservation Corps, which renovated more than 400 housing units over the next two decades. Harenda worked his way up, became the executive director in 1985, and added a master's degree in finance to his résumé.

In 1991, Harenda took over an organization called the Community Development Corporation of Wisconsin. With a seasoned builder at the helm, the organization could bring a project all the way from dream to finished product entirely with in-house talent—acting as developer, construction manager, and general contractor on every project. With a focus on fixing up apartment buildings, CDC of Wisconsin in the mid-1990s tackled a number of notorious apartment buildings that stood along Wells Avenue, a main artery running west from downtown.

That section of Wells was a real estate sinkhole for the community: Absentee landlords let the apartments cycle through an endless chain of transient and disruptive tenants, some departing in the middle of the night, while the buildings crumbled around them. Local gangs, drug dealers, and prostitutes operated out of the apartments with impunity, gaining citywide notoriety. The intersection of 27th and Wells, with its cluster of rundown tenements, formed something of a divider between a stable area to the east, within the orbit of Marquette University, and deepening blight to the west.

Today, that intersection and the blocks surrounding it demarcate something quite different: They now form a clean, handsomely designed gateway to a community rescued by its residents. "In 1989, '90, '91," says Harenda, "you had a lot of boarded up apartment buildings, a lot of people hanging out on street corners. You don't see that now."

CDC of Wisconsin rehabbed six buildings around 27th and Wells that now contain 158 attractive but low-rent apartments. To lure a more stable mix of tenants, they added one- and two-bedroom apartments to what had been single-room-occupancy buildings. They added off-street parking and greenery, ornate fencing, and restored facades. It became a place where working people would want to live. Meanwhile, the YMCA sponsored another large project a few blocks away that now offers another 170 apartments; and another attractive 189-unit development stands nearby.

It's hard to overstate the effect such a large-scale change can have in a concentrated area. These three developments alone represent a renewal of nearly 5 percent of the neighborhood's total housing stock—shifted from neighborhood deficits to assets in just a few years.

"In order to change the fabric of the neighborhood, which is the underlying goal," Harenda explains, "you needed to not do one building, you needed to do a lot of buildings, to have a synergy, so that you can take back the neighborhood. I think that has happened here."

Apparently the broader market agrees. In early 1997, the *Milwaukee Journal-Sentinel* reported that inner-city property values had risen for the first time in twenty years. Studies that tracked an increase from 1994 to 1996 showed that Milwaukee's poorest neighborhoods, which roughly form a ring around downtown, experienced a nearly 8 percent increase in property value—within 1 percent of the citywide average. The conventional wisdom, that these neighborhoods can go nowhere but down and don't respond to boom periods, evidently didn't apply in Milwaukee. Why? Because the neighborhoods themselves were planning, investing, and building. Conventional wisdom normally assumes that that won't happen.

Leo J. Ries, Milwaukee's director of housing and neighborhood development in the 1990s, points to groups like Merrill Park Residents Association and CDC of Wisconsin as essential to the rebound of the city's poorer sections. "There needs to be an investment of public and private effort, plus an indigenous group of residents who are working and fighting not to accept decline, not to accept social disorder in their neighborhood," Ries told the *Journal-Sentinel.* "Together you create neighborhoods of choice, where newcomers choose to become stakeholders, and once you achieve that, the [property] values will go up."

❑

The Bronx, Los Angeles, Milwaukee, Houston, San Diego, Cleveland, San Francisco—the diversity of these cities suggests how broadly the CDC phenomenon is now dispersed, and how rapidly it is growing. How did such an idiosyncratic, local strategy proliferate so quickly all over the country?

The traditional ways of spreading successful local programs weren't available to CDCs. In another time, individual success stories might have become the basis for some massive federal replication program designed at the Department of Housing and Urban Development and wholesaled to states and localities with federal grants attached. But just as CDCs started to become significant players in more than a few cities, Ronald Reagan was elected president, punctuating what in fact had been a long period of mounting disenchantment with big government—particularly the antipoverty kind of big government.

So, in what may well have been a blessing in disguise, CDCs would get no guarantees of federal largesse. Instead they were relegated to what *Business Week* columnist Robert Kuttner called "creative scrounging"—piecing together resources from myriad foundations, banks, local government agencies, special taxing districts, and the occasional federal or state grant. This made the early work of most CDCs far more laborious and chancy, as they methodically cobbled together one small project after another. But in the process, they avoided the "too-much-too-soon" problem that plagued many of the biggest ideas of the Great Society—reasonable plans and young organizations swamped by too many federal dollars before they were ready.

The lack of federal support also meant that there was no federal bureaucracy prescribing what was supposed to happen. CDCs were free to develop and pursue their local agendas. And as they scrounged for dollars and technical help, they were building a web of relationships and a diversified funding base that would be with them for the long term, not for the short cycle of the latest federal program.

Thus what began as a weakness—the absence of large-scale financial support and the consequent meagerness of early results—has turned into a strength, in two ways. First, CDCs in city after city are now raising capital both for projects and for overhead from a wide range of charities, banks and other financial institutions, private corporations, city governments, and increasingly, state governments. This support base now constitutes a formidable constellation of stakeholders, investing, monitoring, and generating results together.

Second, the CDCs were forced to focus tightly on micro-level results—on producing one small success after another—to keep both the neighborhood and citywide support alive. They could not rest complacently on multiyear entitlements, but neither could they often pull off a stunning coup with giant, headline-making projects. We have come to regard their laborious, pointillist achievements in those early years as a "paradox of little victories." It turns out that small but tangible progress was just what neighborhoods accustomed to decades of decline needed: not one grand scheme or a big, dramatic master-stroke (those approaches had already compiled decades-long records of insignificance or outright failure), but step-by-step, visible progress. Organizations built on an aggregation of success tend to be strong, well run, and versatile. In all these cities, the twenty-year accumula-tion of these house-by-house, block-by-block activities are now on display, and the effect is little short of amazing.

The lack of large-scale support had one other salutary effect: a shortage of publicity, and with that, a refuge from impossible expecta-tions. The intractable and intertwined problems of American inner cities had developed over forty or more years of decline. Yet most of that period has seen a chronic—and peculiarly American—yearning for *the answer,* a serial scrambling after some magic pill that would provide an instant (if sometimes fantastically expensive) solution, or else would be just as quickly abandoned. That was, in cartoon form, the story of Urban Renewal, Model Cities, the Office of Economic Opportunity, Section 8, Urban Development Action Grants, and on and on.

Yet CDCs, in their obscurity, had years in which to organize slowly and gather strength without the terrible burden of being that one great answer. With little notice or fanfare (at least until very recently), CDCs have become a force in America—a vast new decentralized ap-paratus for urban neighborhood problem solving. To all but those few who have had a reason to pay attention all these years, they seem al-most to have burst upon the scene.

One sector that did pay attention from the beginning was organized philanthropy, in particular the Ford Foundation. In the late 1970s and early '80s, when federal support for cities began to flag, founda-tions saw the need for a "third partner" to catalyze and facilitate the work of CDCs. Noting the difficulties the federal government had had in selecting and working effectively with local institutions, foun-dations tried setting up private intermediaries—something like chari-table fund managers, where foundations could entrust large grants that would in turn be distributed to the most productive community groups along with specialized project advisers, quality monitoring, and a constant search for innovation and technical improvement. In 1979, the Ford Foundation and several other funders launched the Local Initiatives Support Corporation, or LISC, with $9.5 million of seed money. Its mission was to find 100 exemplary CDCs and give them the financing and technical assistance that could take them to significant scale. In 1982, the celebrated developer James Rouse started the Enterprise Foundation with a similar mission.

Once again, in 1990, foundations gave another powerful boost to the expanding organization and ambition of the community development industry. At the urging of Peter Goldmark, then president of the Rockefeller Foundation, more than a dozen national foundations, both corporate and independent, joined the federal government in creating the National Community Development Initiative, which has since pumped more than $255 million into grant and low-interest loan funds for CDCs in twenty-three cities. NCDI has channeled this money largely through LISC and Enterprise, relying on them to ensure not only efficient investment in significant projects, but the growth, effectiveness, and durability of the CDCs themselves.

Enterprise, LISC, and a host of smaller organizations continue to help CDCs, governments, and private funders interact and form productive partnerships. In New York City, where the productivity of CDCs and other nonprofits has been at the core of the housing production plans of Mayors Ed Koch, David Dinkins, and Rudolph Giuliani, the intermediaries help engineer large transactions—like purchases of major properties, multiple leases in big commercial developments, or syndications of multimillion-dollar equity investments—and put projects and resources in the hands of nonprofit community groups. Intermediaries serve as go-betweens among sometimes recalcitrant public agencies, chary private investors, and wary community groups. They strive to maintain a balance between ensuring that grassroots organizations truly shape and lead the projects and at the same time making certain that all of the participants remain engaged in—and well served by—the work of community development.

Since 1982, Enterprise has committed more than $2.5 billion in grants, low-interest loans, and equity investments for more than 1,100 community organizations. The result: 96,000 affordable homes and apartments. LISC has helped some 1,700 CDCs produce more than 100,000 dwelling units and 11 million square feet of commercial and industrial space, investing more than $3 billion in CDC projects over its twenty-year history. Both organizations have generated unprecedented flows of capital from the private sector into nonprofit grassroots development.

These intermediary organizations have done what none of the assorted players—CDCs, individual funders, nor government—had been able to do alone. They have created stronger organizational and technical capacity among community organizations. They gave grassroots leaders access to new sources and larger amounts of funding, as well as to influential people and agencies. They created opportunities for information exchange and networking among people at every point along the development chain—big capital markets, retail financial institutions, for-profit and non-profit developers, local investors and property owners, elected officials, government planners and service agencies, community groups, home buyers, and tenants. And they have boosted political advocacy, and generally enhanced the credibility and visibility of the CDC movement.

Some years ago, the Urban Institute described this national support system for nonprofit housing developers as "the single most important story of the nonprofit development sector in the 1980s." The Washington-based research and policy organization went on to say:

> Arguably, without this source of support for grassroots development activity, state and local governments would have displayed far less responsiveness to nonprofit developer needs over the decade. Intermediaries as a group have performed three vital functions in the sector: (1) mobilization of capital, including project, operating support and pre-development finance, and critical assistance in financial packaging, (2) provision of technical assistance in both financial packaging, project development and local institution-building, and (3) as a result of the preceding two functions, legitimation of CDCs, enhancing perceived technical competence and reducing risk to both public and private sector funders.

Importantly, the intermediaries provided national support in a way that was not overly prescriptive. Incorporated into LISC's mission statement, for instance, is the view that "CDCs are the most effective vehicle for bringing lasting positive change to inner cities." In effect, these were national organizations bringing flexible support to local organizations, helping to form local partnerships for local action—not a task that any government agency could plausibly have managed.

❏

One accomplishment of CDCs and intermediaries has gone mostly unnoticed, but it's hugely significant: They have fundamentally changed the local politics of community development. Before 1980, many of the groups passing as community development corporations in most major American cities were blatantly political organizations— nonprofits set up by mayors, city councilors, or aldermen for the purpose of receiving and dispensing public funds and patronage. There naturally was little private-sector support for such organizations, and they generated few results. But they controlled the action.

The grassroots development movement, by producing independent, results-driven organizations—many of them church-based—created a formidable alternative to the do-nothing patronage groups. And the intermediaries, by mobilizing private sector support and delivering it to the newer organizations, drove a stake through the heart of community "development" based on politics rather than performance.

In the late 1980s, for example, the Detroit business community, through a civic organization known as Detroit Renaissance, invited LISC to consider opening an office in Detroit. While exploring the possibilities, LISC officials met with then-Mayor Coleman Young. Young evinced support for the program, but made it clear, with trademark bluntness, that he would "control who got the funds." LISC, just as bluntly, replied that, in that case, LISC would prefer not to have a Detroit program. The mayor relented, the program went forward on the normal, independent basis, and the CDCs that were actually producing in Detroit got financial and technical support from LISC and the private sector. Soon, the performing CDCs were getting the lion's share of available public funding as well, with no political strings attached.

This incident illustrates the power of independent, privately backed organizations to challenge the prevailing power structure without acrimony and confrontation, and then to deliver dramatic results. Detroit had deservedly been known as a place where nothing got done in the neighborhoods unless it was political. It now has a thriving, independent community development network attracting significant private-sector support.

The story also suggests that, however grudgingly at first, politicians *will* support projects and organizations outside their direct political control, if they can get credit for the results. For their part CDCs have cemented the bargain by being willing to draw favorable attention and credit to the public officials who help make their work possible.

The change in Harlem was at least as dramatic as the one in Detroit, against comparably bad odds. For more than twenty-five years the state-chartered urban renewal agency known as the Harlem Urban Development Corporation, backed by the neighborhood's antiquated political establishment, had controlled (most would say stifled) social and economic development in the most famous African-American community in the world. But not until the late 1980s did the paralysis and inaction get the attention it needed. By then, in other parts of New York, including the South Bronx and central Brooklyn, neighborhood revitalization efforts by independent CDCs were starting to explode.

By then, Mayor Koch's enormous citywide housing program had begun to take off—including a huge component that relied on housing production by CDCs. To organize and direct that effort, Koch turned to LISC and Enterprise, the two leading national intermediaries. That effort, with all the financial support and favorable public attention it brought, created a huge opportunity for CDCs to accelerate the job of renovating abandoned apartment buildings that the city had come to own, mostly through tax foreclosures.

But amid this explosion of new housing production, Harlem wasn't participating, at least not much. The neighborhood had few credible CDCs—owing directly to the "climate control" that the Harlem Urban Development Corporation had exercised over all development plans in the area. A number of Harlem ministers, seeing how the missed opportunity was cheating their congregations, decided to change the equation. With LISC's help, they organized brand-new, church-based CDCs. One came from the fabled Abyssinian Baptist Church, itself a historic anchor of the community. The church's young, charismatic pastor, the Rev. Calvin Butts, was anguished by the lack of action on housing abandonment, drug abuse, and soaring drug-related crime. Year by year, he had watched the neighborhood all around the church come apart. Meanwhile, he was hearing about all the things community development corporations were accomplishing just across the river in the South Bronx—an area that was actually worse off than Harlem.

Reverend Butts wanted to work with the Harlem Urban Development Corporation—but he was rebuffed. "HUDC gave great lip service," he said later, "but did nothing." So, reluctantly at first, he took direct action by organizing the Abyssinian Development Corporation. A seed grant from LISC let the new organization hire its first staff person: Karen Phillips, a member of the congregation with considerable urban development experience. Within ten years, the group had built more than 600 apartments, renovated 150 brownstones, opened a large Head Start center, and brought a huge full-service Pathmark grocery store into the neighborhood.

A second minister, the Rev. Preston Washington, followed a similar script and organized an equally impressive group, Harlem Congregation for Community Improvement. HCCI has built 1,300 units of housing and 32 retail stores, and brought about more than $300 million in investment in Harlem. "We all found out," Reverend Washington said, "that HUDC was hollow on the inside."

It's worth noting that none of the ministers "took on" the old Harlem UDC. Driven by necessity, they simply set out to do something credible themselves. By accomplishing that, though, they exposed the stark reality of HUDC. When George Pataki, the new Republican governor of New York, abruptly ended HUDC's funding in 1994, there was barely a murmur of protest. The truth was, the organization wouldn't be missed. Harlem was on the move. And CDCs, aided by national and local intermediaries like LISC and the corporate organization New York Housing Partnership, gave it a significant jump-start.

Today, in virtually every major American city, community development is a legitimate partnership of the public, private, charitable, and community sectors. The virtual disappearance of patronage-based community groups and their well-oiled cronies can be credited in large part to CDCs and their intermediary supporters, and it is a huge accomplishment.

❏

None of this implies, though, that most poor communities can redevelop on their own without government support. It's important to point out that neither the Detroit nor the Harlem experience occurred without help from City Hall. Instead, City Hall needed to change the way it gave that help—and the list of people who received it—to respond to success and production rather than to the call of patronage.

That is a profoundly difficult change for governments to make. When they manage, it's usually because they come to rely on intermediaries and private organizations like Detroit Renaissance and the New York City Housing Partnership to help direct resources. That willingness to cede control and trust private partners tends to ebb and flow in most City Halls, depending on who's in charge. But, as we argue in more detail later, the quality of cities' chief executives has improved starkly in recent years. With savvier, more enterprising mayors has come a willingness to support neighborhood institutions when they're productive—and even, more and more, to withdraw support when they're not.

In any case, to accomplish a national task over the long term, government money is indispensable. And that includes a substantial investment of federal dollars. The intermediaries therefore took to Congress and the White House the same message of local control and flexible, market-driven investment that has worked so well in City Halls. They have argued (often, but not always, with success) that local grassroots organizations need federal capital that can be melded effectively with other investment, much of it private, that they raise locally. Raising the necessary money in Washington without creating massive, overweening federal programs has been a constant challenge.

When it works, it is usually because federal money is only part of a broader financing system that includes other, independent investors and contributors. (The main exception has been in housing for the elderly, a constituency with more than the average claim on federal generosity.) Unlike the great federal urban development efforts of the past—say, public housing or Section 8—today's CDC projects aren't overwhelmingly federally funded.

Still, the government role has been crucial: While CDCs (and the intermediaries) were obtaining large amounts of market capital, particularly from banks, almost all that money was used in combination with government and charitable dollars. This mix of private and public dollars created blended interest rates that can work in severely depressed communities. As neighborhoods revived, the proportion of private capital could be expected to rise, as it has.

The problem is that few federal programs are flexible enough to be of consistent use to community-based entrepreneurs, whose success has depended on not concentrating all their projects into the neat, absolute categories popular in Washington: one program solely for homeless families; one just for the elderly; one just for small businesses; another just for apartment complexes. A happy exception has been the Low Income Housing Tax Credit, enacted in 1986 with strong support from the intermediaries. This program offered an income tax credit to corporate and individual investors when they invest in new or rehabilitated rental housing for the poor.

The resulting projects have produced single-family homes and apartment complexes and row houses. They've sprung up in dense, high-rise neighborhoods and rolling rural communities. They've accommodated the working poor next to welfare recipients; single individuals next to families and children. For all its restrictions (it's still a federal program, after all), the Tax Credit has given grassroots developers access to a source of publicly subsidized private capital that can be tailored to multiple needs.

The Tax Credit has spurred the creation of more than a million affordable houses since it started. The intermediaries have assumed a prominent role in packaging and selling tax credits to private investors on behalf of the CDCs. Because they operate all over the national map, they can combine CDC projects into large bundles of eligible projects, in which corporate investors can then buy shares as limited partners. (The CDCs, as nonprofit institutions, have no use for a tax credit, but for-profit investors obviously do.) The shares these investors buy give them the right to subtract the corresponding credits from their own tax bills. Billions have flowed into the neediest neighborhoods as a result of this kind of investment.

The credit is also flexible enough to be useful in a wide variety of renewal schemes—it can be used to rehabilitate abandoned apartment buildings, or to build new townhouses, or even to create service-enhanced residences for homeless individuals. Because of this adaptability, the Housing Credit is by far the most useful federal housing program for CDCs. The strong involvement of private-sector investors has also introduced the novelty of market discipline to federal housing programs: If management of the projects starts to slip, it's typically the private investors who enforce reforms or reorganization, not the slower-moving government funders.

Another legislative success for CDCs has been a block grant program known as HOME, administered by HUD, that was enacted in the early 1990s. This housing-subsidy program joined the older Community Development Block Grants as the only HUD programs of consistent use to CDCs. Their usefulness resides mainly in the wide latitude they give to local and state governments to respond to opportunities that are quite different from place to place. For CDCs, that means their local governments can use the block grants to give them flexible "gap" or "seed" money that can be artfully combined with charitable dollars, other government grants, and private investment, for projects of many kinds.

The problem is that all these programs are tiny. The two block grants together make up just a small fraction of HUD's budget, with the balance going to the usual, categorical, prescriptive programs like public housing, which we discuss further in Chapter 8. Despite their popularity and effectiveness, block grants are unlikely to be expanded. Ironically but significantly, it's the very attributes that account for their effectiveness—flexibility and local decision making—that make them less appealing in Washington, both in Congress and in the Executive Branch. Since local officials have the final word on who gets block-grant money for what projects, national politicians get small thanks for the results. The good results of block grants are often credited to mayors and other ribbon-cutters at the state and local level. The political "credit" problem means that federal decision makers generally think of block grants last when they're dreaming up new initiatives. The few remaining programs do tend to survive, year by year, but they are unlikely to grow.

Perhaps the federal program of greatest value to grassroots groups is not a program at all, but a regulation: the Community Reinvestment Act, which compels banks to extend credit in all parts of the markets they serve. By different routes, for different reasons, CRA does with

private capital something like what block grants do with public dollars. It allows them to flow (and also ensures that they flow) wherever
opportunity and initiative can put them to best use. We discuss CRA
in depth in the next chapter.

In general, CDCs ought to be "direction finders" for federal policy.
They map out ways of doing business (the phrase is significant) in inner cities that were neither traditional nor obvious in public policy before the last few decades. CDCs have a great deal to tell us about what
works. Unfortunately, what works for them at the federal level is a very
short list of programs that shows no sign of lengthening.

Nevertheless, when it all comes together in a single city—a strong
network of thriving CDCs, a broad and diverse support base, political
leadership, and fifteen or more years of patient, methodical effort—
the results are breathtaking. The cities that have invested the most political will and local resources in this process, like Boston and Chicago,
routinely astonish visitors who have been away from their inner-city
neighborhoods for a while, and are unaware of the cumulative transformation.

❑

In the cities where CDCs have been most successful, they are supported by a strong network of diverse institutions that include many
of the key stakeholders in the civic realm and mainstream economy.
Since the mid-1970s, Boston has been a fertile environment for developing such a network, yielding a number of new institutions that have
provided crucial support to the metro area's twenty-five CDCs. Since
1970, these groups have produced more than 8,500 units of affordable
housing in poor neighborhoods across Greater Boston. CDCs in the
Boston area have also developed forty-one different youth programs
serving 3,000 young people.

One of the keys to achieving this level of production in Boston was
getting the private sector, particularly downtown interests, involved
in the renewal of the city's low-income neighborhoods. In the early
1980s, various business, government, and civic leaders came together
to develop a broad agenda for reviving Boston's low-income neighborhoods, which included jobs, education, and housing. One con-

cept that came out of those discussions was the Boston Housing Partnership. The partnership essentially pooled public and private capital to invest in the acquisition and rehabilitation of affordable housing, with CDCs handling the work. The first "round" of the partnership was extremely successful, producing 700 units—200 more than had been promised—and subsequently has been replicated in dozens of other cities.

The housing partnership remains an excellent model for leveraging private capital to revive ailing neighborhoods. The Housing Partnership "put a lot of CDCs on the map as credible community-based developers," says Mat Thall, a veteran of Boston's community development field and LISC program director there since 1991. "It was a very important institution that moved CDCs to a larger scale of production and achievement."

Almost a decade before the establishment of the Boston Housing Partnership, three institutions came together for a series of Wednesday morning breakfast discussions at the instigation of Mel King, a lecturer at MIT's Department of Planning and Urban Studies who later became a state legislator representing a largely minority district in Boston. The discussions grew more and more concrete over time, eventually leading to the formation of a series of local institutions, each supporting a different aspect of the work of CDCs.

One provided capital to invest in firms located in struggling neighborhoods (the Community Development Finance Corporation); another delivered technical assistance to CDC staff (Community Economic Development Assistance Corporation); another allocated direct operational support for CDCs (Community Enterprise Economic Development). The creation of these institutions, all funded in various ways by the state government, acknowledged that CDCs were the government's most effective partners in the revitalization of low-income neighborhoods. It was a level of broad-based public and private commitment to the idea of community development far in advance of the rest of the country.

Other nonprofits contributed mightily to this innovative environment. Carol Glazer, LISC's first program director in Boston, convened a group of foundations and the United Way to raise longer-term support for CDCs' core management and administration—the working capital so scarce in the public and nonprofit sector. Like the housing partnership, the resulting Neighborhood Development Support Collaborative was the first of its kind in the country, and has since been replicated all over the United States.

With so many government, business, and other nonprofit leaders investing energy and money to nourish the entrepreneurship of neighborhood groups, Boston CDCs were finally part of a more organized industry, a phenomenon that in those days was still rare in other cities. From the early '80s, they have been buttressed by exceptional institutional support for their work, and the results have been impressive. In addition to becoming the primary producer of affordable housing in the Boston area for two decades and counting, Boston CDCs changed the face of a number of historically rough neighborhoods, particularly Dorchester, Roxbury, and Jamaica Plain.

"For a lot of neighborhoods, in addition to the immediate direct benefit [of affordable housing]," says Thall, "CDCs have helped to transform both the image and the self-image of the neighborhoods as being hopelessly lost to being neighborhoods where great things are possible."

The rebirth of Boston's Egleston Square neighborhood, a once-troubled section of Roxbury/Jamaica Plain, caught the attention of Charles A. Radin, who wrote a cover story on the neighborhood's comeback in the November 1998 *Boston Globe Magazine*. "Among the areas leading Boston's neighborhood renaissance," wrote Radin, "Egleston Square is perhaps the most interesting, simply because it is so ordinary."

By ordinary, Radin meant that it didn't stand out in any particular way from the rest of inner-city Boston; it had neither "landmark buildings" nor "a well-known history" that can help to generate interest in the revitalization of a particular area. But as Radin pointed out, the turnaround of Egleston Square was neither a miracle nor a twist of fate—it was built on a blueprint that "included effective, imaginative community groups, better policing, improved city services, and a good overall economy."

The rebirth of Egleston Square was the result of the determination and creativity of individuals and institutions who counted themselves as stakeholders in the community, from the residents to business and nonprofit leaders to the police department. It was accomplished by small-business owners like Robert Lawson, who arrived in Boston in the early 1960s from the North Carolina tobacco fields, opened a barbershop, got burned out, bought the fire-damaged building, and persevered through many years without the "privileges" of insurance or bank financing.

It was accomplished by nonprofit leaders like Mossik Hacobian of the CDC known as Urban Edge, whose organization saved a tremendous amount of the neighborhood's housing stock in a long march of grueling, building-by-building battles against slumlords and vandals alike. And it will be sustained by people like Will Morales, a neighborhood kid who went to prison on a cocaine conviction and now, as director of the neighborhood's new YMCA branch, points local youth to a better life.

Nor is Egleston Square's new stability going unnoticed by the private market. A Fleet Bank branch opened there in 1992, a McDonald's in 1996, and a Walgreen's pharmacy in 1997—all at a single intersection where guns and crack had reigned as recently as the early 1990s.

Lest anyone think that Egleston Square is an exception to the rule, Radin asked Police Commissioner Paul F. Evans how Boston's neighborhoods have changed over the years. A native of South Boston, Evans knows the city's mean streets intimately, having come up through the ranks from foot patrolman to top cop. His response: Egleston Square, Dorchester's Codman Square and Uphams Corner, and South Boston's East Broadway—all areas with active CDCs—are now "as good as, if not better than they were thirty years ago."

When sociologist William Julius Wilson wrote his landmark 1996 book on the nature of today's urban poverty, *When Work Disappears,* he settled on Chicago's South and West Sides for the bulk of his research. Many of the neighborhoods that make up those vast areas have struggled under the weight of poverty and political isolation for nearly a half century, some much longer. Yet, over the last two decades, these same communities and scores of others around the city have given birth to one of the largest and most productive community development networks in the country. In the late 1990s, this network is reaching a scale of production that is restoring huge portions of the city to the status of sustainable, working-class communities.

Between 1980 and 1998, more than forty CDCs produced over 10,000 units of affordable housing in Chicago, nearly half of all residential development in the city during that time, representing a net gain of $750 million in new investments in the city's poorest neighborhoods. Chicago's CDCs have also developed more than 1.5 million square feet of commercial or industrial space over the same period.

The effect of such investments is difficult to overestimate, especially in areas like Kenwood/Oakland and Woodlawn. Between World War II and the early 1990s, vacant land and abandoned buildings swallowed 70 percent of the property in those areas. For four decades, not one house was built there for sale at market rates. Today, dozens of new market-rate houses have been built and sold, along with more below-market homes and more than 300 renovated apartments. A rebounding housing stock was one of the key factors in persuading an experienced retail operator to open Lake Pointe Market there in 1999, the area's first new supermarket in forty years.

Chicago neighborhoods with equally mean reputations—Pilsen, Woodlawn, West Town, Chicago Lawn, and the Near West Side—have all benefited enormously from the activity of their CDCs, and dozens of other poor neighborhoods are witnessing steady, if still incremental, improvement. Even in communities where a true "renaissance" seems far off, CDCs have established impressive operations that can easily be credited with staving off wholesale destruction.

Bethel New Life CDC in West Garfield Park is an example. When Mary Nelson, Bethel New Life's veteran executive director, first came to West Garfield Park with her brother in 1965, their car was pelted with bricks. She was helping her brother David move into the neighborhood to take an assignment as pastor of Bethel Lutheran Church, and they had arrived literally in the middle of a riot. Mary intended to stay with her brother only until things calmed down. But by the time that calm arrived (after five more riots in the next four years) she was there to stay. In 1979, Bethel completed its first rehab project with a HUD-foreclosed building, volunteer labor from the congregation, and a tiny investment fund of $9,600, cobbled together from the church and the Nelsons' credit cards.

From that humble beginning, Bethel New Life CDC has become a bulwark against decline in a community suffering from endemic problems with unemployment, broken families, and crime. The CDC's budget alone pumps $10 million a year into a neighborhood where many private investors still fear to tread. The group has built or rehabilitated 1,000 houses and apartments, and has worked with other West Side churches to build 250 more. It has placed 4,000 people in full-time jobs, and continues to do so at a rate of 500 a year. It built a health center that treats 1,000 patients a month and runs a program credited with cutting the area's infant mortality rate by 36 percent since the mid-1980s.

The CDC built a $1.4 million recycling center. It trains mothers on welfare to become licensed day care operators in renovated homes. It helped young people start up and run a credit union, a catering business, and a bookstore. Ever since Bethel New Life and a coalition of other groups protested the planned shut-down of the neighborhood's "El" station, the threatened Lake/Pulaski stop has become the center of a $300 million city redevelopment that includes a shopping center, a bank branch, a day care center, and a police substation. They turned an abandoned hospital campus into a complex that includes housing, offices, retail shopping, a small business "incubator," a performing arts center, and a computer training institute. They have even been known to set up Sno-Cone and hot dog stands on seedy corners, just to crowd out drug dealers with swarms of hungry pedestrians.

❑

How implausible it was that a ragtag bunch of neighbors, in communities deserted by most mainstream institutions, could make such a difference! It was the very modesty of their ambition—not to save the nation or the world, but a house or a block or a neighborhood—the very concreteness, the localness of what they set out to do—that now highlights the stunning scope of their achievement.

Finally, after swimming against the tide for so long, it is lately getting a little easier. As we shall see.

Bayporte Village, a development of new single-family homes in West Oakland, California, where lenders competed to offer mortgages. (Marcia J. Novak/Oakland Community & Economic Development Agency)

PART THREE

Emerging Markets

WEST OAKLAND, California, sits in a tough corner of the less fashionable side of San Francisco Bay, a convenient, if slightly dispiriting, outpost from which to watch the steady climb in personal incomes, architectural glamour, and stratospheric property values just out of reach across the water. With a 1996 median household income of about $10,000, West Oakland is one of the poorest neighborhoods in the Bay Area, and has been for decades.

Any plan for new housing is therefore sure to make headlines in West Oakland, where investors and for-profit developers seldom go sightseeing. So in 1997, it was already big news when two nonprofit development groups formed a joint venture to develop seventy-one single-family homes in the area—three- and four-bedroom houses with two and a half baths and a garage, costing roughly $150,000 each, a big ticket in depressed West Oakland. In that price range, amid financial and real estate markets that had all but evaporated in the 1970s and '80s, the two development groups braced themselves for a fight over financing.

And a fight is what they got. But not the one they expected: Overnight, the project had become the target of a bidding war among the Bay Area's most prominent banks, all competing for a piece of the

deal. Sumitomo, Home Savings, American Savings, Norwest, Coun-
trywide, Wells Fargo Mortgage Corp., and Bank of America each tried
to outdo the others with offers of favorable pricing and flexible underwriting. Bank of America won, in the end, with an offer that one developer paraphrased as "send us a warm, breathing, blood-running
body, and we'll write a mortgage." Every house in the first phase of
construction was sold, most to buyers who had never before owned a
home. The remaining phases are under way as this is written.

In the high-growth years of the 1990s, more and more such stories
became the stuff of amazed news reports telling tales of the rebirth of
slums: banks competing to make residential and even business loans
in the former moonscapes of Detroit, Cleveland, Chicago, Milwaukee, and dozens of other cities where the credit well had long ago
dried up. And where credit was starting to flow again, it was largely
following an earlier stream of equity: years of public, and later private,
investment in housing at all income levels, and a trickle of retail and
service-industry investment, lately widening into a small river.

Like the credit markets, retail returned warily to inner cities, beginning with a few pioneering outposts in the 1980s—a new Winn Dixie
supermarket in a Miami riot area (a store that quickly became one of
the chain's most profitable); successful Pathmark supermarkets in
Brooklyn, Newark, and other hardscrabble markets; Goldblatt Broth-
ers' discount stores in Chicago and Stop & Shop in Boston; and Payless ShoeSource stores around the country. But the success of this advance guard, and a growing body of business and economic literature,
is making the case that inner cities are not just high-risk niche markets
where only a few specialty operators can survive. On the contrary, as
the business-minded policy group Social Compact has pointed out,
some of the most concentrated spending power in the country is in
low-income areas—precisely where retailers have been scarcest.

Social Compact is a coalition of corporate executives promoting investment in lower-income neighborhoods. In those neighborhoods,
Social Compact has shown, families spend a high percentage of what
they make, and there are many more families per acre than in wealthier neighborhoods and suburbs. So although median incomes are
high, for example, in Chicago's prosperous Forest Glen neighborhood,
the per-acre spending power is nearly three times greater on the other

side of town, in the poorer, mostly minority neighborhood of Little Village. Not surprisingly, once they have a chance to think it over, retailers have been heading for Little Village.

And for the first time in decades, there is now enough credit there for investors small and large to move in, set up shop, and expand. Inner-city markets, at least in some places, have had potential for years, most of it untapped. And when it was tapped, the source of capital was often informal—family members or other social groups, often immigrants from a single place of origin, lending to one another and sharing risks and expertise. Where those informal sources of capital were lacking, hardly anything occurred. Until the sudden awakening in capital markets at the end of the century.

A Detroit developer, reflecting on a late 1990s development of luxury homes on the Detroit River, succinctly described the importance of this change in the urban credit market: The project, he observed, "sits on an island with fantastic views of the river, Canada, and downtown Detroit. It's got good access to downtown, plus the quiet and security of an island. Why didn't anyone put housing here twenty years ago? Same river, same views, same security. But one thing you didn't have was credit, and now all of a sudden, it's there."

Credit for small businesses, for housing, and for consumers has all been on the rise in the 1980s and '90s. And the consequences are everywhere. Minority home ownership has skyrocketed. Boarded-up commercial strips in threadbare neighborhoods are stirring back to life in record numbers. As Federal Reserve Governor Laurence Meyer put it, "you can feel the electricity on the streets in these neighborhood markets."

The story of the rebirth of markets in long-desolate neighborhoods is really four stories, woven together. Thus far, we have discussed mainly the first one: Thirty years of pioneering public and private investment in housing. Here, we take on two others that are just as important: a slow but strong regulatory nudge to draw banks into neighborhood residential and business lending; and most recently, the discovery by major retailers that it is possible—sometimes even easy—to do business and turn a profit in the inner city. The fourth element—a steady supply of new residents and customers, especially from abroad—is more perennial, almost a mainstay of urban lore.

But because it remains controversial, we revisit it briefly at the end of this section.

But these four stories of market rebirth—about renewed housing, the flow of capital, the retail revival, and the fuel supply of new populations—are usually told piecemeal, if at all. And all too often the telling comes with an idle shrug of bafflement, like the spotting of some rare bird far from its natural habitat, or with the sentimentality of a parent displaying kindergarten artwork. The surge in new inner-city investment trespasses all the comforting boundaries of ideology (a triumph of capitalism borne on the shoulders of government regulation and grassroots activism), and thus tends to be dismissed either as a quaint curiosity or a trifle.

It is neither. In fact, it is this very indifference to ideology that has made the rebirth of urban markets so powerful and potentially so durable. Tax-cutting Republicans and social-activist Democrats can conspire on tax incentives or regulatory changes to spur inner-city development precisely because it offends neither and, sometimes in different ways, appeals to both. Like crime reduction and school reform, the passions surrounding inner-city capital and markets are the passions of opportunity, community, and quality of life.

The previous chapter sketched out how a firestorm of grassroots development sparked—or at least contributed to—the explosion of new and renovated housing. Here we turn to other market forces that this renewal of housing and residential neighborhoods has unleashed: first the credit revolution, then the return of retail and services. Some of the individual stories may be familiar, at least in part. But the unifying patterns among them—and the sheer volume of what they represent—is both surprising and, at least for now, still poorly understood.

Chapter 5

THE CREDIT REVOLUTION

T O A CASUAL reader skimming the headlines of the late 1990s, it might have seemed as if America's soberest financial institutions had suddenly gone bingeing on skid row. Here, all at once, were some of the most famous names in banking, flashing their wallets on the poorer side of town like sailors on shore leave. This announcement, on May 4, 1998, was merely the latest in a chain (and far from the last), but at that point it was surely the most amazing:

> NEW YORK—Citicorp and Travelers Group today made a ten-year, $115 billion commitment to lending and investing in low and moderate income communities and small businesses. *This pledge is more than double Citibank's $56 billion of domestic deposits*—the largest such community commitment as a percentage of deposit base ever made by any institution. [emphasis added]

Admittedly, the arithmetic wasn't nearly as outlandish as it seemed on first glance. The promise stretched out for ten years, while the deposit base was only some of the money available at any one time. More to the point, institutions of Citibank's and Travelers' size routinely tap vast outside sources of capital that dwarf even the biggest banks' domestic deposits. Even so, this had to be the first time a bank boasted that it would invest *twice as much* as it held in deposits solely to benefit low- and moderate-income communities and small businesses.

Yet leaving aside the remarkable size of the Citi-Travelers' commitment, it was far from unique. Announcements of this sort had become almost commonplace by mid-1998. When First Union absorbed CoreStates in 1997, it trumpeted a nearly $14 billion, five-year commitment to affordable housing, community development, and small business loans just in CoreStates' market area. When Wells Fargo acquired First Interstate the year before that, the combined institutions pledged $45 billion in such loans over ten years. Merging New York giants Chemical and Chase Manhattan Banks pledged $18 billion in community investments and another $70 million in charitable contributions. The merger of Great Western and Washington Mutual in 1997 brought a $120 billion lending commitment over ten years, and the 1996 marriage of NationsBank and Boatmen's Bank produced a $200 million pledge just for St. Louis, Missouri, and its environs.

Granted, these giant numbers were carefully qualified and footnoted, and some of them may prove chimerical. But they presented in aggregate a single, vivid benchmark for dozens of new phenomena that residents and small entrepreneurs in poor and minority neighborhoods had been reporting for several years: new easy-application programs for lower-income mortgage-seekers, with special ways of qualifying. Bank-sponsored training programs to help small businesses and first-time home buyers submit successful applications. Whole new underwriting departments in the bigger banks, dedicated to adapting traditional products and services to the special needs of poor neighborhoods. New, flexible lines of credit for community-based developers building or renovating big housing and commercial projects.

It was as if the flat earth of retail banking had suddenly found its Columbus. Banks by the hundreds were planting new flags in the former terra incognita of the inner city.

For anyone wondering where these institutions had acquired their sudden zeal for social investment, Citicorp and Travelers helpfully supplied an explanation in the second paragraph of their May 4 press release:

Citicorp and Travelers Group have announced plans to merge. Citibank, which refers to Citibank N.A. and seven other banking subsidiaries of Citicorp, is subject to the community lending requirements of the Community Reinvestment Act.

To say the least of it, the Community Reinvestment Act, or CRA—one of the most vilified and misunderstood pieces of banking legislation since the New Deal—does not require banks to make these outsized commitments to affordable housing, small businesses, or any other particular class of borrower. It has nothing whatsoever to say about charitable donations. It doesn't even require that banks single out low- or moderate-income people for special treatment. It simply requires every bank to "[meet] the credit needs of its entire community, including low- and moderate-income neighborhoods, consistent with the safe and sound operation of such institutions."

Or else what? On that subject, the act falls practically silent. It merely instructs regulators to "take account" of the bank's fair-lending record when deciding whether to approve an application for a new charter, a merger or acquisition, or the opening or closing of branches. It doesn't even say that regulators, after taking such account, necessarily have to disapprove applications from banks with bad records. And banks that do not apply for these things face no consequences whatsoever. The whole act is barely 700 words long—scarcely the length of a foreign dispatch in *USA Today*.

Yet in practice, CRA has placed enormous pressure on banks to extend more credit to low- and moderate-income areas than they otherwise would have. The vagueness of the legislative language has been cleared up over the years by reams of regulation, requiring government examiners to inspect how much banks market and extend their services to poor neighborhoods, minorities, small businesses, and community groups. And despite its lack of explicit penalties, the act has come to be enforced most vigorously and publicly just at the moment when banks are the most vulnerable to public and regulatory pressure: when they seek permission to expand, merge, or otherwise change the scope of their charter.

Hence, Citibank's and Travelers' brief but significant explanation for their burst of commitments to inner cities. Put less subtly, it amounts to this: "Our merger plans require the approval of the same regulators empowered to enforce the CRA. So before they start their review, we're making sure the deal isn't held up by complaints about Citibank's community-investment record."

That is one important reason why the 1990s were so rich with colossal CRA commitments. At a time of massive consolidation in the industry, when every day's news brought another merger or buy-out among big national and regional institutions, all of which first had to pass muster with regulators, it was small wonder that the papers were filled with record-breaking commitments to community reinvestment. The mergers are not over, at this writing, and can probably be expected (at a slower pace) for the first few years of the twenty-first century.

Whatever the motivation, the Citibank-Travelers commitment surely seemed elephantine compared to anything that had gone before. Yet records are made to be broken. Barely two weeks later, enter NationsBank again, this time in a bid to merge with California behemoth BankAmerica. The announcement:

MAY 20, 1998—NationsBank and BankAmerica today unveiled a *$350 billion,* 10-year commitment to community development lending and investment, by far the largest and most comprehensive program ever for community development lending by a United States bank. ... As part of this unique commitment, the new company pledges to *acquire, build or rehabilitate* 50,000 affordable housing units during the next 10 years. [emphasis added]

Not only would the newly merged BankAmerica double the new Citigroup lending commitment, but the bank would actually *build some of the houses* on which it would then write mortgages. The only thing left would be to provide a car service to get buyers to the closing.

David Coulter, who was chairman and chief executive officer of BankAmerica at the time of the merger, has for many years been among the industry's liveliest advocates for community-reinvestment lending. There's little doubt that he believes such investments are not only socially equitable but economically sound. All the same, part of Coulter's remarks in the merger announcement made it clear where some of the impetus for such an enormous commitment came from.

"It's worth noting," said Coulter, "that our commitment roughly equals the combined total of all community lending goals made by the rest of the banking industry since the Community Reinvestment Act became law in 1977."

So sweeping and so profound has been the banks' change in approach to inner-city markets that today many of them angrily insist that legislative and regulatory pressure had little or nothing to do with their community lending programs. One banker, insisting on anonymity, said,

> We make loans in the inner city markets not because of CRA or the regulators, but because there are good loans to be made there. That took us a while to figure out—and a lot of that was figuring out how to recognize market potential that isn't captured in traditional measurements, so you really have to get to know the markets firsthand. But the regulations didn't make us do that; good business did.

Maybe. But for whatever reason, "good business" took a long time—more than two decades in most places—to work its good effects. And in the meantime, you have to wonder what induced so many lenders to "figure out how to recognize market potential" and "get to know the markets firsthand." Even assuming that many lenders no longer need any regulatory pressure to pursue business opportunities in poor and minority communities—an assumption that belies the language of their own press releases—it still seems likely that the initial pressure of CRA brought many bankers back into neighborhoods where they previously preferred not to stray.

❑

Controversial as CRA remains today—it narrowly survived its latest and most serious assault in Congress in late 1999—there is little to match the cries of alarm rising from Congress when the act was first passed. In more recent years, the act has come to be remembered wrongly, at least by critics in the GOP, as one of the Democrats' *causes célèbres* at the height of their post-Watergate exertions. Yet among many Democrats at the time, the passage of CRA was barely a cause at all, and its passage proved to be anything but célèbre. Had it not been for the zealous relentlessness of its sponsor, Senate Banking Committee Chairman William Proxmire of Wisconsin, the idea would have been highly unlikely to pass at all, at least in 1977, and probably not for years.

At that point, a minority report of Proxmire's banking committee, signed by opponents from every ideological corner except the confirmed Left, predicted that CRA's antiredlining rules "will discourage the free flow of funds and disrupt the flow of credit from capital-surplus areas to capital-short areas." It would, North Carolina Democrat Robert Morgan cried, raise the cost of mortgages, proliferate bad debt, corrupt the capital markets, and scare conscientious banks away from the very inner-city neighborhoods it was meant to enrich. Republicans, by and large, were less optimistic.

To many of its most dedicated supporters outside Congress— mainly grassroots organizations from low-income neighborhoods— the provision was a small (some said timid) attempt to compel banks at least to give less-affluent communities fair consideration for credit. It did not require banks to make any particular loan that they would otherwise responsibly have turned down, and certainly not any unsound or unprofitable loan. It simply required that banks demonstrate that they extended their marketing and services fairly to all of the communities where they were chartered to do business. They did not have to lend equally in all areas, just prove that they had offered their services aggressively and given equitable consideration to every customer who applied.

The penalty for not complying was subtle and (it turned out) more potent than it first appeared. As long as a bank didn't open or close branches or contemplate a merger, it could thumb its nose at CRA with impunity. And at first, fooled by the law's seeming toothlessness, many did. Only later, when a consolidation fever gripped the industry, did CRA develop a bite even nearly comparable to its bark.

Yet despite the law's apparent mildness, opponents initially saw in CRA the heavy, unwashed hand of government performing surgery on a vital organ of the free market: the one through which, at that time, most Americans saved and borrowed. Many lawmakers in 1977 were of an age to remember the bank failures of the 1930s. More than a few of those senior members, in good conscience, were disinclined to meddle with a regulatory system that had ensured safety and soundness for forty-plus years.

(Ironically, within a dozen or so years, some big banks and many savings institutions were indeed failing once again, in the fabled S&L crisis of the 1980s, and government policy was in fact at least partly to blame. Changes in the tax code, in deposit insurance, and in accounting and auditing practices were all part of that story, as was some out-and-out mismanagement. But CRA had no part of it, as even its fiercest critics conceded. The ruins of the industry, in fact, were bestrewn with gilt-edged paper from celebrity golf courses, exotic resorts, luxury condominium complexes, and—aptly enough—high-stakes casinos. Throughout that time, and even to the present day, community reinvestment loans have routinely outperformed other parts of the banks' real estate portfolios. For all the bile and bluster expended on CRA, not one financial institution has ever failed—or even suffered a bad night's sleep—because it overextended itself in poor or minority communities. The resorts and casinos, it need hardly be said, were mostly located elsewhere.)

For many members of Congress, the origins of CRA's legislative language were hardly reassuring. Much of that language arose from the grassroots experiences of firebrand community activists in Chicago, led by the formidable Gale Cincotta. With an alliance of grassroots guerrillas from around the country, Cincotta's protest group, called the National Information and Training Center, had drafted much of the act's language on the floor of a hotel conference room blocks away from Proxmire's Capitol Hill office.

Like most of the early fair-lending advocates, Cincotta had learned about the practice known as "redlining"—refusal to offer loans or other bank services in poor or minority neighborhoods—the hard way:

> When my grandparents retired and moved in with us—my mother and my father, my uncle, my dad's brother—we had four generations of people in the one house. So we got this two-flat [a house containing two apartments] and the only way you could get mortgages was, say, if the house was worth $20,000—it sounds funny now—you maybe could get a $10,000 loan and then the person who sold it to you had to

finance the difference. That was the only way you could buy a house in the city. Yet you go driving to the suburbs and you'd pass billboards offering loans for 5-percent down. I later talked to people in other areas of the city who couldn't get a loan at all, or the costs were sky-high. Seemed to me something was wrong.

My parents had a restaurant, and I found out the way they got money for supplies and working capital and everything is what they referred to as "juice loans"—supplier loans. The person who brought you in the juice or the side of beef or the crates of tomatoes also lent you money—at a very high interest rate. No banks would talk to you. From listening to their friends, people who owned laundries and grocery stores and all that, I learned that there weren't loans going much of anywhere in our area. That's how I learned about redlining.

For Cincotta and for Proxmire, the goal wasn't to force banks to relax their lending criteria. The goal was to get them to *apply* those criteria in older city neighborhoods in the same way as in suburbs. The whole industry, Cincotta discovered, was geared toward fueling the explosion of subdivisions that eventually suburbanized America. New, standardized homes, their values bolstered by seemingly endless demand, were easy collateral for simple, by-the-books home mortgages. Why, bankers seemed to be asking, should we take the extra trouble to make comparable loans in the idiosyncratic markets of the inner city, where every block told a different story and values went down as well as up?

Cincotta thought the answer was obvious: Not just out of fairness or justice. "But because if they didn't we were going to lose the cities. You could already see it happening."

❑

For most of this century, like it or not, Congress has been a prime mover in deciding where credit would flow in metropolitan areas. Politicians' pristine desire not to meddle in the "allocation" of credit has a polite ring of philosophical purity to it, but it bears no relation to reality. Throughout the great flow of new credit into the American suburbs after World War II, the roots of the banks' behavior lay not solely in their boardrooms, but squarely in Washington.

A big part of what made suburban housing so easy to finance and develop was that the government was quietly underwriting much of the cost. Not only was the federal government steadily writing checks for new highways, water and sewer lines, and other basic infrastructure that made subdivisions possible, but it was subsidizing the mortgages themselves, generally through the mortgage interest deduction, but also quite specifically through the Federal Housing Administration (FHA). And it had been doing that since the earliest days of the New Deal.

Federal lending programs, in fact, did not merely subsidize suburban development, they explicitly and aggressively blacklisted inner cities. In his landmark book *Crabgrass Frontier,* Kenneth T. Jackson unfolds some of the evidence of longstanding federal lending discrimination—practices that, if they occurred in any private-sector bank today, would be grounds not just for regulatory enforcement, but criminal prosecution.

Jackson describes the early appraisal procedures of the Home Owners' Loan Corporation (HOLC), a New Deal precursor of FHA that laid much of the technical groundwork for the modern mortgage. Among HOLC's "technical" innovations was the literal practice of redlining—of laying out elaborate, color-coded maps of metropolitan areas across the United States, with their neighborhoods graded according to their suitability for mortgage lending. In the worst areas, typically shaded in red, HOLC noted "detrimental influences" including the "infiltration of a lower-grade population" or an "undesirable population." In these areas, HOLC normally declined to accept any mortgages at all.

FHA, founded in 1945 after a dozen years of HOLC map-making, carried on the tradition. The new agency was in many ways a technical improvement on HOLC's relatively primitive operation (FHA insured mortgages, rather than refinancing them, thus relieving the federal government of having to supply huge amounts of capital directly to the mortgage market). But in one respect FHA made no attempt to improve on HOLC: It continued to redline, as historian Mark I. Gelfand put it, "vast areas of the inner cities, refusing to insure mortgages where the neighborhoods were blighted or susceptible to blight," no matter how bankable individual properties within those neighborhoods might still be.

In a red-coded area, for example, a subset of stable, well-maintained houses could no more qualify for financing than could other structures that might have been abandoned or run-down. These areas, needless to say, were most likely to be occupied by African Americans, immigrants, or other minorities—though as Cincotta learned, white native-born Americans were hardly exempt. "This action," wrote Gelfand, "practically guaranteed that these districts would deteriorate still further and drag cities down with them."

Private lenders had thus been schooled for decades on methods of redlining that were not just permissible under federal rules, but were largely *engineered* by the federal government. Seen in this context, the criticism that CRA would be an "interference" in the private credit market seems at least peculiar, if not flatly hypocritical. In reality, the act was a modest, indirect attempt to undo generations of destructive lending practices that Washington itself helped invent. Consequently, to view the modern mortgage industry as an immaculate offspring of the unfettered private market—one whose dainty virtue was now threatened by an unprecedented federal groping—was disingenuousness raised to the level of parody.

Perfect, in other words, for a congressional debate.

❑

CRA finally slid past its bipartisan opposition—though narrowly, and mostly through procedural maneuvers. Only five votes kept it from dying in the delivery room, when an amendment to delete it from that year's Housing and Community Development bill failed on the Senate floor 40 to 31, with both Republicans and Democrats voting for deletion. In the House of Representatives, the measure was never so much as introduced. Only Senator Proxmire's adroitness in the House-Senate Conference Committee nudged the measure into law, over howls of dismay from Wall Street, economists of various schools, and, naturally, the heads of banks and thrift institutions coast-to-coast.

Even then, the struggle was barely half over. Next, the four fiercely independent agencies then regulating various parts of the banking system—the Federal Reserve, the Office of the Comptroller of the

Currency, the Federal Deposit Insurance Corporation, and the Federal Home Loan Bank Board—had to agree on a single set of regulations that would bind the whole industry. It didn't help that many on the staff and board of the Federal Reserve felt the law was dangerously misguided.

It had a champion, though, at the Federal Home Loan Bank Board. Anita Miller, a former community activist herself, and later a senior program officer at the Ford Foundation, had been appointed to the Bank Board in the late 1970s, and promptly took responsibility for the board's community lending efforts. To Miller, CRA was a simple necessity, long overdue. But enacting the law would be a hollow victory, she reasoned, if the regulations didn't give bank examiners clear, uniform, fair, but powerful authority to hold banks accountable for what the law required. She recalls:

> CRA required all the Federal regulatory agencies to come out with one set of regulations. You can't underestimate the complexity of that. It had never happened before. So the heads of all these [bank regulatory] agencies, people in key positions, had held hearings all over the country, but after months and months of negotiations, they couldn't come out with the regulations. One of the big problems was that nobody in these agencies really understood the subject very well. The other problem was that, in those days before Paul Volcker [became Federal Reserve chairman], the Fed was so conservative and so hostile. It changed later on, but at that time, the Fed was so tied into the major banks in the country that they didn't want any part of CRA, and they didn't want any regulations, and as far as they were concerned the least that was done would be too much.

Writing the regulations therefore turned into what then–Bank Board attorney Sandra Rosenblith later described as "something like World War I, where whole battles were waged over a few inches." As she remembers it:

> One typical issue was small business lending. We argued meeting after meeting over whether that meant loans to small businesses, small loans to any businesses, or small loans to small businesses. The statute just

said "small business lending." The whole statute was very short, so it was subject to a lot of interpretation, but this shows the depth of detail in our arguments, that we went back and forth *for weeks* over just those words. It ultimately came out to "loans to small businesses," which had been the logical interpretation all along. But it took weeks to get to that obvious point, and every other phrase ended up leading us to another protracted negotiation just like this one.

Miller's high-level lobbying, and the dogged negotiating tactics of staff-level champions like Rosenblith, eventually produced a consensus document that, whatever its ambiguities, made one point clear: Banks would do well to learn how to lend fairly in low-income markets, and every regulatory agency in the industry would be watching. In quiet times, admittedly, the penalties for failure would be few. But in times of change, every attempt at mergers, branch closings and openings, or other changes in business scope would screech to a halt for banks whose community-reinvestment record was poor. And eventually, by the 1990s, the day would come when mergers and other changes in scope would be matters of life and death for America's most prominent banks.

❑

Since the late 1970s—and most especially in the '90s—whenever banks consider merging, buying, selling, or opening and closing branches, one of their first questions has been "how will we do on CRA?" If their record is poor anywhere, even in one neighborhood, they can expect community leaders or advocacy groups to file a "comment," or challenge, to their application. Opinions from community groups and members of the general public are specifically invited in the CRA regulations, and all must be reviewed before regulators issue any approval or denial.

The review may consist of a painstaking examination of bank records, one or more public hearings, lengthy closed-door meetings, and most often, all of these in combination. Banks often find it necessary to respond in writing, and may need to negotiate with the "commenting" organizations and other community groups before responding. Meanwhile, other authorities may comment further, and all the while a complex and sometimes sensitive merger, acquisition, or expansion sits on ice, while the regulators, bankers, and advocates bicker about community reinvestment.

A senior official of one large bank—an institution with a generally well-regarded CRA record—described the frustration this can cause:

> We had a lot of pressures from various groups in merger and branch applications, conjuring up a lot of statistics, even against our record in the inner city—which afterward, when the TV lights went out, they would always tell us was the best in the industry. But on the record, they'd argue we were redlining, and they'd pressure us to do a lot of things that went way beyond lending—including change the makeup of our board of directors, make donations to their organizations, what have you. Leverage was being used in the process that went way beyond questions of fair lending, and everybody knew it. That's just how the game was played.

Significantly, the banker who raised these concerns would discuss them only on condition that his name, and the name of his bank, not be used. "There's still a lot of distrust around this issue," he said. "It's gotten a little better over the years, but it'll never go away completely."

In the first, and still extremely rare, example of how badly all of this can go, regulators turned down the Greater New York Savings Bank's request to open a new branch in 1979, specifically on CRA grounds. A handful of other major denials (there have been no more than half a dozen in the whole history of CRA) have served as double-edged reminders: first, that occasionally banks may face the extreme penalty; second, and conversely, that any reasonable effort to accommodate the demands of CRA will probably clear the regulatory obstacles from a bank's path.

In the Federal Reserve's annual community-reinvestment reviews, between 90 and 95 percent of banks generally get ratings of "satisfactory" or "outstanding." "Out of tens of thousands of CRA exams," says John Taylor of the advocacy group the National Community Reinvestment Coalition, "the number found unsatisfactory is infinitesimally small, and they're always tiny institutions in the middle of nowhere. And rare as a dodo bird is the denial of a merger application as a result of a CRA challenge."

Why, then, if CRA demands so little, have banks' community-reinvestment commitments added up to more than $1 trillion as of 1998? One reason, say Taylor and other advocates, is that the commitments actually conceal tens of billions of dollars in routine business that banks would have done anyway. The commitments frequently include, besides genuinely new activity, some "no-brainer" loans to wealthy minority customers, ongoing credit-card services, and the processing of conventional home loans that are almost immediately sold to national mortgage institutions. Others include highly subsidized, insured, or richly collateralized loans to nonprofit agencies backed by government programs.

Still, when community organizations complain that CRA enforcement hardly ever leads to severe penalties, they overlook the preemptive nature of most CRA enforcement. The penalties aren't necessary because banks either have learned to live by the act's rules, or else they quickly find ways of doing so once the regulators are pounding at the door. Most banks, as the escalating press releases of the 1990s have proven, will go to great lengths to prevent a CRA challenge by demonstrating (or at least promising) an aggressive community lending program in low-income areas.

The results are by now beyond dispute, as Taylor and many others willingly acknowledge. Something astonishing has happened in inner-city credit markets across the United States. Not only have community-based organizations found it vastly easier to line up financing and equity investments for their projects, but millions of individual borrowers and home buyers have found credit where for decades there had been only rejections.

Mortgages to low- and moderate-income neighborhoods surged by nearly 26 percent between 1993 and 1995, according to the Reinvestment Coalition, and by close to 10 percent from 1995 to '96. Home ownership among African Americans and Hispanics has climbed steadily through most of the 1990s, and in some years jumped sharply. Total lending in low-income communities has increased from an average of $3 billion a year between 1977 and 1989 to $43 billion a year as of 1997.

A June 1995 report by the Chicago Federal Reserve estimated that some $8 million in lending per metropolitan area, an average of roughly 100 loans per market, was attributable primarily to CRA. That hardly seems like a lot, except that a loan attributable "primarily" to CRA would be a significant loan indeed—one, in short, that could not otherwise be explained by conventional criteria, even in the expanding markets of the mid-1990s.

Finding and counting such loans is hardly a precise science (or even, some would say, much more than guesswork). But however they are counted, such loans are only the most extreme evidence of the effectiveness of CRA. If there are $8 million in loans per year per city resulting *just from CRA*, how much more lending may be the result of ordinary economic decisions—ones that are responsible and defensible by conventional rules—but that otherwise might have been back-burnered, quietly discouraged, or overlooked, except for the goading of CRA? On paper, those don't look like unusual or exceptional loans, and they consequently aren't counted as "attributable" to CRA. But judged from an inner-city residential street or a barrio commercial strip, they may seem remarkable indeed.

Unmotivated by law or regulation, many bankers admit (off the record) that some institutions have avoided market areas that they perceived to be "more complex" or "higher risk," even though it would probably be possible to make sound loans in those areas with a little extra effort. One senior banker described the reasoning this way (again, on condition that his institution not be identified):

> You don't want to take on high-risk loans in an area you're not already familiar with. That isn't a racial decision, it's an economic one. If you're not doing much business in a particular neighborhood, and the data on the surface look bad, are you going to spend the time it takes to ferret out the few strong opportunities from the overly risky ones? How much time and research is it worth investing for a few small loans in a place where you don't really understand the risk factors, and the chances for a bad decision are high?

Bankers were not alone in making this calculation. In its published guidelines for loans on apartment buildings and other multifamily developments, the Federal National Mortgage Association (commonly known as Fannie Mae) as recently as 1990 was still telling bankers: "Lenders should originate loans in stable *neighborhoods of good or better quality*, or ... where the economic trend is positive, strong, demonstrable, and continuous" [emphasis added].

This was the world's largest mortgage institution talking—the fourth largest financial company in the United States—from whom most banks drew a huge percentage of their capital for residential lending. The skittishness wasn't merely a matter of published guidelines: A banker in Miami recalls the day when a whole delegation from Fannie Mae canceled a planned visit to Miami's Liberty City neighborhood when someone informed them that the area had been the site of a recent riot. The visit was never rescheduled.

As long as Fannie Mae was saying, in effect, "stay out of risky neighborhoods," bankers would have to find other sources of capital when lending money for apartment buildings and other multiunit complexes. Unlike banks, of course, Fannie Mae is legally a "government-sponsored enterprise" not subject to CRA.

Six years later, though, a new CEO at Fannie Mae wrote that these "non-racial" arguments still led to a result that was not visibly different from explicit racial redlining. As a result of fair-housing legislation to correct the problem, James A. Johnson wrote proudly that "the home-ownership rate for native-born young black American households increased from 31 percent to almost 44 percent between 1980 and 1990. For native-born young Hispanic households, the rate increased from 38 to 52 percent."

This hardly sounded like the same Fannie Mae. And sure enough, behind the scenes, some important factors had changed. In 1992 Congress enacted new rules that subjected Fannie Mae, the Federal Home Loan Mortgage Corporation ("Freddie Mac"), and other "government-sponsored enterprises" to a few provisions similar to CRA. That, and the arrival of James Johnson, signaled a new day at the core of the home-lending industry. (Still, at the beginning of 2000, fresh allegations of lending discrimination by Fannie Mae and Freddie Mac had reached the Justice Department, which is still investigating as this book goes to press.)

Yet just as the flood of new capital was finally being heralded by scholars and pundits, taken up enthusiastically by investors and home buyers, and touted in the banks' own press releases, CRA's opponents in Congress were arming for their greatest assault ever. The first rumblings came in 1998, when New York's veteran Republican Senator Alfonse D'Amato, chair of the Senate Banking Committee, lost a reelection bid and the committee gavel passed to Texas Senator Phil Gramm.

D'Amato, a confirmed conservative, had been a passionate and skillful defender of CRA. A few New York State Democrats even worried publicly over his defeat, knowing that they had lost the Senate's most valuable friend of fair banking. Worse, the incoming chairman was certain to take the opposite tack: Gramm is so ferocious an opponent of CRA that he has compared it to slavery, and called it (without so much as a nod to the actual institution of slavery) "the greatest national scandal in the United States."

That kind of talk from some other member of Congress might simply have invited ridicule. But from the chair of the Banking Committee, at this moment in history, it fell like a hail of artillery. For more than twenty years, bankers, economists, regulators, and other business leaders had been pushing legislation that would undo some of the banking restrictions passed during the Great Depression. The reforms they were advocating would let banks sell insurance and deal in securities, and permit companies in those three fields to merge. For most of its history, the proposal had fallen prey to infighting among insurance companies, commercial banks, and investment banks. But late in the 1990s, the three sectors had finally managed to agree on a single proposal, and by 1999 the Financial Services Modernization Act was finally headed for approval—just as Phil Gramm took charge of the Banking Committee.

No reform legislation would make it through that committee, he flatly declared, unless it also undid some key elements of CRA, particularly its main enforcement mechanism: the process by which community organizations can "comment" on proposed mergers, when they believed a merging institution had failed to serve the community fairly. Because this process sometimes delays mergers—and can induce institutions like Citibank and Bank of America to fork over huge sums for social-investment purposes—Gramm considered it "an extortion racket." Of course, twenty years' experience had proven that, without the "comment" provisions, there were virtually no penalties for ignoring CRA. Eliminate those, and you vaporize the act—which was exactly what Gramm intended to do.

The banking reforms were, according to one bank lobbyist, "probably the most heavily lobbied, most expensive issue" before Congress in a generation. Banks and other financial services companies had spent some $30 million to press their cause in just the first three quarters of 1999. They were not about to do anything that would jeopardize passage of the bill they'd worked so hard (and so expensively) to promote. But neither did they have anything bad to say about community reinvestment, even off the record. "The effort by Mr. Gramm to limit the community lending laws," the *New York Times* reported in mid-1999, "does not appear to have the support of the majority of the banking community, which has profited handsomely from making loans to the disadvantaged and underserved." But just in case bankers were tempted to speak up on the subject, Gramm warned them privately to bite their tongues. Any kind words for CRA, and he'd kill their bill.

In the House of Representatives, where Banking Chairman Jim Leach was determined to craft a bipartisan bank-reform bill, there was little debate about community reinvestment, and what few issues arose were quickly resolved. The few mentions in the final House bill actually had the effect of strengthening the act in small ways. And Republicans there (including many with conservative credentials every bit as solid as Gramm's) were apparently content to leave CRA more or less as they found it. Thus it was that, once again, the fate of community reinvestment was going to come down to one senator's maneuvering in a Conference Committee. Only this time, the senator in question had a knife in his hand.

In the end, for reasons partly concealed in the final closed-door negotiations, Gramm flinched. All other differences had been reconciled, the financial industry had a bill it deeply wanted, and the president was willing to sign it—provided it left community reinvestment largely intact. It seems likely that, in these final hours, Gramm found himself isolated—staring down powerful financiers, exhausted colleagues, and a presidential veto threat—and decided not to risk their unanimous wrath on this issue. He insisted on a few face-saving provisions that together weaken the act only slightly. The enforcement provisions, in any case, are largely intact.

The bank-reform battle was the most profound political test of CRA, and of the principle of fair banking, since the day Proxmire introduced the issue in the 1970s. Despite the fevered opposition of the most powerful politician in the field, despite a starkly muted defense (at best) from the industry, and despite almost zero involvement of mass public opinion, CRA survived, pretty much intact. After sneaking its way into the law books, the twenty-two-year-old act found itself backed by a broad, energetic defense on Capitol Hill. That defense happened solely because, in those twenty-two years, the law had proven itself not only fair, but fantastically profitable to some of the most desperate places in the country—while doing zero harm to the banks whose interests Phil Gramm was so keen to defend.

The most effective argument in defense of CRA, it seems, came from the Leadership Conference on Civil Rights, a trade group of the country's major civil rights organizations, as well as from community development and advocacy groups. Community reinvestment, they argued all over Capitol Hill, is a crucial avenue to the economic mainstream for members of minority groups and working-class white Americans who are finally making it as businesspeople, home owners, and investors. Minority neighborhoods are turning around, minority entrepreneurs are finding capital for new ventures, and minority families are starting to think of banks as places where they can do more than just cash checks. That progress was not the result of "banking as usual." It was, in fact, the opposite of the "slavery" to which Gramm tried to compare CRA. It was the combined effect of effective regulatory pressure and intelligent bank response. The Leadership Conference made that case loud and clear, and—against long odds—Washington listened.

❏

Although there is no database that measures exactly where banks' commitments have flowed, anecdotal evidence is that, at the beginning of CRA's third decade, more institutions are more responsive to more credit needs in more urban neighborhoods than at any time in living memory. In 1998, analysts at the Urban Institute found increased lending in the low-income areas of twenty-two out of twenty-three cities they studied. In eleven of those cities, they found "significant improvements."

The National Community Reinvestment Coalition—a collection of neighborhood-based community-reinvestment leaders from around the country—has kept a tally of banks' CRA commitments over the years. In the fourteen years between 1977 and 1991, they reported a total of $8.8 billion in aggregate commitments. In the next six years, new commitments added more than $388 billion to that total— enough, for example, to put nearly 4 million people in new or renovated homes (though it will surely be used for more things than housing). But then, that entire twenty-year amount was instantly dwarfed by the announcements made in just the first *six months* of 1998. After promises of that scope, the odds are surely good that some of this money, at least, will flow as new credit to capital-hungry markets. And increases in credit to inner cities and rural communities seem to bear that out.

Chapter 6

NEW STORES —
AND NEW CUSTOMERS —
ON MAIN STREET

THUS FAR, the great mass of renewed inner-city credit has flowed primarily into residential mortgages, far more than, say, small business or other commercial loans. For one thing, mortgages are relatively easier for banks to issue, largely because national institutions like Fannie Mae provide most of the capital and absorb the lion's share of risk. Meanwhile, federal policies like CRA and the Home Mortgage Disclosure Act have put most of their regulatory ammunition behind fair lending in the residential market. And in any case, businesses are inherently riskier things to underwrite than home purchases.

This predominance of home-mortgage lending in inner cities has made an easy target for critics of both federal policy and neighborhood-led development. These critics argue, reasonably enough, that houses, unlike businesses, don't create jobs (apart from the short-term construction work associated with building or renovation). For those who have been impatient for the kind of lending that attracts investment capital and builds employment, residential development has seemed like little more than community beautification.

In the early years of neighborhood revitalization, that view was understandable, if a little myopic. But after twenty years of renewed residential lending, something far more fundamental is changing in inner-city communities where renovated housing and ancillary improvements have reached a critical mass: Businesses, particularly retailers, are coming back—not because of inducements from lenders or government policy, but because the environment is now more conducive to doing business. There are two parts to this conduciveness: First, investments in housing, increased home ownership, and the attendant reductions in decay and crime now make many residential neighborhoods inviting for customers again. But the improved environment has also made it possible for businesses to notice and act on a crucial second factor: *There is disposable income in these neighborhoods.* Quite a lot of it, in fact. The density of inner-city neighborhoods makes up in volume what those neighborhoods lack in individual earnings or wealth. And in these neighborhoods, more of the family income tends to be spent locally, on daily necessities like food, household goods, and medicine—provided there are local stores in which to spend it.

No one has made this argument more persuasively, or from a loftier vantage point, than Michael Porter, the Harvard business professor who first made his reputation studying competitive advantage among private companies, and later among nations. In a now-famous 1995 article in the *Harvard Business Review,* Porter turned his attention to the competitiveness of the American inner city. From that seminal article, and volumes of subsequent writing by Porter and others, a whole body of theory, experimentation, and spirited debate has flowed. Among other things, the research that underlay that article also helped fuel the Initiative for a Competitive Inner City, a nonprofit group that Porter founded and still leads.

For Porter, one of the youngest tenured professors ever at Harvard Business School, the transition from dissecting corporate strategy to building inner-city neighborhoods was like a leap into a professional abyss. Criticism flew from both sides: Some B-school colleagues rolled their eyes at what they considered a woolly-headed social mission unbecoming a business scholar. And more than a few veteran urbanists scoffed at someone they saw as a corporate and academic naïf wading into the social and political swamps of urban policy. "His program," wrote Merrill Goozner in a 1998 article in the *American Prospect,* "is essentially a jazzier version of the ghetto bootstrap capitalism that has proved so difficult to put into practice."

But Porter's arguments have proven to be both subtler and tougher than his critics recognized. Economic development programs as successful and respected as Cleveland's and Boston's have looked to Porter as a guide, with stunning results. In mid-1999, President Bill Clinton set off on a national "new markets" tour of redeveloping areas—advocating investment tax incentives with speeches drawn point-by-point from the writings of Porter and his disciples. And the evidence that these ideas can work has been strongest in precisely the area that Porter's Initiative for a Competitive Inner City targeted as its richest opportunity: inner-city retail markets.

"Could it be," a front-page *Christian Science Monitor* article asked in 1998, "that some of America's seemingly destitute inner cities are

Michael Porter and merchant Eduardo Cruz in Roxbury, Boston, 1994.
(Michael Quan/NYT Pictures)

actually untapped gold mines of consumer desire—that they're ready to hand a handsome profit to retail stores willing to venture into struggling neighborhoods?" Yes, it could be. As the Initiative for a Competitive Inner City documented in a 1997 study, inner-city retail markets account for 7 percent of national spending, with some grocers capturing, on average, up to 40 percent better sales per square foot in inner cities than in their metropolitan areas as a whole.

Retailers have known this, at least intuitively, for some time. Several, like Payless ShoeSource, have built whole growth strategies around inner-city communities, carefully picking sites in communities that, while often poor, offered enough stability and safety to attract customers. Others, though, needed persuading. Finding those stable, safe neighborhoods is a science, and the penalties for mistakes can be high. Discount retailers like Payless and fast-food franchisers like McDonald's have become experts at it; others needed time to learn the ropes. And many have waited, while others tested the water and their own opportunities clarified.

"Generally when people look at the inner cities they see challenges," Pathmark senior vice president Harvey Gutman said in 1998.

> They see expensive land assemblage, difficult approval policies, higher operating and distribution costs, taxes, and crime. But some of the more astute retailers are seeing opportunities as well—emerging and regrowth in inner-city locations, a need for modern supermarkets, and in many cases government incentives or encouragement or both to make the stores a reality. Stores that closed down in the 1960s and '70s are starting to look at the equation again, and they've found it's shifted.

It's shifted slowly, to be sure. Pathmark's own experience in Harlem, where it now has a hugely successful new supermarket, illustrates just how stubborn the old barriers to investment still can be. When the chain set out, in 1995, to open a new supermarket in East Harlem, the result was a classic New York City neighborhood trench war. But instead of the usual clash of militant residents against the "suits," this was a war of business against business. Harlem residents were just as eager as Pathmark to see a convenient supermarket in their midst. In fact, it was two residents' groups, the church-based Abyssinian Development Corp. and the nonprofit Community Association of East Harlem Triangle, that were seeking to develop a new shopping plaza for the supermarket to occupy. But small merchants in the vicinity, fearful of losing their captive market to a national competitor, organized to block the project.

"It is comforting for the oppressed to rail against the oppressor," veteran urbanist Louis Winnick wrote in the *New York Times* some years later. "But in Harlem, who was the oppressed and who was the oppressor?" Thus did the tidy ideologies of the old urban politics run headlong into the new politics of inner-city markets. The "oppressor" in this case was a phalanx of low-income minority consumers, fed up with crossing the East River or heading downtown on a bus every time they wanted a supermarket's variety and low prices.

The self-described "oppressed" were owners of neighborhood convenience stores and small markets. They resisted the project fiercely (often ingeniously), and managed to baffle their local politicians enough to delay it for years. In the end, the supermarket squeaked past its opponents by a single vote on Manhattan's chief planning board. On the day of its opening in 1999, the dais proudly featured the African-American and Hispanic leadership of the sponsoring community groups next to their mostly white partners from Pathmark, with the Republican governor of New York State presiding in between.

But behind the happy ending is a perfect illustration of why retailers have been slow to discover the unparalleled opportunity of an inner-city location. If they're willing to put up with the suburban competition, both for customers and for workers, companies can close on several store locations in a matter of days, just by doing business with one big mall developer. In Harlem, one store took months of executive time and trouble—stretched over a period of years—plus an occasional black eye in the local press.

As with all New York City development disputes, plenty of favors had to be passed around Harlem to pacify various disputants. But after the dust had settled, residents had their supermarket, plus a new bank branch, drugstore, and parking garage. And a ramshackle commercial strip along East 125th Street at last had an economic anchor.

The struggle was well worth it for Pathmark, too, according to Gut-man. But you can see why at least some retailers still view the whole thing with a mixture of curiosity and distaste.

Still, what happened *next* in East Harlem helps explain why the market explosion in inner cities can't be understood just through the lens of individual projects, no matter how impressive or difficult those might be. Within weeks before the Pathmark formally opened, the *New York Times* reported that other local grocery stores were redesign-ing their shelves and facades, stocking fresher produce, and expanding their inventory. Another proposed supermarket site, in Central Harlem, was now drawing competing proposals from experienced op-erators, including one from Pathmark.

Even as the Pathmark turf battles were raging, a retail and movie-house complex, with basketball superstar Magic Johnson as a prime investor, was in development just blocks away. Farther east, another developer prepared plans for yet a third retail development, with a competing complex of movie theaters by United Artists. When the lat-ter plans were unveiled, the *New York Times* quoted market analyst Ken Smikle as saying that companies like United Artists would never have considered this neighborhood if pioneers like Magic Johnson hadn't prepared the way. "It took someone who understood the com-munity to recognize that there was more to profit from than to fear," Smikle said.

Pathmark likewise had made a science out of "understanding the community," well before tackling the political morass of East Harlem. A supermarket chain that operates only in northeastern states, Path-mark was one of few supermarket companies never to give up com-pletely on inner-city markets—not because of social concerns, but for business reasons. "A great percentage of the population here," says Gutman, "is in inner cities. We could still have focused only on the suburbs, but that by definition would have limited our growth oppor-tunities. A few of our competitors now are seeing the success that we've had and are starting to put a toe into those same waters."

The changing equation evidently became clear to many retailers in the mid-1990s, about the same time Porter was turning his attention to urban neighborhoods. In 1996, Harvard Business School produced the first case study focused on inner-city supermarkets, concentrating on examples from Harlem, Cleveland, and Newark. That same year, the *Boston Globe* reported on its front page that "three decades after fleeing the poor central city, corporate America is making its first tentative return."

> With the suburbs commercially saturated, supermarkets, pharmacies, clothiers, video stores and movie houses are beginning to fill the storefronts that once housed only bodegas and pawnshops. They are being accompanied by banks, insurance agencies, even some manufacturing and service companies, which, if they ever operated in low-income communities, joined the white flight of the '50s and '60s that decimated much of the nation's urban landscape.

Note that there are two parts to this equation. Yes, the economic opportunity of inner cities has become clearer, as more and more cities and neighborhoods have taken steps to control crime, improve physical conditions, and stabilize residential markets. But a second factor is just as important: Suburban markets are increasingly saturated, and many consumers are beginning to chafe at the predictable, arid environment of suburban shopping plazas and malls.

A consumer reaction, slow but perceptible, has started to take shape—what *Women's Wear Daily* called an "overwhelming consumer interest in neighborhood shopping." "Retailers and consumers are demanding [a neighborhood] environment," retail developer Ken Himmel observed in 1997. "They are saying they want a better shopping experience. Mall traffic is off, and it's telling retailers that people are looking for something more."

In fact, as *Women's Wear Daily* reported in the same story, research is showing that consumers are spending less and less time in malls, sales there are down, and the average number of trips to malls has declined in the 1990s. The point is not, of course, that consumers prefer to shop on the South Side of Chicago or in Newark's North Ward rather than in upscale suburbs. The point is that the opportunity for retailers to continue developing in suburbs and to increase revenues there is drying up.

Meanwhile, the consumer demand for local shopping in inner-city neighborhoods is overwhelming. It's not just the convenience. A lack of quality neighborhood retail outlets imposes a real cost on people who must choose between high-priced convenience stores and a long trek to remote shopping centers for groceries. When Shaw's Supermarket opened a new store in New Haven's Dwight neighborhood, resident Michele Chichester told a local reporter that, until that day, she'd had to take a taxi to buy groceries. The trip added an average $9 a month to her grocery bill.

That's $9 she wasn't spending on food or household necessities. That money wasn't just flowing outside of her community, it was draining her quality of life. By opening a store in Dwight, Shaw's supermarket gave Michele Chichester—and a great many of her neighbors—the equivalent of an after-tax raise in their paycheck. Generous? Not really: As Ms. Chichester told the reporter, the odds are rather good that Shaw's will see most or all of that $9 a month coming straight back into its till. But the Chichester family will now have something to show for it: There will be up to $9 worth of additional merchandise in the family pantry.

What some supermarkets, fast-food, and discount retailers discovered first, other businesses are starting to learn as well. In 1998, the pharmacy chain Rite-Aid announced a $230 million investment plan for "economically depressed urban areas," featuring thirty-seven new Rite-Aid stores, seventy-three relocations, and seventeen remodeling projects across twenty states and the District of Columbia.

Although Rite-Aid chairman and CEO Martin Grass was subsequently feted at the White House and honored by community groups, the point of the "development plan" was not philanthropic. True, Rite-Aid included civic participation and local hiring among the responsibilities of its inner-city stores. But as Pathmark's Gutman pointed out, that's simply an essential part of successful urban retailing: "You don't succeed anywhere unless you understand your market and limit your risks," and doing that requires working with local people and organizations, being perceived as a good neighbor and a community asset, and taking part in civic projects that are good for the whole community, including the store.

For Rite-Aid, as for most of the advance guard of retailers returning to the inner city, the main calculation is finding opportunities for growth to replace the choked commercial strips of an overbuilt suburbia. Compared to its potential locations in suburban Los Angeles, for example—with their miles upon miles of megastores, discount outlets, shopping plazas, and other hubs of competitive ferment—the sparkling new Rite Aid in South Central LA is the only drugstore for two miles. Which location seems riper?

Even more upscale retailers are coming back, though more often to downtown stores than to residential neighborhoods. The hip clothing chain The Gap, for example, in the late 1990s not only opened stores in minority markets coast to coast, but launched a nationwide print and TV ad campaign featuring hip-hop artists decked out in Gap jeans and accessories.

But even in downtown locations, retailers insist on more than just inexpensive space and a lively market. "Absent other urban economic initiatives," a Federated Department Stores spokesperson said in 1997, "many downtowns cannot sustain a retail base." The key "urban economic initiatives" that most retailers want to see are local magnets for pedestrian traffic: a dense and lively residential neighborhood, or a consumer gathering spot like a stadium or transportation hub. Cities are rich in these assets—and in consumers eager to spend time and money closer to home. What has been lacking, until recently, is the "economic initiative" to develop or stabilize such magnets, and make them safe.

When Pathmark located in two of New York City's toughest neighborhoods—first in Brooklyn's Bedford-Stuyvesant in 1979 and then twenty years later in Harlem—the company didn't go in alone, but looked first for a community organization with popular and government backing. The partnership with residents and city government, Gutman says, was essential: "When the community shares the ownership of the store, there's going to be a greater measure of safety. Knowing that caused us to learn a lot more about the inner city." And it led to explicit partnerships with community-based development groups, including an equity stake for those groups.

That is Rite-Aid's approach as well. But it's not everyone's, and for some businesses it probably isn't essential for success. What is essential, as Porter and others continually emphasize, is a concentrated residential base of consumers in reasonably safe, stable housing. Core cities, with federal help, have labored for more than two decades to establish or reestablish those kinds of communities, often with strategies that focused on little or nothing besides better housing. Yet those strategies have in fact created the consumer base and the hospitable environment for what *Women's Wear Daily* later called "a newfangled brand of urban renewal."

It's actually nothing of the kind. The restored commercial markets in inner cities are in fact merely the latest stage of the oldfangled brand of community and residential development. First came the capital, then the houses, then the stores. It wasn't fast or easy, but it wasn't especially "newfangled" either. It simply took time, labor, and capital to bring back to neighborhoods the economic engines that had built them in the first place.

But look at what that combined, sustained effort means for those neighborhoods, and for the city around them. Return, for a moment, to that Shaw's Supermarket in New Haven—in a place where for years neighbors have labored to repair and renovate housing, boost home ownership, and generally improve the physical and social atmosphere of the neighborhood.

The aggregate effect of all that effort, though measurable in property values or resident opinion polls, became magnificently more obvious when the community was drawn together by the centripetal pull of a new shopping plaza. Both the store's owners and its customers now talk enthusiastically about the community's stake in this development and its determination to keep the store's environment safe and clean. One neighbor who had recently bought a home near the market said, "I feel like they just built an extension on my house—like I got something now that the previous owners didn't have, and that I didn't know whether I was going to have."

The social magnet of that development—and its solid affirmation that life in this community is sustainable and improving—amounts to an explosive economic force as well as a social one. The message is: This is once again a neighborhood with large-scale pedestrian traffic to feed other businesses, with community assets that benefit residents and call forth their vigilant protection, and most of all, where owning real estate starts to look like a promising investment as well as a route to better housing. Those are the essential messages for attracting further investment to the area. Without them, the neighborhood remains a charity case. With them, it becomes a market and an enterprise.

The inner-city investment boomlet isn't limited to retail stores. In its May 1999 issue, *Inc.* magazine devoted its cover story, the editor's essay, and a lengthy series of profiles to what it called the "Inner City 100": high-growth companies of all kinds that chose an inner-city location not for lack of alternatives, but for its advantages, and now are thriving there. "Far from being liabilities," the magazine effused, "these potentially precarious areas have actually become a key competitive advantage ... whether because of proximity to customers and suppliers, the ready availability of an untapped local labor pool, or the cost advantages of the real estate."

The hard work of creating this "competitive advantage" began, in significant degree, with the first stirrings of the credit revolution of the 1970s. The re-creation of healthy retail markets, with all their attendant benefits in social vitality, employment, and security, was the next essential step. But for these rejuvenating forces to work, neighborhood markets still need the most basic resource of all: people—especially working-age people. And in inner cities, it turns out, that, too, can be partly a matter of government policy.

The New (Urban) Americans: A Postscript

Among the last stories anyone would have expected to see a decade ago was this curious item, which showed up on the *New York Times'* front page in early 2000:

> NEWARK, March 9—Soaring home prices. Sclerotic traffic. The maddening roar of new construction. Too many people, not enough room.
>
> Ah, the woes of a booming economy.
>
> But in an unlikely tale for flush times, the locale in question is not Manhattan or Westchester County, but a corner of Newark, a city left for dead after the 1967 riots, where almost a third of the residents still live in poverty. The Ironbound section, long a bastion of Portuguese immigrants and more recently a magnet for Brazilians and other Latin Americans, has become one of the hottest swaths of real estate in the region. ...
>
> The Ironbound's main commercial artery, Ferry Street, is lined with restaurants and bakeries, its sidewalks thick with pedestrians. "I defy you to find an empty storefront on Ferry Street," [Newark historian Charles] Cummings said.
>
> On weekends, thousands of Brazilians, Portuguese and other visitors from the metropolitan area flock to Ferry Street, snarling traffic and

double parking on side streets. On most afternoons, the desperate honk-ing of blocked-in drivers fills the air.

For business owners like Jose Moreira, the throngs are good news. "On weekends you can't even walk around in here," Mr. Moreira said on a recent Sunday as he held court at his restaurant, Casa Nova.

The news isn't all rosy. The *Times* story carefully points out that this massive new vitality is not general to Newark—a city still struggling back from years of mismanagement and inflamed race relations. But the Ironbound covers a large and by now well-known swath of the city, luring tourists from elsewhere in New Jersey and New York and providing Sharpe James, Newark's enterprising reform mayor, a com-petitive asset with which to attract investors to his city.

Yet this story of fantastic strength in one of America's toughest places is not a story of wise philanthropy, or planned redevelopment, or suc-cessful government initiative—or, for that matter, of any urban "pol-icy." It's a story about people moving to this country and finding an urban neighborhood they consider congenial (in this case, largely be-cause the Ironbound's Portuguese heritage made it easy for Brazilian newcomers to do business in their own language). The Ironbound isn't especially attractive or strategically located—its name comes from be-ing ringed in by railroad tracks. It had just one major asset: a welcom-ing ambience for a particular group of immigrants. And that—plus the entrepreneurship of the new arrivals—launched a rocket of economic growth for the neighborhood and the whole city.

If urban neighborhoods are becoming attractive to some American middle-class families once again, as it seems they are, it is still unre-alistic to expect inner cities suddenly to become prime destinations for the mass of upwardly mobile families now moving to suburbs. Someday, as those families grow weary of suburban monotony and multihour commutes, and as metropolitan areas learn to practice smarter growth, the outward pull to suburbia may actually turn around in force. But that is at best a long time off. Meanwhile, inner-city neighborhoods—especially the poorest ones—need fresh sup-plies of people willing to plant stakes, take entry-level jobs, start small businesses, and repair and maintain property. People, in other words, like the Portuguese and Brazilian residents of the Ironbound. The world is richly supplied with such people. The question for

American cities is whether these would-be residents will be allowed into the United States.

As in the formerly mean streets of Brooklyn, Chicago, and Oakland—in fact, the vast majority of recovering central-city areas—neighborhoods have proven that it's possible to build stable, tranquil, safe communities without obliterating poverty. A successful neighborhood doesn't necessarily have to be one where the poor are displaced by the better-off. It can simply be a place where a mix of incomes, widely accepted social norms, and a concerted effort at self-improvement have taken root. But wholesale vacancy, chronic joblessness, and an exclusively elderly population is not tenable, no matter how well behaved and self-motivated the remaining populace is. Neighborhoods need working people—people raising families, buying goods, populating the streets and parks, demanding results from schools. Where such people do not now exist, they need to be supplied.

For most of our history, in city after city, immigrants with small means and only basic skills have settled in such neighborhoods, done well there—and in a generation or so, like most Americans, moved on, replaced partly by newcomers much like themselves. Now, there is surely no more hardy perennial in our national political conversation than whether immigration is a good thing for America. That is a macroeconomic argument well beyond our scope here (although others have made an affirmative case persuasively and in depth). There is almost no question, in any case, about whether immigration is good for *cities,* or about whether many inner-city markets will reach their full potential without it.

One small example of the favorable macroeconomic evidence: A 1998 study by the National Academy of Sciences concluded that "due to immigrants who arrived since 1980, total gross national product is about $200 billion higher each year." The academy went on to forecast that immigrants would add $2 trillion to the nation's GNP by the end of the '90s. Michigan Senator Spencer Abraham, quoting the study approvingly in the *Wall Street Journal,* proudly declared that it "confirms what most Americans have known all along: Our tradition of welcoming immigrants pays off—for the immigrant and for the rest of us."

Yet plenty of Americans would no doubt dispute the claim that they have known this all along, or even that they believe it now. As a result, "our tradition" of welcoming has been highly intermittent, and the interruptions have had dire consequences for the American city, periodically choking off its vital supply of new residents, consumers, and investors. Conversely, though, the fact that immigration has lately been more open has played a considerable role in the revival of inner-city neighborhoods and markets.

In his 1990 book, *New People in Old Neighborhoods,* historian Louis Winnick writes:

> Congress did not foresee when it lifted America's immigration gates in 1965 that it was legislating, de facto, a far-reaching urban program. ... Mass immigration has advanced any number of goals congruent with the social agenda of the '60s. Included are urban renewal and richer ethnic and racial diversification of schools and neighborhoods. ... One of the more beneficial of the new-immigration social reshapings is the restoration of life to the decaying and depopulating neighborhoods in many of America's ebbing industrial cities.

The 1965 law brought to an end the lengthy and destructive—at least for cities—period of tightly restricted immigration, a spell born of disillusionment with World War I and the nativism and xenophobia of the 1920s. For more than forty years, the federal government had enforced strict "national origin" limits that sprang from widely accepted theories about racial inferiority (which had far more disastrous effects on the other side of the Atlantic) and from corresponding American fears about degrading the Anglo-Saxon gene pool.

Before that sudden constriction, as Thomas Muller points out in his pathbreaking book *Immigrants and the American City,* "much of the nation—particularly its industrial cities—[had] benefited from large-scale entry. As immigrants took bottom-level jobs, employment opportunities for skilled native residents increased. The cities of the Northeast and Midwest that became world-class industrial centers during the 19th Century owed much of their growth to these immigrants." Renewed immigration after 1965, he writes, has

> facilitated urban renewal by strengthening small businesses, providing low-wage labor, and maintaining the population base necessary to sustain a high level of economic activity. The new immigrants—unskilled

workers, professionals, and entrepreneurs—have encouraged the flow of investment, furnished workers for factories and service industries, and helped revive deteriorating urban neighborhoods.

Is it then too much of a stretch to argue that at least some of the negative forces we described in Chapter 2—the inner-city population declines, the vacancies and slum conditions, the disappearance of jobs and business activity—might have *something* to do with the scarcity of new immigrants in the 1950s and early '60s? Yes, technological and market changes played a huge role. But Muller evidently sees a connection to immigration as well: "Until the 1930s," he writes, "immigrants replaced natives leaving the urban core. The post–World War II boom in suburban residential construction, fueled by rising income, allowed the middle class exodus ... to resume. This time, however, there were few immigrants to take their place."

Winnick puts it even more strongly:

Congress did not foresee that when it lowered the gates, by creating a demographic hollow, it was imposing a penalty on America's older cities. Inadvertently, it abruptly excluded a flow of community builders who for successive generations had nourished the growth and strengthened the quality of urban areas. ... It is a reasonable supposition that the course of urban events during the '50s and '60s would have been much less troubled had that demographic discontinuity not occurred.

Certainly the constriction after 1924 was severe. Quotas based on national origin allowed only 6,000 Russians to enter in the next five years; 270,000 had come the previous two decades. Before 1924, 17,000 Greeks had come every year; the new quota allowed merely 100. In total, between 1930 and 1945 fewer than 700,000 immigrants came, compared to 5.4 million in the previous fifteen years. Today, the numbers are up again—nearly a million new bodies a year—bringing an attendant energy and ambition that has had striking effects in countless rebounding neighborhoods.

The point would be easy to overstate. We are not suggesting here that demography is destiny. There were many other factors at work in shaping the image and reality of the American city in the late twentieth century. But many of these factors were negative, as we discussed earlier in this chapter. Perhaps surburbanization was a "natural" phenomenon—rising incomes allowing formerly huddled masses in city neighborhoods to breathe free on green lawns and leafy cul-de-sacs. But we will never know how natural it was, because of the massive federal subsidy that eased and accelerated it, in the form of tax, transportation, and housing policies. Meanwhile, behind that outward push, the central city was feeling the inner crunch—the outrageous constriction of credit, both private and public, that hastened the decline.

The final indignity, unrecognized at the time, was the cutting off of the cities' supply of new people who could have replaced those departing. Without them, the cities' descent grew steeply worse. More immigration might not have prevented the worst urban problems of the 1950s and '60s, but it might have made the damage less total, and recovery therefore quicker.

Even in hard times, immigration is good for cities—though not equally good for all cities. So-called gateways like New York, Los Angeles, San Francisco, and Miami benefit the most. Others that attract fewer newcomers—Cleveland, Pittsburgh, Philadelphia, and Buffalo, for example—benefit least, and in fact continue to lose population. In some of these cities—Cleveland, for example—civic leaders have pursued years of growth and rebuilding policies, sometimes to great effect. Yet, thanks to the virulent politics of the issue (especially in older industrial cities), few if any have sought to market their cities to immigrants. A top executive of the corporate recovery group Cleveland Tomorrow, which takes deserved credit for much of that city's recent vitality, confessed that many of the group's governing members would privately have welcomed an immigrant influx. But in a heavily unionized city, partly dependent on the internationally embattled auto industry, no one dared even to raise the issue. "It's practically the only thing that could have helped us that we didn't consider," says a former player in the organization.

The popular argument against immigration, whether in Cleveland or Detroit or even in immigrant-rich Los Angeles, is that in places where jobs are scarce, it is socially and economically destructive to bring in more and more job-seekers. Looking at the job market as static (or, more commonly, as shrinking), these observers in effect believe that populations must fall to suit the current job base. That's a recipe for spiraling decline.

In neighborhoods like Queens, New York, or central Oakland, California, by contrast, the influx of new populations has added both consumers and investors to neighborhoods starved for both. Immigrants have opened businesses of their own and spent money in existing neighborhood shops, bolstering the real-estate market, paying taxes, and contributing to the circulation of money, goods, and traffic in the community.

This works, of course, only if the wider regional economy offers enough jobs to employ those not running their own businesses or working in the immediate neighborhood. In areas where the metropolitan job market is fundamentally in crisis, new populations probably won't help much, nor will they stay long. As Winnick puts it: "It would be folly to assert that the consequences of immigration are invariably positive. ... The history of American immigration is strewn with the sequelae of failed immigrants who cursed their luck and died as unfulfilled as when they came, or who added to the travails of the host society." But where there are local and regional strengths to build on—that is, in most metropolitan areas—an infusion of immigrants can significantly tip the scales in favor of inner city growth.

More recently, it's true, some groups of better-heeled immigrants have headed directly to suburbs, without so much as pausing inside the city limits. And those who do settle into city neighborhoods are sometimes desperately poorer, and far more socially disadvantaged, than the low-income Americans who live there. In the prosperous years of the late 1990s, when more and more Americans were working, demographers began to notice a "foreignization of poverty" in the harsh conditions of recent, often non-English-speaking immigrants. None of this suggests that foreign arrivals offer a simple, unmixed blessing for cities. Yet to concentrate on the least well-off, or the least urban, of the immigrant flow is to miss the main, and largely positive, story: Most immigrants, even poor ones, contribute materially and quickly to the urban and national economies. And in the process, they provide desperately needed tenants, home buyers, shoppers, and active neighbors to the streets and markets of inner-city neighborhoods.

Admittedly, for the least-skilled Americans, the arrival of ambitious, sometimes experienced or well-educated foreigners is hard to view in a positive light. The National Academy of Sciences, in the study cited earlier, found that native-born Americans who did not finish high school earn about 5 percent less than they would without immigration. But as the study later points out, 90 percent of Americans are not high-school dropouts, and the number of dropouts is annually falling. What a mistake it would be to hamstring the future of whole, fragile communities so as to apply an indirect salve on problems that should be tackled directly, through the school system.

For both good and ill, the story of American cities and immigration policy has been a case of largely unintended consequences. Neither the restrictions on immigration nor the opening of the gates was ever debated with the effect on cities in mind. (When was the last time any secretary of Housing and Urban Development or big-city mayor identified immigration as the key to urban vitality?) Yet the sine curve of immigration policy has perhaps driven the fate of urban communities more than almost any so-called urban policy ever has or will. Like many of the issues we raise in these pages, it is not part of the official urban policy of the United States—which has actually had little to do with the fate of cities, except where it has done material harm. But it is one of the levers of official power that can spur or retard urban growth more certainly than any War on Poverty, no matter how artfully waged.

Just as immigration has provided human fuel to local markets, the credit revolution has provided capital, and the retail revival has provided goods, services, and a renewed "sidewalk economy." All these things lie, to some degree, within the influence of government policy. Sources of credit, in fact, have needed some gentle coercion from federal regulators to find their opportunities in the inner city. Retailers, especially small ones, needed some of the resulting capital. But mostly they needed an advance regimen of public safety and neighborhood stability, along with friendly regulations from City Hall. And the doorway for immigrants is almost entirely in the hands of Congress.

These are elementary market forces, not the rigged equalities favored by the more dogmatic liberals. But neither are they the "unfettered" free market beloved of strict conservatives. Used deftly, and with restraint, government policy in each of these areas can play a material role in improving and renewing urban markets. And in fact, whether by coincidence or design, in the closing years of the 1990s, that is precisely what has begun to happen.

William Bratton, foreground, upon his resignation as New York City Police Commissioner, with Mayor Rudolph Giuliani in the background. (Chester Higgins/NYT Pictures)

PART IV

Public Order

A YOUTH CRIME wave convulsed Boston throughout the late 1980s. It reached its apex in 1990, when the city cut a dubious notch in history: 152 homicides, an all-time record. Most were gang-related.

Somehow all that carnage prepared no one for what happened on May 14, 1992, at the Morning Star Baptist Church in the Mattapan section of Boston. During a memorial service for a slain gang member, with 300 people in the pews, one group of youths set upon another in a violent mêlée. One teenager was stabbed repeatedly—right in the sanctuary of the church. The teenager survived, but the message could not have been clearer or more graphic: *There was no sanctuary* from youth violence in the black community of Boston.

The next few days were entirely predictable. The newspapers and local TV stations sounded the alarm and urged action in repeated editorials. Coalitions and committees formed, mass meetings were convened, and the mayor held forth. What could not have been predicted is that the city, shocked at first into an all-too-usual frenzy of condemnation and introspection, would soon produce the most successful and sustained anti–youth crime campaign in America. Though the effort was focused primarily on curbing gang violence, the magnitude of the success drove *overall* city crime rates to historic lows. The combined effect illustrated the powerful nexus among gangs, guns, and the general state of public safety in the inner city.

In the 1990s, Boston's homicide rate has fallen farther and faster than any city's in the nation—a plunge of 61.2 percent from 1990 to 1996. In 1998 there were 35 murders, down from 152 in the 1990 orgy of bloodletting. The turnaround was so abrupt and decisive, and so tightly correlated to a series of measures undertaken in Boston, that the city has since become one of the two national meccas for crime-fighting pilgrims looking for new ideas. The other is New York City.

New York, much bigger and more richly supplied with news outlets, has had more publicity for its anticrime battle, and got it sooner, than did Boston. Mayor Rudolph Giuliani, a former federal prosecutor elected in 1993, seemed at times almost to be a single-issue executive, creating a powerful identity for himself as America's preeminent urban crime-buster. And he got results. In a city about fourteen times the size of Boston, homicides dropped 58.7 percent between 1990 and 1996, most of that occurring after Giuliani's election (though some important police reforms began under his predecessor, David Dinkins).

Just as in Boston, the correlation of these achievements with a series of dramatic changes in police strategy—many of them engineered by Giuliani's hand-picked police commissioner, William Bratton—seemed to argue that the city had done something special. New York has since entertained a flattering stream of visitors from the media and other police organizations throughout the late 1990s, seeking whatever magic has evidently taken the rot out of the Apple.

As this is written, the New York crime miracle has been tarnished a bit, owing to some widely publicized incidents of police brutality and apparent excessive force, against a backdrop of historically poor police relations with the minority community—even though many of the largest crime reductions have occurred in poor minority neighborhoods.

Nevertheless, New York's achievements are enormous, as Eli Silverman describes in his book *NYPD Battles Crime: Innovative Strategies in Policing:*

New York City's 12 percent crime decline in 1994 (compared to a national drop of less than 2 percent) grew to 16 percent in 1995 and remained 16 percent in 1996. *These decreases accounted for more than 60 percent of the national decline.* Over a five-year period, overall rates for murder, rape, robbery, felonious assault, burglary, grand larceny, and motor vehicle theft plunged 50.5 percent. New York can justifiably claim to be the major force driving down the nation's crime rate. [emphasis added]

Boston and New York soon had some company, as many cities joined the dropping-crime parade in the '90s. Between 1990 and 1996 homicides fell in Houston (54 percent), Los Angeles (27.9 percent), Philadelphia (17.7 percent), and even ill-managed Washington, D.C. (15.9 percent). As the 1998 statistics became available, headlines like the following became commonplace: "Upbeat Data on Crime and Youth" *(New York Times),* "Study Shows Decline in Violent Crime" *(USA Today),* "Violent Crime Decreased to Record Low in 1998" *(Boston Herald),* and so on. Violent crime in 1998 had fallen to its lowest level since 1973, the first year the Justice Department tracked that statistic. The national homicide rate actually decreased to the 1967 figure of 6 per 100,000. And in one especially good sign for the inner city, the sharpest downturn was in youth homicides (halved between 1993 and 1998). Among these, the declines for young black males were the most pronounced.

If these trends persist—and whether they will remains a subject of hot debate among baffled experts—the implications for cities and their most troubled neighborhoods are almost incalculable: What if, at long last, older and poorer urban areas were no longer frightening and chaotic, but simply poor? They might then be able to attract and retain residents and businesses, and to encourage investment, at least as well as lower-market suburban areas where commuting distances are longer and entertainment opportunities fewer. Remove the element of fear from people's residential and investment decisions—or even just reduce it—and just about everything changes.

Making that happen is a challenge much like the others we have discussed so far: rebuilding dilapidated housing stock, organizing residents, and attracting capital and commerce. It starts with treating neighborhoods as places where people care what happens, and where both residents and government are mobilized to fight disorder root and branch. It starts with creating an environment where a single broken window (whether literal or metaphorical) is treated as the beginning of chaos, and is swiftly repaired.

If that sounds like nothing more than obvious common sense, read on.

Chapter 7

TAKING BACK
THE STREETS

A MONG ALL the late '90s headlines about falling urban crime
rates, one from the *Washington Post* seemed to signal something
less than a consensus about where all this progress was coming from:
"FBI's Report of Falling Crime Greeted by Applause, Debate." Actually, what followed seemed more like a collective head-scratching than
a real debate. Even as an assortment of pundits and politicians were
showering praise on officials in New York and Boston, others were less
sure that local engineering played any role at all. Yet they were just as
unsure about what *did* play a role. Attorney General Janet Reno took
the ecumenical approach: "It's because of more police officers on the
streets, tougher sentences, more prosecutions, better prevention programs, a healthy economy, and a new approach to crime-fighting that
involves a close working relationship between communities … and local law enforcement." Yet at the same time, the FBI, which reports to
Reno, said that it had "no idea" why crime rates were falling so fast.

This could not have pleased the attorney general's boss, President
Clinton, who was at that moment taking credit for more cops on the
street, tougher sentences, the robust economy, and tighter control of
handguns brought about by the new Brady law. And in what could
only be seen as a setback for the whole concept of social "science,"

Fox Butterfield wrote in the *New York Times* that "crime has declined dramatically for six years, but new studies prepared for a national conference of academic experts on crime suggest that criminologists are no closer to understanding the reasons than when the downturn was first detected."

The article went on to note that the academic papers "restated most of the favorite explanations offered for the drop in crime: improved police tactics, more criminals behind bars, a better economy, and a re-vulsion by young people in the nation's inner cities against the culture of drugs and guns that spawned much of the violence of the late 1980s." Unfortunately, the conference participants were reluctant to allocate any particular fraction of the improvement to any of these po-tential causes.

Still, a close inspection turns up some intriguing patterns in all of this, even if those patterns failed to rise to the academic standard of "conclusions." One professor, for instance, pointed out that there were two trends in homicides, one for those over twenty-five and the sec-ond for young adults and adolescents. It turns out that homicides committed by the over-twenty-fives had been going down since 1980. On the other hand, coincident with the crack epidemic, murders by young people had soared through most of that period. They spiked (by more than 100 percent) between 1985 and 1994, and plunged only thereafter. So the big gains in overall crime rates, as Boston saw most dramatically, owed much to the change in youth crime.

It would seem to follow, then, that the key to the future tranquillity of the inner city rests largely on keeping youth- and gang-related vio-lence low. Can it be done? The experts disagree, and many doubt that local policing strategies make much difference. In fact, at the same conference Jeffrey Fagan, a Columbia University criminologist, and Franklin Zimring of the University of California at Berkeley shrugged off Giuliani's whole anticrime record as "a pleasant mystery."

One thing that is not at all mysterious is the staggering benefit this crime drought has brought to the inner cities. Out-of-control crime was the nearly universal expectation for the inner city. Any other pos-itive trend there, including several we discuss in this book, was sharply hemmed in by the prospect of continued crime and, just as important, an all-but-unshakable fear of crime. Conversely, the repair of residential communities and the reintroduction of commerce obviously proceed exponentially faster without the virulent toxin of street violence and chaos. The pace and scale of the urban rejuvenation of the 1990s is therefore intimately connected to the rise in public safety. And while the fumbling debate over cause and credit will no doubt continue, no one disagrees that the benefits for cities in this period have been incalculable.

In fact, the change in New York was so profound that even the local TV news broadcasts and tabloid newspapers began to take notice. Long driven by the unspoken maxim "if it bleeds, it leads," local TV news outlets in New York had persistently devoted 30 to 40 percent of their airtime to ghastly crime stories. This went on well into the period of significant crime reduction, prompting the *New York Times* to complain in 1996, "Crime is Down Everywhere Except on your Local Nightly News." Yet just a year later, the *Times* could announce, "As the City Grows Safer, Crime Loosens Its Grip on the News." The volume of crime reporting was sharply down, and there were even a few evenings where "crime news was relatively brief and came late in the programs."

Admittedly, local news would be the last place to register this kind of social improvement, for obvious reasons. *Boston Globe* columnist Derrick Jackson reported in 1999 that a University of Miami study of local news in New York, Los Angeles, Chicago, Miami, Indianapolis, Syracuse, Eugene, and Austin found that 29 percent of newscasts on average were devoted to crime. Another study showed 33 percent for Baltimore and Philadelphia (in fairness to local TV, crime increased in Baltimore throughout the '90s). "It is no wonder, then," Jackson surmised, "that despite the highly publicized drop in national crime, a Gallup survey last fall showed that 56 percent of Americans felt there was more crime than five years ago, compared with 35 percent who felt there was less."

Nor was local TV the only culprit. The *Los Angeles Times* reported in August 1998 that between 1990 and 1995, network news coverage of crime actually went up by 336 percent, while the national crime rate dropped 13 percent over the same period.

Clearly, for these and other reasons, actual crime reductions don't readily equate to commensurate drops in fear. And fear in turn retards progress and investment that cities need, besides preserving destructive stereotypes. But here again, the New York story is encouraging. Because perception is finally catching up with reality in New York City, tourism and business investment, and consequently the city's economy as a whole, are booming. And at least one TV network can even claim some of the credit for this perceptual turnaround. One of America's shrewdest urbanists, Mayor Richard Daley of Chicago, often says that NBC's *Today* program, by opening up its broadcasts "to the street"— training its cameras on throngs of smiling tourists from middle America—has done as much for the image of New York and other big cities as anything those cities could have done for themselves.

Yet even in the midst of these amazing achievements, local police and public safety activists now face the same academic caviling as the community development pioneers we described in Part 2. Thus far, at least, scholarship cannot or will not confirm that their activities are the independent variable (or even one among several) that's turning the tide. Wider trends, say the learned skeptics, may account for whatever progress cities claim to have made—it could all be the result of social zeitgeists, shifting demographics, an upbeat economy, the petering out of the crack trade, the El Niño weather system, whatever. Their corollary argument is that other, contrary trends may shortly engulf the cities' meager efforts and throw the whole public-safety parade into reverse.

Thus have cities and their crimefighters borne a load of carefully reasoned condescension from the thinking classes. Yet the idea that the turnaround in urban crime is merely a fantastic coincidence of favorable vapors stretches the imagination. To begin with, the cities that have made the most far-reaching changes in their police strategies are also the cities with the best results. That certainly doesn't *prove* that their changes were the main cause of falling crime rates, but it hardly points to El Niño, either. Everyone, surely, has benefited from a stronger economy and all the other universals. Yet cities like Philadelphia and Baltimore that came late to the anticrime party have meanwhile suffered from crime rates that stayed amazingly resistant to all the positive ions in the social atmosphere.

In any case, like activists in any field, the advocates of better crimefighting refuse to be deterred by the alleged global inconsequentiality of what they do, or the diffidence of the academy. Animated by passion, confirmed by anecdote, they soldier on.

In that light, the experiences of Boston and New York particularly commend themselves to closer examination, for several reasons. First, as we have seen, these two cities accomplished the biggest and fastest reduction in crime in the 1990s—an achievement that appears to have flowed at least partly from comprehensive new approaches to law enforcement that were dramatic departures from the past. Second, the Boston and New York strategies, though different, both represented the application of giant doses of common sense and pragmatic good judgment. Third, both cities unwittingly borrowed an enormous store of insight from the on-the-ground experience of the grassroots community development movement.

In our view, a national obsession with the experience of these two cities is in order. What they have done, and the parts of it that can be applied or adapted elsewhere, seem to offer the best hope of sustaining most of the recent progress in reducing urban crime—pending, of course, a big shift in those pesky wider trends.

❏

It is now enshrined in lore and legend that the New York policing revolution began, of all places, in the highbrow magazine *Atlantic Monthly,* which in March 1982 published an article by James Q. Wilson and George Kelling called "Broken Windows." Sixteen years later Wilson self-effacingly told the *New York Times* that he didn't consider the piece his "finest literary moment." But few magazine articles have had more influence on social policy.

The article's title refers to an experiment conducted by Stanford psychologist Philip Zinbardo thirteen years earlier, in 1969. Zinbardo left two cars on city streets, one with a single broken window and the other intact. The first was quickly stripped and destroyed, but the second remained untouched for a week. When the researcher broke a window on the second car, it too was promptly vandalized.

Kelling and Wilson used the "broken windows" metaphor to stand for a set of broader observations about the relationship of all manner of physical disorder and crime on city streets. "At the community level," they wrote, "disorder and crime are usually inextricably linked, in a kind of developmental sequence." Deteriorating physical conditions, they believed, spawned further disorder, which in turn licensed certain kinds of antisocial behavior, which in turn actually attracted more serious crimes.

> We suggest that untended behavior ... leads to the breakdown of community controls. A stable neighborhood of families who care for their houses, mind each other's children, and confidently frown on unwanted intruders can change, in a few years or even a few months, to an inhospitable and frightening jungle. A piece of property is abandoned, weeds grow up, a window is smashed. Adults stop scolding rowdy children; the children, emboldened, become more rowdy. Families move out, unattached adults move in. Teenagers gather in front of the neighborhood store. The merchant asks them to move; they refuse. Fights occur. Litter accumulates. People start drinking in front of the grocery store; in time, an inebriate slumps to the sidewalk and is allowed to sleep it off. Pedestrians are approached by panhandlers.

According to Kelling and Wilson, disorder produces fear, and the inevitable response to fear is withdrawal and often flight from the neighborhood. "Such an area is vulnerable to criminal invasion. ... The citizen who fears the ill-smelling drunk, the rowdy teenager, or the importuning beggar is not merely expressing his distaste for unseemly behavior; he is also giving voice to a bit of folk wisdom that happens to be a correct generalization—namely that serious crime flourishes in areas in which disorderly behavior goes unchecked." In other words, there goes the neighborhood.

The striking thing about this is that it is precisely this "spiral of decline" that in most cases activates the citizens who have formed the thousands of community development corporations across the nation. These groups are alive to the negative multiplier of blight, in both perception and reality, and so they focus their development efforts on those targets.

It may be that few of the grassroots activists who founded community development corporations ever read "Broken Windows," or Northwestern University Professor Wes Skogan's important book, *Disorder and Decline: Crime and the Spiral of Decay in American*

Neighborhoods. But their street-level tactics represent an implicit and overwhelming confirmation of those authors' theoretical insights. Skogan writes:

> This condition, which we will term *disorder,* has a social and a physical dimension. Disorder is evident in the widespread appearance of junk and trash in neighborhood lots ... in decaying homes, boarded-up buildings, the vandalism of public and private property, graffiti, and stripped and abandoned cars in streets and alleys. ... What these conditions have in common is that they signal a breakdown in the social order. ... Sometimes, disorder propels people to act—if they are fortunate enough to realize it is evidence both that their community is in decline, and that it will cause further trouble in the near future. [emphasis in original]

Most CDCs are born with the understanding that disorder is both a symptom and a cause of neighborhood decline. Evidence of decline is in fact what prompted many of them to form in the first place. Since the blight often manifests itself first in abandoned or neglected housing (with its rich store of literally broken windows), CDCs have often concentrated on building or renovating affordable housing first—not necessarily out of a primary concern for sheltering needy people, but rather to fight decay and disorder. Reasonably enough, they regard boarded-up buildings, blighted housing, and weedy vacant lots as sores on the body politic. Seeing a neighborhood as a living organism, which it is, makes it easier to identify these open wounds as a breeding place of social infection that in time takes the whole community down.

In effect, thousands of CDCs have proceeded on these assumptions without ever having the benefit of a thoughtful articulation like "Broken Windows." It has been based mostly on intuitions or "folk wisdom" that are obviously widely shared. The policing revolution, on the other hand, is far more traceable to a body of theory, first glimpsed publicly in the *Atlantic Monthly.* One of the authors, James Q. Wilson, has written and been influential on a wide array of subjects. George Kelling, on the other hand, has devoted himself, as both researcher and consultant, to the policing implications of "Broken Windows" with the single-minded energy of a zealot.

Many think of Kelling as the father of "community policing" or "problem-oriented policing" or "order-maintenance policing"—all of which derive intellectual fuel from his work. ("Community policing" aims at building more responsive connections between local police and residents at the street level; "order-maintenance policing" concentrates on controlling minor crimes that create a climate of menace and disorder; "problem-oriented policing" focuses on crimes of whatever level that approach a critical mass in certain places. The three approaches are all distinct in some ways, but all of them upend the longstanding strategy of concentrating most police resources on "serious" or violent crime, to the relative neglect of everything else.) But perhaps Kelling's greatest achievement lay not in the purely intellectual sphere, but in recruiting a tough and ambitious Boston cop, William Bratton, to his ideas.

That alliance between theoretician and practitioner proved to be the "Broken Windows" idea's big break—eventually giving Kelling's ideas a tryout on Broadway. Bratton also, incidentally, provides the critical link between the two flagship cities: At pivotal moments he was head of transit police and chief of police in both Boston and New York.

Bratton describes his arrival in New York to be interviewed for the transit job, beginning with a seminal ride across the Brooklyn-Queens Expressway into Manhattan:

> In 1990 I can recall coming in from the airport ... and coming down that highway. It looked like something out of a futuristic movie in terms of graffiti on every highway wall, dirt on rubber tires that looked like they had not been cleaned in years, burned-out cars, litter everywhere. Welcome to New York. Then when you reach the first stop light in New York City, you see the official greeter for the City of New York. You know, the guy out there in baggy dirty clothes with a rag. Or the more sophisticated might have a squeegee. ...
>
> Then there was the subways. ... I can remember going through the first turnstile array and watching people leap over turnstiles, crawl under them, anything but pay the fare. Every platform had a cardboard city on either end of it where the homeless had taken up residence. This was a city that had really lost control of itself and its subways.

Bratton aptly captures the feel of New York in those days, and the palpable sense of menace that went with it. He and his boss, transit chief Bob Kiley, set out to recapture the subways. Their first assault was an unstinting commitment to eliminate all graffiti from subway cars, and keep it off, and to end fare-beating—the two loudest signals of disorder in the public view of the subway system. The graffiti came off, and fare beaters were relentlessly arrested, usually by plainclothes cops. (Meanwhile, Kiley and metropolitan transit chairman Richard Ravich were engineering less visible infrastructure improvements that eventually brought about a monumental turnaround in the whole system's performance, including the literal elimination of its many broken windows.)

Bratton soon got an unexpected bonus from his crackdown on "nuisance" crimes—and a perfect illustration of the Broken Windows hypothesis that "little," "cosmetic" things can lead to big changes. Collaring "petty" offenders suddenly led to a harvest of arrests of serious criminals. One out of ten fare beaters turned out to be wanted on a felony warrant, and many others were carrying illegal firearms. In one stroke, Bratton had not only eliminated an appalling spectacle that was frightening the public and costing the transit system tens of millions in lost revenues annually, he was bagging large numbers of wanted felons in the bargain. As a billiard player would say, a three-cushion shot. Crime in the subways fell off a cliff. Between 1990 and 1994 felonies dropped 75 percent, robberies by 64 percent.

After cleaning up the subways, Bratton briefly returned to Boston as superintendent of police (the Number 2 position) where he began Boston's transition to Broken Windows policing. But he was quickly summoned back to New York by newly elected Mayor Rudolph Giuliani, where he would have a chance to try in the wide-open city an approach that worked so well in the closed system of the subways.

As the world now knows, his approach worked the same rapid wonders all over New York. "Order policing" was applied with a vengeance against the whole spectrum of antisocial behaviors, not only the famous squeegee men (who often proved a good deal more violent than the cute name implies), but also public intoxication and urination, and even playing loud boom boxes in residential neighborhoods after dark. Orthodox policing had said: Don't sweat the small stuff, go after "serious" crime (of course, after it was committed). Giuliani and Bratton turned that orthodoxy on its head by deliberately obsessing over the small stuff. In so doing they transformed the whole environment, which according to Kelling and Skogan was causing the serious crime to occur in the first place. And they reaped the dual benefit of safety and the appearance of safety.

Bratton did two other revolutionary things: He devolved real authority and accountability to the precinct level, and he developed a now widely copied crime-tracking system called Compstat, which produced twice-weekly updated crime statistics at the neighborhood level, to replace the three- to six-month-old data the department had grown accustomed to. Compstat data formed the basis for the new precinct level accountability for visible events on the street. From that platform, Heather MacDonald of the Manhattan Institute argues convincingly that the real revolution Bratton and Giuliani worked was one of rising expectations. No longer would the reigning idea be that all the police could do was contain crime, which after all was really due to "root causes":

> The real Giuliani crime revolution consisted of rejecting this fatal quiescence even more than in launching the celebrated quality-of-life and "zero tolerance" campaigns. The police would and could defeat crime, declared William Bratton. … Only commanders committed to double-digit crime reduction could hope for promotion; those who did not succeed were out. The rest is history. From 1993 to 1998, homicides in New York dropped 70 percent, and major felonies 46 percent, transforming the city.

Most people want to make a difference; Bratton and Giuliani convinced New York and its police department that the police could actually reduce crime, and then did it. The morale of the department and the whole city soared.

On January 15, 1996, New York's police chief was on the cover of *Time* magazine, and shortly thereafter departed for a lucrative private-sector career. New York, one of the world's largest cities, had proved too small for the outsized egos of the police commissioner and his boss the mayor, who regarded showcases like the *Time* cover as his own exclusive real estate. Bratton's rising national acclaim didn't help their relationship.

But the positive trends Bratton set in motion continued under his successor. Unfortunately, a troubling new trend also turned up: a series of highly publicized cases of excessive force, particularly among officers of the elite Street Crimes Unit, the Green Berets of Bratton's crime-reduction campaign. The public reaction highlighted Giuliani's failure (or unwillingness) to build the kinds of bridges to minority leaders that should have carried him through the rough patches. Kelling soon worried, on the opinion page of the *Wall Street Journal,* that the bad publicity might cause the NYPD "to revert to the 'stay out of trouble' mentality. ... [I]f a new [police] commissioner backtracked on maintaining order, ... control of public spaces could quickly be lost." At this writing, Kelling's fears appear to be justified, even without a change of commissioners. A few unofficial reports in 1999 (some apparently originating with the police officers' union) suggest that officers were starting to hold back—whether for fear of condemnation, or from mere pique over recent scandals—from making difficult arrests in potentially controversial circumstances.

Yet the connection between undue force and street-crime enforcement is neither universal nor necessary. Boston achieved nearly identical eye-popping crime reductions while actually *improving* police-community relations in minority neighborhoods. It is no accident that, when *Newsweek* did a major 1998 story on Boston's crime success, it was neither a cop nor a mayor, but a black minister who appeared on the cover. Gene Rivers, an alumnus of a Philadelphia street gang who went on to attend Harvard, was one of the several hundred ministers who met in the wake of the tragedy at Morning Star Baptist Church. Out of that group a few leaders emerged: Rivers, Bruce Wall, Jeffrey Brown, and Ray Hammond. Most were ministers from the Roxbury and Dorchester neighborhoods, where Boston's African-American population and much of the youth violence were concentrated. They proceeded to form what they called the Ten Point Coalition, dedicated to taking their ministries to the street to meet the kids where they were, and to forging a new relationship with the criminal justice system. This became the basis of a remarkable, and now justly famous, police-community partnership.

A 1999 article in the *Public Interest* argued that the coalition had

played a critical role in Boston's sharp drop in youth violence ... by changing the way the police (and other elements of the criminal justice system) and Boston's inner-city community relate to each other. In its

intermediary role ... the Ten Point Coalition balances the community's
desire for safe streets and its reluctance to see its children put in jail. It
has created ... an umbrella of legitimacy for fair and just policing.

That legitimacy permitted, among many other things, an intense
and unrelenting pressure by law enforcement on the gangs. Unrepen-
tant gang members who perpetrated violence felt the weight of the law
round-the-clock, a campaign in which all segments of law enforcement were marshaled in coordinated action—another novelty for fractious big-city crime bureaucracies. Not only police, but probation officers, youth workers, justice officials from all three levels of
government, and even Harvard University's Kennedy School of Government joined with the ministers.

According to Orlando Patterson and Christopher Winship, Harvard
sociologists who analyzed the program, there were four principles at
work. First, the Bostonians, like their New York counterparts, rejected
what they called "root-cause liberalism." Violence was to be dealt with
as crime, and not excused away by the usual litany of urban ills. Second, virtually all players agreed that the lion's share of the violence
came from a tiny group of hard-core gang members, and that the community had a duty to help law enforcement identify them. Third, the
church leaders were given a behind-the-scenes but material role in de-
termining which youths would be arrested, and which ones slotted
into programs that might help them. Finally—and this was critical—
the principle of zero tolerance applied not just to criminals but to the
police: There would be no tolerance for excessive force and indiscriminate stop-and-frisk tactics based on racial profiling.

The whole process was helped immeasurably by the conciliatory per-
sonalities of Mayor Thomas Menino and his police chief, Paul Evans, a
self-effacing street guy who came up through the ranks. Their lack of
flamboyance and their willingness to share credit helped create the
right atmosphere for unprecedented cooperation among agencies, jurisdictions, and constituencies. And Menino, unlike Giuliani, had built
strong political support from the ground up in the black community.

The achievements were remarkable. Among all the gaudy statistics,
one stands out: for an astonishing twenty-nine-month period that
ended in January 1998, there was not a single teenage murder victim
in the whole city, and only four since.

The acclaim has been widespread. The *National Journal* said in early 1999, "Boston's experience sets a resounding example that crime deterrence can indeed work where agencies cooperate extensively at all levels of the criminal justice system and with community organizations." The same year, the *Economist* pointed out that citizen complaints against the police in Boston were dropping almost as fast as the crime rate.

By contrast, in New York at that point, complaints were headed in the opposite direction. Urbanist Fred Siegel, despite being one of Mayor Giuliani's more persuasive fans, had to concede that the "underside of the Giuliani-Bratton-Kelling achievements was that the flush of success obscured the ongoing problem of excess police force used against minorities."

It should be pointed out that if positive police community relations can be achieved in Boston, it probably can be done anywhere. Harvard scholars Patterson and Winship again:

> Given Boston's less-than-perfect race relations—and the deep distrust rooted in the school desegregation battles of the 1970s—its recent success is especially telling. ... It helps prove that there is no inherent conflict between effective police work and respect for the freedom and dignity of individuals.

"Order policing" and the creative, systematic use of timely management data pioneered in New York, combined with the unusually sensitive community partnership displayed in Boston, are, or at least ought to be, the twin waves of the future. But there is another, as yet almost wholly unacknowledged aspect of both the New York and Boston stories. Through the same period of dramatic crime reductions, *both cities were making more progress than virtually any others in eliminating blight in their toughest inner-city neighborhoods.*

❏

Shortly after his tenure as New York's police chief ended, William Bratton was invited to address a group of grassroots housing activists. He opened his remarks by graciously applauding their progress in refurbishing New York's abandoned housing. But practically in the same breath he went on to add: "Of course, absent what we did in reducing crime, fixing up the housing would have relatively little positive effect on the city." Even forgiving a human tendency to put one's own efforts at the top of any list, Bratton's remark missed the main point by a mile. He had overlooked, apparently, some of the fundamental implications of the very theories that had propelled his own meteoric career.

In the purest version of the "Broken Windows" argument, it is the physically deteriorated environment that licenses antisocial behavior—which then begets more serious crime. The boarded-up houses, vacant lots, and abandoned cars provide the spawning ground; physical rot is the fundamental precipitating condition. For all their effectiveness in cracking down on a wide range of antisocial behaviors, the New York City police never repaired a single broken window, fixed up a single house, or cleaned one vacant lot. They could deal only with the social manifestations of the deteriorated community. That was indispensable, and it went a long way toward implementing the more general notion of "Broken Windows." But by itself, better policing alone might not have brought about the phenomenal success accomplished in New York.

Fortunately for Bratton and the police, they didn't have to fix up houses, because it was being done for them, big time, courtesy of Mayor Ed Koch's massive housing investment program. Launched in 1986, the city committed $4.2 billion of its own money over ten years to build or renovate 150,000 houses and apartments. Continued subsequently (though on a shrinking basis) by Mayors Dinkins and Giuliani, the effort has thus far carried on for thirteen years and amounted to well over $5 billion. Annual expenditures reached their zenith in 1989 at $850 million and have since tapered off to about $250 million a year. The *New York Times* likened the scale of the undertaking to the construction of the Pyramids. By 1997 16,000 new homes had been completed, 44,000 abandoned apartments "gut" renovated, and another nearly 100,000 units "moderately" renovated.

We described the effect of Koch's program on the South Bronx in Chapter 1. But other damaged areas of the city—notably Harlem and central Brooklyn—have been massively altered as well. Many of these communities resembled limitless oceans of blight in the late 1970s and early '80s. Now in some places there is scarcely an abandoned structure or a buildable house lot to be found. In the first ten years of the plan, according to Alex Schwartz of the New School for Social Research, New York's city-owned inventory of abandoned housing units went from 48,987 to 8,177—a cut of 83 percent.

Over this period, New York outspent the next fifty largest American cities combined on housing. Boston didn't have the benefit of that kind of investment, but it's a much smaller place. And more to the point, Boston was the first city to be fully committed to a strategy of supporting community-based development corporations. Now after nearly twenty years of patient, methodical effort, the CDCs of Boston have virtually ended blight. Only Dudley Square, in the heart of Roxbury, still contains a significant collection of abandoned buildings, and all of these are slated for renewal. Indeed, the main housing problem in both cities today is a terrible scarcity of *any* kind of housing—and rapid price escalation in both the home ownership and rental markets.

Can it be just a coincidence that the two cities that did the best job rejuvenating their neighborhoods also lowered crime the most? Logic suggests that the "Broken Windows" theory works both ways. That is, if physical deterioration leads to crime, physical revitalization may well be making its own distinct contribution to pushing crime back. By that light the thoroughly uncredited crime-fighting heroes are Ed Koch in New York and the CDCs and nonprofit housing groups in both cities.

Even if rebuilding neighborhoods makes its own contribution to public safety, it is still just one element of the crime-fighting equation, not the whole story. Bratton might have been closer to the mark if he had said, "neither our crime-fighting work nor your housing work would have been as effective in isolation." Implicitly acknowledging that truth, many CDCs in both Boston and New York were pushing beyond bricks and mortar into direct crime-fighting efforts of their own.

A survey of nonhousing activity by CDCs, undertaken by the Local Initiatives Support Corporation in the early 1990s, revealed how far these organizations were reaching into the social cleanup of their neighborhoods, even as they were fixing crumbling houses. Besides organizing block clubs and citizen crime watches, these groups were carrying on a dizzying variety of so-called "community building" efforts: refurbishing pocket parks, planting community gardens, organizing arts festivals, and creating sports leagues and other youth activities.

Some were reengaging, or trying to, with their local public schools. And a few others were starting charter schools of their own (a topic covered more fully in Chapter 12). All this activity was so widespread that it belied the image of CDCs as "developers" concerned just with housing and other physical construction. Instead, the pattern showed a keen appreciation that you can't save a neighborhood with buildings alone. *Social organization had to accompany physical revitalization* if there was going to be any lasting success.

In 1990, about the time William Bratton was riding down the highway to an interview for his first job in New York, a seminal community organization in the South Bronx was making its first overture to the local police station for what would become a historic partnership between a precinct and a CDC. Ralph Porter, president of the MBD Development Corporation (formerly Mid-Bronx Desperadoes) remembers calling together the heads of nonprofits, youth programs, government agencies, churches, and block associations to meet with the local police brass—one of those routine public-relations meetings police hold all the time, jawing about local problems with little long-term effect. But this one, dubbed the 174th Street Leadership Council, turned out to be different.

This time, for starters, the major community organizations weren't merely mouthpieces of local discontent. They had *done* things of monumental importance in the neighborhood—built housing, brought in business, helped rein in delinquency and vandalism—things that in turn had made the police's work more effective. Meanwhile, police had come a long way from their embattled "Fort Apache" days, and were prepared to believe—well before Bratton's arrival, and ahead of much of the city—that the decline in "broken windows" and progress against crime were intimately connected.

Second, residents were prepared to overcome years of distrust of the Bronx police, and to furnish valuable information, at considerable personal risk. The Leadership Council arranged secret meetings with narcotics officers, for instance, at which residents could furnish information on the still-flourishing drug trade. Getting vulnerable people to turn in heavily armed neighbors took courage and trust—things the New South Bronx was still getting used to. But as Porter put it, "people know what destroyed their community in the past, so therefore their tolerance level for crime and negative activity is much shorter."

The Leadership Council's story is still unfolding—a fact that is remarkable in itself. A police-community conversation that in most places would have lasted (at best) a few months has instead carried on and expanded throughout the 1990s, and shows no sign of winding down. "They've seen concrete solutions," says Porter about both the police and the neighborhood's residents. "Where there used to be a drug den, now there are two-family homes. And people feel they were a part of that."

On Chicago's embattled South Side, a community group joined forces with police in a different way: by literally taking back a street that police complained was the epicenter of neighborhood crime. Father Michael Pfleger, longtime pastor of St. Sabina's Catholic Church, made the first foray to precinct commanders in 1993, the peak year for violent crime. As he recalls it:

> We went to the commander of the district at that time and asked "what is the worst time for crime, and where in this district?" He told us, "79th Street, Friday nights between 9 at night and 4 in the morning, it's just open fire and anything goes." So, we went to the church the next Sunday morning and told [the congregation] that's the greatest time for crime and that's the greatest area, then *that's where we need to be*. We started the following Friday night, meeting [at the church] at 9 o'clock, and we would be out on 79th from Ashland to Vincennes. We would be out there every Friday night from 9 p.m. until about 12:30 a.m.

The congregation poured out onto the sidewalks every Friday night, in numbers ranging from 100 to 300 people at a time, approaching young people with information about available jobs and training programs, offering rewards for information on guns and drug-trafficking, and passing out a hotline for kids who want to escape the gang culture. They stopped in every store, encouraging shop owners to call the police with information on drug sales and other illegal activity in the area. To the gang leadership, it must have looked like an invasion. Within eight weeks, crime was down 50 percent on the 79th Street beat.

The gangs fought back, of course, increasing their own numbers on the street at times, and operating on the edges of the volunteer phalanx. To prove there would be no "give," Father Pfleger and his troops persisted *for years*, maintaining an incontrovertible community control over 79th Street. It was a beachhead—a strategic victory, but not complete. In 1998, a full-scale gang war erupted, affecting the whole neighborhood. Father Pfleger turned up the heat:

We went to the gang leader's houses. One night we had 300 men, plus the alderman, the local police commander, the superintendent of police, and the attorney general, and we all went to their houses and called them from megaphones, saying that this was not acceptable that there had to be a cease-fire. We wanted to help them and work with them, but we were not going to tolerate violence or the loss of life. We went to their mothers. We went to their girlfriend's houses. Eventually they came to us. I met with a number of them first, and then we brought in the police commander of this area as well as the alderman, to sit down and work out some cease-fire truces.

From that point, it became clear who was in charge in the Saint Sabina's area, and it was not the youth gangs. The community had been willing to fight for years (and continues to exert a visible presence on the streets) to regain control of their streets.

If that were the end of the story, it would be an encouraging little epic of local determination and pluck (plus singular leadership). And it would surely confirm the part of the "Broken Windows" doctrine that Bill Bratton embraced in his remarks to the New York housing activists: Crack down on street-level crime, and many other things become possible.

But in fact, the story did not begin and end with community crime fighting and better cooperation with law enforcement. In both these neighborhoods, as residents tackled crime, they were also repairing the physical environment. Ralph Porter's nonprofit organization built and restored so much real property that it is now among the biggest and most respected development companies in the city. In the Saint Sabina's community, the anticrime campaign coincided with a period, first, of strategic demolition of abandoned and unsafe structures, and later, of new investment, including $7 million worth of new housing for the elderly, a new police station, and half a dozen new businesses, in just the church's immediate area.

At the core of the "Broken Windows" strategy are two complementary messages: a negative one—making clear what will not be tolerated—and the positive message that (in Kelling and Wilson's phrase) somebody "cares what happens" and is fixing things up. In this strategy, the methods of development and crime-fighting converge.

❏

Crime is a particular concern for CDCs, not just because it under-mines the community and endangers its residents, but also because CDCs have become major-league property owners, thanks to their taking over so many apartment and commercial buildings. They are now responsible not only to neighbors, tenants, and new home own-ers, but to expanding ranks of private and public investors and lenders who underwrote all these projects. Though the CDCs are nonprofit, they are not immune to financial failure. And a number of venerable CDCs in New York, Chicago, Indianapolis, and other places did col-lapse—most often because they had not been able to re-create a civic realm that kept pace with their development successes. So the prob-lems of the chaotic streets invaded the newly fixed-up buildings: ten-ants who didn't pay their rent, vandalism, drug-dealing, and then, sometimes, violence.

So CDCs had powerful incentives to make the *people* side of the equation work. Often they took preemptive steps: They would rent apartments only to tenants they deemed "responsible," by conduct-ing thorough interviews and even home visits. This struck some as heartless.

"You mean you *turn people away?*" one foundation executive asked incredulously.

"You bet we do" replied Genny Brooks, the founder of the Mid-Bronx Desperados, which played so central a role in saving the South Bronx. "We're doing enough, turning this neighborhood around. Don't ask us to take people who won't contribute."

The executive persisted: "But what happens to them?"

Brooks's reply: "I don't care."

This exchange took place during a foundation tour of the South Bronx in the early 1990s. While applauding the housing accomplish-ments, the visiting philanthropists were clearly discomfited by the CDC's hard-nosed approach to tenant screening. Brooks was un-apologetic—even to an audience she had every reason to please.

Among this crowd were some of the richest and most consistent of Brooks's private supporters. Some of them, she knew, were losing in-terest in the South Bronx, a cause some considered by now happily ended. And to be fair, it was easy to see how someone might feel that way: Streets bustled, buildings sparkled, flowering trees lined tidy sidewalks. One longtime contributor publicly worried that further grants to the South Bronx could be akin to "gilding the lily." Brooks therefore needed this meeting to convey how fragile the Bronx's progress against social disorder—and therefore *all* disorder—still was. In building after building, she pointed out, lived the children of single working mothers, many of them newly off welfare and some still on it, dependent on scarce day care to supervise their children while at work or in training. In the children's world, popular music glorified violence and sex; drugs could still be bought in school, and negative peer pressure was everywhere.

The community was fantastically calmer and more upbeat than at any time in the past two decades; but the journey back from oblivion was only half over. Brooks wanted them to understand that the consequences of chaos engulf the poor first, and are not conquered solely because the environment becomes attractive again. Just as Bratton seemed to believe that police tactics alone could restore public order, the foundations seemed to believe that physical reconstruction alone built stable communities. The CDC was seeking to reestablish civic norms in a community that had been shattered, physically and socially, and had to be reconstructed almost literally from the ground up.

Hence Brooks's dangerously tough—but thoroughly sound—answer to the foundation officer's question. In the first instance, rebuilding the social order means insisting that people living in fixed-up buildings must behave themselves. More ambitiously, it means refashioning what political scientist Richard Nathan calls a "mutual obligation society"—the web of reciprocal responsibilities and expectations that mark any stable, healthy community. Like the Boston ministers who founded the Ten Point Coalition, CDCs like Brooks's widely believe that compassion dare not take the form of indulging destructive behavior, or the whole community unravels.

❑

Given that CDCs are such an effective force both for social cohesion and physical revitalization, with such obvious implications for crime fighting strategies, you'd think they might have come to the notice of at least those urban police departments that are the most committed to "Broken Windows" policing. Not so.

In June 1993 the Police Executive Research Forum (a leading trade organization of big city police chiefs), the Local Initiatives Support Corporation, and the Criminal Justice Program at Harvard's John F. Kennedy School of Government brought together a select group of police chiefs and some of the CDC directors from their respective cities. The chiefs had to be introduced, not just to the people representing the community groups, but to the concept of the CDC itself. They had no idea such a thing existed.

When the CDCs began to explain themselves—how they could turn crack houses into home ownership opportunities for first-time buyers, for example—the chiefs got interested. And from that interest a fascinating experimental program was born—an idea that just may describe the next frontier for community policing nationwide.

CDCs have for years forged informal working relationships with local police at the street level. That part wasn't particularly new. What made the demonstration ambitious and important was that it would test whether *formal* cooperation between CDCs and police—cooperation that would affect how both parties did business—could make a bigger difference. CDCs would bring their street savvy, knowledge of neighborhood problems, and ability to redevelop troubled property to the community-policing table. The parallel universes of community development and community policing would for once converge.

So would the sometimes divergent schools of police reform traveling under the respective banners of "community" and "order." Critics of "community" policing sometimes complain that close relations between law enforcers and neighborhood groups make for good public relations, but don't necessarily reduce crime. Many of these critics feel more warmly toward "order" policing—pursuit of lower-level criminals who contribute to an atmosphere of chaos that invites more crime. But as the Harvard conference made clear, the two elements are mutually dependent. Good "order policing" needs the cooperation of residents to identify trouble spots and root out criminals and gangs; good "community policing" needs the accountability and concreteness that come from measurably cleaning up disorderly, crime-ridden streets. Kelling emphatically embraces both, as did the Harvard conferees.

Dubbed the Community Security Initiative, the resulting program got under way in target neighborhoods in Kansas City, New York City, and Seattle. There were many difficulties—in creating a common vocabulary between the two sides, in building trusting relationships, and in overcoming decades of disillusionment. But all three partnerships persevered, and appear to have generated important results. Other cities are now adopting the approach.

In each of the three pilot cities, the community and the police worked out a set of mutual responsibilities that reflected a strong perceived link between physical and social disorder and crime. Under Seattle Police Chief Norm Stamper, the results were particularly significant: a 39 percent crime reduction in the target area, compared to a citywide reduction of only 9 percent. (Stamper resigned at the end of 1999, after Seattle hosted a ministerial meeting of the World Trade Organization, and massive street protests drew what some considered an intemperate response from police. Nonetheless, his effectiveness in the CDC partnership remains a national model.)

Beyond the nose-diving crime statistics, the *Seattle Post Intelligencer* summed up the social consequences this way:

> To see how a partnership between police and community can change a neighborhood, hit the streets of the International District [the partnership's target neighborhood]. Start at Hing Hay Park, where the aromas of roasted duck and steamed dumplings have replaced the pungent odors of urine and booze that once dominated. Seattle police and community members got merchants to voluntarily stop selling high-alcohol wine and fortified beer. They put in tree lights, a restroom, and game tables in the park and reduced public boozing, brawls, and urination. These days, the park is a place where the elderly play Chinese chess and residents practice Tai-Ch'i.

The Seattle police and the local CDC, the Chinatown/International District Preservation and Development Authority, put their policing and community development programs together, and the result was a transformation—both in the community and in the cultures of the two organizations. They concentrated police resources in the right places, cracked down on disorderly behavior, and fixed up derelict properties. No one should underestimate the organizational and personal commitments required for such a partnership. As the *Seattle Times* described it: "Magnifying the accomplishment is the fact that it follows decades of troubled relations between Seattle police and the Chinatown International District, because of real and perceived transgressions and cultural and language barriers."

The kind of alliance forged in Seattle's International District, however difficult, could make the most of both community policing *and* community development. Do that in more cities, and suddenly the idea of stability in low-income neighborhoods becomes more than just a pious ideal. For too long, supporters of grassroots organizations (including the foundations to whom Genny Brooks gave a dose of reality) have referred to this dream of "stability" as if it could be accomplished by goodwill, compassion, and civic beautification alone. Law-and-order types, meanwhile, tend to speak of "stability" as if it were something that can be achieved solely by force. No one at the front lines takes either point of view seriously any more—least of all police and CDCs. Yet in the policy-making arena, the rhetoric lives on. And the two sides' political allies consequently tend to speak past one another.

That these two movements have accomplished so much separately is already cause for optimism. But as in so many other fields (including those in the coming chapters), their successes have tended to be heralded separately, in unrelated news accounts or policy analyses that look narrowly at one set of achievements and ask, in effect: "How much farther can this go?" The answer may often be: "Not much farther—unless it starts making connections to the other advances in other areas."

Better policing is a remarkable achievement. By itself, it won't save the cities. CDCs are an invaluable engine of redevelopment. Alone, they won't save the cities either. On the other hand, strategic alliances between these two—and with other forces detailed in the coming chapters—just might. From here, we turn to those other necessary elements, where remarkable progress is also under way—mostly, still, in isolation.

A new park fronts one of the remnants of Chicago's Cabrini-Green public housing project. The high-rise is slated for demolition to make way for smaller buildings. (Helen Berlin)

The transformation of Cabrini-Green quickly gave rise to neighborhood improvements. This new shopping center is directly across the street from the public housing site. (Helene Berlin)

PART V

Deregulating the City

THROUGH MOST of the twentieth century, cities have been both blessed and cursed with powerful friends in Washington bearing bold solutions to all their worst problems. And quite often, the older, more cash-strapped cities were just desperate enough to take the bait—to welcome any dollar, and embrace any corresponding regimen, that came wrapped in the promise of a turnaround in their toughest areas.

But time after time, the promised solutions turned out to be rigid, uniform, abstract, unyielding, and—even in the face of proven failure—pretty much irremovable. Time after time, individual cities discovered that their latest team of rescuers had given barely a thought to the distinctive circumstances of each place, were uninterested in the unintended difficulties they were causing, and had no time for suggestions and changes based on actual events.

Now and then, these schemes were colossally destructive: roadway plans that obliterated historic residential communities; transportation, infrastructure, and mortgage programs that subsidized suburbs and effectively redlined inner cities; welfare and housing schemes that made social leper colonies out of formerly mixed neighborhoods. Each of these things was cooked up in some laboratory or academic conference, in Washington corridors or itinerant "hearings," on planners' tables or campaign whistle-stops, and then sold wholesale to cities of every size and description, as the one, overarching, take-it-or-leave-it solution to the decline of urban America. And time after time, the decline continued unaltered. Except when it accelerated.

The authoritarian mindset from which all these dictates sprung had become, by the late 1990s, the object of much hand-wringing and recrimination in Washington and a number of state capitals—as if politicians and planners had awoken one morning to the consequence of all their excesses, and (like Claude Rains in *Casablanca*) could only proclaim themselves shocked—*shocked!*—at what they saw. One can't help suspecting a certain amount of posturing in all that, the usual strutting-and-fretting typical of the late twentieth-century culture wars. Yet there is by now too much consensus about it—a broad base of New Democrats and Old Republicans speak of these things in much the same terms—for it all to be mere Beltway performance art. Something else, more important and maybe more cathartic, is afoot.

That something has been building for years: A mounting frustration, tinged here and there with real anger, over the immovable, unresponsive, draconian mandates and failed institutions that hem in the revitalization of cities and their neighborhoods. The most obvious of these, because they consist of physical structures, are public housing and public schools: supposed "community assets" that have done more to destroy America's least-affluent communities than an army of vandals and youth gangs.

Another of these, the erstwhile Aid to Families with Dependent Children, has done more behavioral than structural harm, though it, too, has carved a few physical gargoyles into the structure of urban neighborhoods. Welfare processing centers, for example, with their armies of eligibility processors, auditors, case workers, counselors, and back-office personnel, helped to create kernels of blight in neighborhoods where the cities' poorest residents were drawn by administrative edict to be processed, reviewed, and recertified for eligibility—meaning they were mostly left waiting for hours on end.

But far beyond the physical burden it placed on a few neighborhoods, the welfare system's most destructive legacy lay in the social isolation of the poor—an organizing principle enshrined in all sorts of government service and relief programs whose benefits are available only to the most destitute. The "means-tested" entitlement—born of a reasonable desire to direct resources toward the greatest need—in practice built a walled-in compound for the dependent, to which people were more or less consigned indefinitely. Like certain quarantine camps in the more benevolent dictatorships, the "means-tested" protectorates of public assistance gave their residents a guarantee of survival (if just barely), but otherwise cut them off from the normal commerce of ordinary society.

These complaints demand an important but subtle caveat: The problem with welfare, public housing, and other federal programs in aid of the poor (we will treat schools next) is not in the aid they dispensed, which materially relieved the suffering of millions of needy people over the years. The problems lay in the ironbound rules and bloated bureaucracies they imposed uniformly on every locality, the passive fealty those bureaucracies cultivated among their "clients," and the programs' passion for amassing poor people into supposedly cost-efficient clusters—creating magnets of dependence usually visited only on communities that were already poor, abandoned, and struggling.

The great environmental cleanup of these toxic systems began in the 1990s. Its success is by no means certain, nor is it yet clear just how reform will work in all cases. But the welfare reform act of 1996 and a series of changes in public housing, culminating in a sweeping 1998 overhaul, unquestionably promise profound change. Most important, it is a change in favor of local determination, market responsiveness, and individual responsibility.

It is necessarily hard to say, just yet, how well the new changes will work. The reforms may go too far, or not far enough; they may need to be re-reformed; or they may point the way for further steps down the same road. It is precisely because recent reforms do *not* spell out all the answers that they have some chance of succeeding. But whether that chance will be realized is among the great questions facing the initial decades of the twenty-first century.

❑

Raising public schools in this context might seem a digression. Public schools are not a system of nationalized poor relief, but a universal entitlement under local control, the great Enlightenment monument to social equality, fundamental to the very idea of American democracy. To this, the only informed response can be: If only it were so.

It's true that public education is not fundamentally a system of federal diktat (though elements of it fit the pattern). In most other respects, however, it bears an eerie resemblance to the welfare and public housing systems—governed by entrenched, Kafkaesque bureaucracies beholden far more to internal stakeholders, like teachers, principals, administrators, and their unions, than to their putative "clients."

Worse, in poor neighborhoods, this education machine *behaves* almost exactly like welfare and public housing programs: It compels poor families to cluster in huge numbers into uniform systems that demonstrably fail, year after year, to meet any articulated goal, but that succeed in one unintended but supremely well-organized social purpose: keeping a well-regulated fence around those who don't have the financial means to escape. Their "means test" is invisible because it is negative: You don't have to be poor to get into an inner-city public school, but you usually have to be better off (or extremely gifted) to get out. And in the poorest areas, usually, most people want out.

Yes, some schools in poor communities rise above this norm, sometimes spectacularly, year after year. But almost all of them do it by way of exception—by doing things differently from the rest of their school systems. In nearly every case, they excel by means of deviations from, variation on, or flat-out exemption from the rules by which the majority of schools must struggle and fail.

The persistent failure of public education in inner cities has imposed, much like welfare and public housing, another grim, immovable obstacle to the self-determination of those communities. In city after city, older, central neighborhoods have emptied out as neighborhood schools deteriorated, and public bureaucracies allowed children no affordable alternative to attending those schools. Except in a few remarkable jurisdictions, the unmistakable message was: If you want better schools, move to the neighborhoods (or suburbs) that have them. You cannot live near a poorly performing school and expect a free education of any quality for your children. If you want to live in these neighborhoods and raise children, you had better be wealthy enough to pay private tuition.

So sure enough, in the older, central neighborhoods where incomes and markets *are* improving, who are the residents who are moving back in? By and large, they are childless or, somewhat less often, higher income. They are empty-nesters or other couples without children, very young couples with pre-school-age kids, single people, or childless gays and lesbians. Some are elderly people who never left the neighborhood, because their children made it through the system when the schools were still adequate. But the leadership in nearly every older city and neighborhood will tell you, first off, that the principal barrier they face in keeping current residents in inner-city neighborhoods and recruiting new ones is the schools.

Cracks in the public schools' bureaucratic monolith have been slow in appearing, but like many structural cracks, they show signs of spreading. Experiments with charter schools, beacon or magnet schools, and the riskier gamble with vouchers, all demonstrate a presumption that the old system is coming to an end. The feudal monopoly of the geographically segmented school district offers too little choice and accountability to be tolerated much longer. Already, those who have any economic choice have stopped tolerating it. The question now is: When will the rest of the population be given the same choice, and when they get it, how will they use it?

❑

It is impossible to discuss any of these issues at the moment without stumbling on the ideological trip wire of late twentieth-century social politics. The philosophical fringes of both parties, with their penchant for partisan saber-rattling and idiotic sound bites, have gone great lengths in poisoning any discussion about these issues. In a debate fought mainly between armed orthodoxies, there is little room for subtlety, and a minefield where there should be middle ground. Start talking about the nuances, and you lose your audience; use plain language, and the ideological speech police move in from both directions.

This chapter (perhaps this whole book) willingly runs those risks. Happily, it is not alone in doing so. More and more, a cadre of mostly local politicians—the "localness" is hugely significant in this context—

have thrown over the shackles of their parties' antiquated ideologies and bravely faced life as unclassified champions of their (mostly non-partisan) local interests. In this regard, Democratic mayors and former mayors Ed Rendell of Philadelphia, Anthony Williams of Washington, D.C., and Richard M. Daley of Chicago are little different from Republicans Steve Goldsmith of Indianapolis or former mayor, now senator, George Voinovich of Cleveland.

What do these temperate politicians see in the hot-button issues of public housing and public schools? Why, for example, would Mayors Daley of Chicago, Michael White of Cleveland, and Dennis Archer of Detroit all *ask for* control of their seemingly intractable school systems? Schools are an issue that many mayors—Rendell among them—deliberately shunned for years, fearing a quagmire of recriminations, feuds, and failure, without any reasonable hope of progress. (Rendell, it should be noted, instead took on a similarly harrowing challenge, Philadelphia's deplorable public housing, and set important changes in motion there.) Now, as the century turns, suddenly very prudent politicians are taking up lances against the mile-high windmill of public education. Why?

One reason, surely, is that the cumulative frustration and anger flowing from all the "grim immovables" are finally breaking down the political fortress that had surrounded them. Teachers' unions, welfare advocacy groups, public housing bureaucracies, all find their defense of the status quo more and more untenable. Both at the grass roots and, increasingly, in the federal and state capitals, demands for thoroughgoing reform are everywhere.

In all three areas—public housing, welfare, and schools—it is too soon to say whether the initial reforms are sufficient or on the right track. The next few years could prove all of them fantastically misguided. But the first sign of encouragement in them is that they take their cue from the operations of the private market. They are based on principles of competition, customer satisfaction, diversity, and constant adaptation—the same principles that underlie success in the ordinary lives of most Americans, whether in business, social life, or the family.

We look with particular attention in this chapter at the change in public housing—where the path to success is by now the clearest, even though progress toward that end is still modest. We look next at public education and then at welfare, where the "solutions" so far are almost certainly unsatisfactory, but where the elements of true reform are at least starting to become clearer. We end with a brief chapter on the political sea change that is making all this talk of reform both more welcome at City Hall and more likely to make a real difference in urban neighborhoods.

The implosion of part of the Pruitt-Igoe public housing project, St. Louis, Missouri, 1972. (The St. Louis Post Dispatch)

Chapter 8

THE FALL (AND RISE)
OF PUBLIC HOUSING

Most of you are afraid of our neighborhood.
But did you know? So are we.
But we are here, you see
Not because we want to be.
— from an anonymous poem,
posted in a building at Cabrini-Green,
a Chicago public housing complex, 1981

CHICAGO MAYOR Jane Byrne," opined the *Cincinnati Enquirer* in March 1981, "is a lady with a lot of guts. She'll need them where she is going."

Where she was going, in the tactful language of a *Chicago Tribune* page one story, was the "troubled North Side [public housing] project" known as Cabrini-Green. On March 21, 1981, the diminutive mayor and Doris Day lookalike told a stunned Chicago press corps that she was moving in to one of the most feared addresses in America, a place where even Chicago's Finest were known to huddle in the shadows and pray for their lives.

It was a half-mile-square war zone: 3,500 apartments in twenty-three slab-style buildings rising as high as nineteen stories, plus forty-four ramshackle row houses, all stuffed into a space half the size of the National Mall in Washington. Nearly every building bore the scrawl of one or another of the ruling drug gangs, which collected up to $30 a month in protection money from every tenant. "People who don't live or work there avoid it like a leper colony," wrote *Tribune* reporter Stanley Ziemba. "Many would agree with one tenant who described it as 'hell on earth.'"

At practically the same moment as Byrne's press conference, federal agents were forming a task force to combat the illegal arms trade at Cabrini-Green, where the reigning Black Gangster Disciples and Cobra Stones were armed like dueling Balkan republics. "We're seeing high-powered rifles and automatic weapons in the hands of children," said an agent of the U.S. Bureau of Alcohol, Tobacco, and Firearms. The latest wave of carnage at the complex had produced ten corpses and more than forty injuries in just the past two months. Drug sales were rampant, robbery and burglary had become routine; rapes and stabbings each were numbering around ten a week. In some buildings, garbage in jammed trash chutes was backed up all the way to the ninth floor.

"Something has to be done," the mayor told a mob of reporters in the living room of her tony Gold Coast apartment, barely a mile from the looming colossus police called "The Rock," which would soon be her new home. "I truly believe," Byrne said, brows knit, "when a mayor is there, everything works better."

From that simple, daring act of faith sprang one of the twentieth century's more intriguing—if occasionally bizarre—experiments in the limits of power.

If Byrne hoped that everything at Cabrini-Green would work better for the mayor, she soon found that matters would not be so cooperative for the mayor's husband. Riding up to inspect their new fourth-floor apartment, Byrne's political adviser and First Spouse Jay Mc-Mullen got stuck for fifteen minutes in a stalled elevator. (The couple was also considering a sixteenth-floor unit, but after the elevator episode, that plan was scrapped.) When he eventually arrived, he discovered that a last-minute barrage of insecticides had not been enough to clear out the fourth-floor cockroaches. Hundreds were unexpectedly on hand to welcome the new tenant, and most never got around to relocating.

Byrne had planned her move to coincide with a full-scale assault on the complex's chronic problems: Beefed-up police patrols under elite command; a flurry of eviction notices; sweeping renovations and repairs; and an Armageddon of pesticides. But things got off to a bumpy start.

The retired general and former Green Beret whom the mayor tapped to head the anticrime team promptly told the newspapers that he wasn't sure he had the stomach for the job. A dramatic late-night gun raid, in which 150 uniformed officers swarmed over 235 apartments, basements, rooftops, and laundry rooms, ended up yielding one shotgun barrel, a load of drug paraphernalia, and a dog. Most of the first wave of evictions turned out to involve rent delinquencies, not lawbreaking ("They're throwing out the wrong people!" a distraught resident told the *Tribune*). The NAACP immediately threatened a Civil Rights action.

Nothing new there. Much of the history of public housing, especially in Chicago, is written in the stilted euphemisms of legal action. Thanks to volumes of court decrees and judicially-concocted tenant entitlements, it had become nearly impossible to evict anyone from Chicago public housing. Practically any applicants, no matter how manifestly antisocial, were entitled to move in, if they simply waited their turn on the 13,000-member waiting list. "A family has to have an awful bad record—so bad, really bad—before we won't let them into Cabrini-Green," the building's manager told the *Washington Post*.

Yet even without changing the project's disastrous concentration and incendiary tenant mix, the mayor's move and the accompanying cleanup programs did have some effect. Rival drug gangs called a truce the day before she moved in. In the three weeks following, police made some 360 arrests and seized forty-one guns. Some windows and doorways were repaired. And with sixty-seven full-time officers, teams of reporters, and a mayoral entourage crawling all over their turf, the teenage mobsters had to move their retail operations underground, or divert them off-site. One month later, declaring herself pleased with the "improvement" in the complex, Mayor Byrne moved back to the Gold Coast.

Despite some cynical press coverage a year or so later ("Fear Returns to Project Where Mayor Stayed," intoned the *New York Times*), the fact is that Jane Byrne did make a difference at Cabrini-Green. As the anniversary of her temporary relocation approached in 1982, homicides were down 25 percent, aggravated battery down nearly 40 percent, and robberies (at least the reported ones) had fallen nearly three-quarters.

The trash chutes were still jammed, the halls still reeked of vomit and urine, and many of the new windows were smashed again. But life was statistically safer.

Unfortunately, too few tenants at Cabrini-Green were statisticians. "The gangs are back," said Jesse White, a state legislator and head of a community center near the project, ten months after Byrne's departure. "They are extorting and intimidating as they did in the past, although not to the degree they did back in the summer." The assistant principal at the local elementary school reported that fewer of her students had been shot in recent months, and reports of gang rumbles were down. Still, she said, gang activity was so prevalent in the school that "the boys must go to the washroom in groups escorted by a teacher."

In other words, after the intervention of federal law enforcement agencies and scores of uniformed Chicago police, plus many more undercover officers and detectives, after hundreds of evictions and the opening of a whole new courthouse just to prosecute those arrested at Cabrini-Green, after the mayor herself moved in amid a cloud of bodyguards and drivers and aides and reporters, after the full exertion of all the official power available to the city of Chicago and its chief executive, the end result was that people were still gunned down in the place where they lived—but in smaller numbers.

Protection and drug rackets still flourished. Children were still conscripted into gangs. Whole families were still compelled to wear only those colors approved by the local hoods. Girls aged six and seven were taught precautions for reducing the risk of rape. That is what life amounted to *after* Cabrini-Green had been massively—and *palpably*—"cleaned up."

In 1981, Cabrini-Green achieved its fifteen minutes of fame. But it was far from the only (or even, by many standards, far from the worst) public housing disaster in America. More than six years earlier, the country's then-most-notorious public housing complex, the St. Louis leviathan known as Pruitt-Igoe, was deliberately imploded on national television—largely because no one could see any reason to leave so grotesque a failure standing.

Yet what were the consequences of the spectacular destruction of Pruitt-Igoe? On the national level, what difference did it make that St. Louis felt no choice but to blow up $36 million worth of federally subsidized housing? About as much difference as Jane Byrne and the mobilized authority of the city of Chicago made at Cabrini-Green. A few things changed on the surface, heads wagged and hands wrung, but otherwise everything went on as before. Federal public housing policy, even under the cinematically indignant Ronald Reagan, remained essentially unchanged.

Meanwhile, despite thousands of decent projects and several good citywide systems (including the hugest of them, in New York City), the majority of big inner-city public housing developments had become a social Chernobyl, stifling the lives within and radiating blight on the neighborhoods beyond. Nearly everything about them seemed engineered for self-destruction: irrational tenant selection and eviction rules, hideous design, neglectful maintenance, and a deliberate concentration of poverty that Blaine Harden of the *Washington Post* described as "stacking poor people in human filing cabinets."

"Cabrini is an isolated, strange place," said Janice Todd, assistant principal at the nearby elementary school. "You are hard-put to find black persons who are successful by any yardstick. And this makes it hard to back up what you tell students about the possibility they may do well by staying in school."

❑

Looking through Mayor Byrne's fourth-floor window at Cabrini-Green, it would have been impossible to envision how public housing could ever form part of the solution for Chicago's (or any city's) neighborhoods. Yet not so many years later, that is precisely the prospect suddenly before American cities, thanks to a steady accumulation of public outrage and, albeit belatedly, an unexpectedly smart government response. To understand how this happened, it helps to scan the missteps and false starts that characterize the last thirty years of federal public housing policy.

But first, to get a preliminary glimpse of the revolution now under way—a transformation that one public housing director compared to the fall of the Berlin Wall—look no farther than, of all places, Cabrini-Green.

In 1995, Housing and Urban Development Secretary Henry Cisneros seized control of the Chicago Housing Authority and turned over its management to Joseph Shuldiner, a veteran manager who had run far better authorities in New York and Los Angeles. Shuldiner in turn took advantage of the first stage of the federal government's far-reaching public housing reforms, HUD's "Hope VI" revitalization and restructuring grants. Fifty million dollars from Hope VI would ultimately go to Cabrini-Green alone.

At about the same time, Congress's new Republican leadership began imposing a tough "viability test" on public housing authorities where 10 percent or more of the apartments were vacant. Show us, Congress said in essence, how renovating and operating these derelict apartments would be less expensive than simply giving people vouchers to move out into private apartments. Otherwise, call in the wrecking ball.

Shuldiner saw a historic opportunity in that threat, and he seized it. Nearly 16,000 apartments in Chicago's public housing inventory failed the congressional test. But instead of simply printing vouchers—on a scale that the private market would be unlikely to absorb in a short span—the newly visionary Chicago Housing Authority came up with a better plan.

Let us go ahead and demolish 11,000 units, the Authority proposed, but also revolutionize the ones that remain and build replacement developments that are smaller, economically integrated, and aimed at helping tenants move up out of poverty. And the model for this transformation will be Cabrini-Green.

In the former no-man's-land around Jane Byrne's temporary dwelling, half the new units will now be privately-owned housing, 30 percent renovated apartments for traditional public-housing tenants (screening out those likely to be disruptive), and the remaining 20 percent affordable homes for low-income families that are not quite as poor as those now in public housing. For those current tenants who can't be accommodated in the new mix, the Authority will issue rent-subsidy vouchers. Although the plan is thoroughly consistent with what is now federal policy, it took Washington two years to approve its far-reaching provisions.

Up to this point, the story might simply amount to a bit of unaccustomed good news for a few thousand terrorized tenants. But look at what the news has meant *beyond* Cabrini's walls: Practically from the day the plan was announced—even well before any demolition had begun—new development was starting to stir on the project's periphery.

Dozens of new homes and a planned grocery store provided an instant market reaction to the elimination of Chicago's most famous eyesore.

The plan became one piece of a nationwide reform effort, finally embodied in a landmark 1998 compromise between congressional Republicans and the Clinton administration. The '98 act allows housing authorities not only to demolish units, issue vouchers, and restore a mixed-income tenancy, but also to contract out the management of public housing to community groups or private management companies—or even sell it to experienced landlords who agree to operate it in accordance with local and national rules.

The approach, to be sure, raises important questions about where and how the families with vouchers will live, and about the long-term availability of housing for the poorest of the poor. Those are honest questions, and they have yet to be sorted out adequately. Not every problem has been solved here, and some will continue to haunt Chicago and Washington and plenty of other cities still searching for better ways to aid the poor.

But there is little dispute that the future of Cabrini-Green and the rest of Chicago's miserable public housing—indeed, the future of all of the worst public housing in America—is one of radical change from this point forward. The debate has shifted, as it had to, from naive tinkering with maintenance and management rules to a complete reconfiguration of a failed vision. Under Hope VI, the Clinton administration undertook to demolish 100,000 units of derelict public housing—more than 7 percent of the total 1.4 million units nationwide—and replace it with mixed-income and mixed-use developments managed, in many cases, by community organizations unfettered by public housing's calcified national bureaucracy.

For decades, public housing was one of the grim immovables—entrenched barriers to revitalization, surrounded by moats of federal law and regulation that no amount of rational argument or advocacy could bridge. It imposed what seemed a permanent ceiling on local property values and a stern warning against any hope of mixing incomes and housing styles, integrating better shopping and recreation, or accommodating new populations and shifting residential preferences—a fortification, in other words, against change.

Now, all at once, public housing itself is changing, and in ways that seem capable not just of allowing neighborhood improvement, but actually contributing to it. "This is an unprecedented moment," former HUD Secretary Henry Cisneros said in 1998, speaking of the Clinton administration's overhaul of public housing. "Both the ideas and the money are there to do something for the first time in decades."

How that can happen, and the odds of its really happening, are among the most important questions facing both American housing policy and America's urban neighborhoods. But to appreciate how difficult and how supremely necessary all this will be, it is best to start with the depths to which public housing policy first had to sink before the "unprecedented moment" of reform dawned in Washington.

❑

The case against public housing, as it arrived at the end of the twentieth century, had grown so fundamental and far-reaching that a great deal of persuasive writing on the subject ended up simply arguing for abolition: an end to all government-owned housing through a combination of privatization and demolition. To cite just one recent example, in a carefully reasoned article in the *Public Interest* in 1997, Howard Husock of Harvard's Kennedy School of Government concluded that

> Six decades after embarking on our first Federally funded housing projects, our goal should not be to save public housing, but to acknowledge its essential flaws: Those with enough income do not need it and will avoid it; and those with little income are ill served by it—both because public authorities make bad landlords and because public ownership undermines the sort of social fabric that the poor need if they are to advance. ... Our continued efforts to save public housing have failed: We have simply created new and worse slums. The time has come for us to let people build the best communities they can, for themselves.

Like most of the public-housing abolitionists, Husock stands on the conservative end of the political spectrum, a goodly distance away from center. Yet the national exasperation with public housing comes not just from hardened opponents of all government social investment, but more and more from people who would have preferred to be supporters, and at other times have been: enterprising mayors and neighborhood leaders, some advocates of the poor, and even many people who have themselves worked or lived in public housing. If the recent outpouring of contempt for government-owned housing in the 1980s and '90s was a depressing overreaction—and it surely was—it was nonetheless a broad-based and well-informed one, and it continues to deserve a careful hearing.

To be sure, public housing had its defenders even in the worst of times. And among the most common defenses of the program, one is indisputably valid and, in a way, genuinely amazing: In a system so hamstrung by bizarre federal rules and impossible revenue structures, a surprising number of local public housing authorities have operated with efficiency and integrity. As recently as 1992, President Bush's National Commission on Severely Distressed Public Housing found that an impressive 94 percent of the nearly 14,000 public housing developments in the United States were providing "decent, safe, and sanitary housing at an affordable price."

Impressive as that finding is, reasonable people could disagree about its implications. For starters, it counts developments rather than units—Cabrini-Green counts as one development and so does a tidy, twenty-five-unit enclave in rural Vermont. The commission's number also includes all the special-purpose public housing developments that accept only elderly tenants—nearly 40 percent of the total—where maintenance costs tend to be lower, social problems fewer, and disruptions necessarily less threatening than in housing for families. Then, of course, there is the question of relative standards.

It's a good deal easier to find these complexes "decent" and "safe" if you do not live in or near them. A scorecard compiled by community or tenant organizations in Chicago, Washington, Philadelphia, Detroit, and other big cities might have produced a considerably lower percentage. The fact is that, especially in large central cities, even decently maintained public housing tends disproportionately to be poorly designed and, in the parlance of the trade, "functionally obsolete"—too small, dense, or cheaply built to pass muster by today's standards.

It is simply not responsible to make any case for saving public housing without first acknowledging the essential accuracy of its critics. To begin with, as Husock put it, many public authorities *do* make bad landlords. Operating a disciplined, efficient apartment-management program in a civil-service environment demands extraordinarily sophisticated leadership and exceptional labor relations—demands that seem far beyond the capacity of a great many local governments. (Though not all; New York City's housing authority, for instance, managed for decades to resist the barrage of federal regulations that bankrupted and destroyed public housing in other cities, and continued operating a balanced, widely respected program. Today low-income New Yorkers will wait years for the privilege of paying slightly *more* for a housing-authority apartment than for their current housing—partly because they find the management more responsive and the property better maintained than much of the housing available on the private market.)

And when public housing is poorly managed, it *does* undermine the social fabric of the luckless communities on which it encroaches. This is perhaps the most damning thing that can be said of the worst public housing: It doesn't simply make life miserable for the unhappy tenants. It corrodes the surrounding neighborhood as well, where those who have alternatives move away, and the rest wall themselves off from the government-sponsored blight in their midst.

The result is divisiveness for the neighborhood and isolation for those in the "projects." In far too many neighborhoods, public housing tenants and other neighbors hardly ever interact, eyeing each other from a distance and warily, if at all. The reasons aren't mysterious to anyone strolling past the worst of these projects: The general atmosphere of indifference and disorder tends to waft over the surrounding neighborhood like noxious gas. Those in the complex, surrounded by crime and chaos, dare not venture too far out of their units. Those beyond are likely to wander in only when looking for trouble.

Public housing's corrosive effect on neighborhoods isn't universal, but it is by no means limited to the biggest and meanest projects of the worst big-city housing authorities. Amid the generally well-managed public housing of Richmond, Virginia, for example, residents of the Blackwell neighborhood can tell a story that sounds in many ways like a miniature version of those in Washington, Philadelphia, or Chicago.

When public housing came to Blackwell in the late 1960s, the Richmond Housing Authority already knew enough to avoid the high-rise monstrosities popular in other cities over the previous two decades. Richmond demolished enough run-down or vacant housing in the Blackwell neighborhood to build some 440 units of new low-rise public housing on several sites, with even a few privately-owned properties scattered among them. There was no discernible boundary between the public housing and the remaining 560 or so conventional houses in the neighborhood. So far, so good.

The design, unfortunately, was still the deadly slab-style architecture that drained the soul out of government housing for more than twenty years (more about that in a minute). And worse, federal tenant selection rules required Richmond, like virtually all public housing authorities, to accept only the poorest and least independent tenants—a responsibility that turns public housing management into perpetual crisis management. As a result, the Richmond Authority had neither time nor resources to devote to the courtesies of being a good neighbor in Blackwell.

The problem, significantly, was not about race. Blackwell was already a mostly African-American neighborhood, and it had its share of poverty. But the new residents—who eventually constituted more than 40 percent of the neighborhood—were far less likely to be employed, to have stable families or well-supervised children, or for that matter, to share the local home owners' sense of responsibility for tranquillity and safety in the neighborhood. It was not their neighborhood, after all; it was someplace the government put them.

Nor did most housing authorities in those years regard it as their responsibility to be concerned about these issues—to worry about employment or day care for residents, to participate in surrounding neighborhood organizations, or generally to build bridges between public housing tenants and other residents of the community. Neither they nor the majority of their tenants were functioning at that level of social nicety.

Richard Gentry, who ran the Richmond Housing Authority through much of the 1990s, says that the Blackwell project "created negative economic value in the neighborhood."

It was decent, safe, and sanitary—the usual standard you hear all the time. It was decently well managed, but because it was developed the way it was, so ugly, so badly designed, and because it was a poor neighbor, it decreased the property values between and around the public housing. When a neighborhood declines, first, people stop keeping their houses in good condition, and second, when they leave, the property becomes abandoned because nobody wants it. That's what happened in Blackwell from the late '60s to the late '90s. Residents of Blackwell from way back when still complain today that public housing destroyed their neighborhood.

❏

How did it get this way? When public housing was created, in the second wave of Franklin Roosevelt's New Deal, it was meant as a weapon against the Great Depression, putting unemployed builders to work and offering some temporarily destitute families a place to live. The federal government paid only for capital costs—the buildings' operating expenses had to be covered by tenants' rents. As a result, most public housing tended to be a way station for working- and middle-class families who had fallen, like much of America, on momentarily hard times.

That began to change after World War II, when the federal government set off on a two-track housing strategy that has lasted nearly the entire balance of the twentieth century. On one track were federal programs like the Federal Housing Administration, the Veterans' Administration, and the giant mortgage institutions like Fannie Mae (which began as a government agency but is now a private corporation operating with an implicit government guarantee). These programs helped middle-class and upwardly mobile families buy new homes—most often in new suburban developments, where they could escape city life and the company of their poorer neighbors.

The other track was for the poor, and especially for minorities. The Housing Act of 1949 transformed public housing from a mainstream support for the temporarily down-and-out into a slum-improvement program, where residents of the poorest and most run-down urban neighborhoods—especially the waves of African-American immigrants from the rural South—could escape the squalor of tenement life and live decently at low rents. The act required, among other things, that cities building new public housing demolish one "slum dwelling" for every new unit of public housing they built.

At best, many cities saw this as a way of transforming the poorest neighborhoods into "modern" environments that would somehow uplift and improve poor families' lifestyles (even as they set about razing the social and economic anchors of community life, like shops and restaurants, social clubs, and churches). At worst, as in Chicago, cities used public housing, in tandem with the Urban Renewal program, as a way of bulldozing black neighborhoods and concentrating their residents into tidy new ghettos, where federal subsidies would, in effect, pay them to remain.

Meanwhile, beginning in the 1940s and '50s, new fashions in architecture were wafting in from Europe, most famously the severe skyscraper slabs championed by Swiss-born modernist Le Corbusier. The vision of a "contemporary city" full of "vertical neighborhoods" spread like a biblical plague through the public housing boom of the 1950s. Quite apart from the style's European cachet, federal planners saw in it an appealing (if simplistic) thrift: Cramming hundreds or even thousands of units into a single construction project, they reckoned, would surely offer enormous economies of scale. (Wrong. As bitter experience would prove, they were more expensive than lower-rise projects at every stage, from construction, through operation and maintenance, even up to their often merciful demolition.)

As if their grim design and costly construction weren't bad enough, the proliferation of these gargantuan projects coincided with a period of increasingly garbled public policy and merciless cost inflation. Historian Alexander von Hoffman gives this summary:

> When Federal authorities held down unit costs [in the construction budgets of public housing], local housing authorities compensated by increasing the number of apartments in high-rise complexes. ... To make matters worse, landholders, contractors, and unions progressively inflated their charges in every large project. Caught between stingy Federal unit-cost ceilings and skyrocketing project costs, the authorities skimped, eliminating such basic construction and safety elements as

insulation for heating pipes. ... The open spaces [designed as play-grounds and "communal areas" among the modernist high-rises] evolved into dangerous no-man's-lands.

Even then, not all had been lost. If the social philosophy of this phase was patronizing at best and segregationist at worst, and if the esthetics were frequently execrable, at least the approach to management was reasonably sound. Rents still had to cover operating costs, and federal regulators still required local housing authorities to include a "socioeconomic cross-section" of the eligible population on their rent rolls. That was one way of ensuring that the housing authorities served poor families in a stable social mix, while making certain that average rents were high enough to cover costs. Since most applicants for public housing were among the very poor, this requirement had the effect of giving an edge to those with slightly higher incomes, so as to maintain the required "cross-section" and keep up the average rents.

And in any case, even the poorest families had to meet a minimum rent threshold. In general, the goal of federal policy was for working families to pay between one-sixth and one-fifth of their incomes on rent, depending on family size. Yet many of the poorest families were really paying as much as 40 or 45 percent, just to meet the minimum (there was also a maximum to protect families at the higher end of the payment spectrum). That was hard on the tenants, certainly, but it demonstrated a reassuring command of arithmetic: Operating expenses had to be paid from operating revenues, and if those expenses were not going to be subsidized, then they would have to be met entirely from rent receipts.

But even the iron laws of arithmetic were no match for federal housing policy. In an eminently well-intentioned piece of legislation at the end of 1969, Congress abolished the minimum rents, and with them the elementary equation that for three decades had balanced costs against revenues.

The new law, sponsored by Senator Edward Brooke of Massachusetts, the Senate's first African-American member, mandated that no family would have to pay more than 25 percent of its income to live in public housing. That would have been fine, and for some families a godsend, except that for the next three years Congress failed to appropriate a subsidy to make up the lost revenue. Richard Gentry, who went on to run successful housing authorities in Austin, Texas, and Richmond, Virginia, was working at HUD at the time, and remembers the effect of the Brooke amendment this way:

> Suddenly, between 1970 and '75, every public housing authority in the country was bankrupted. With all the best intentions, Congress managed to do something good for the tenants and broke the system in the process. Up to that point, the system had been one of great financial integrity. But beginning in the 1970s, housing authorities went on the dole, and all sorts of problems followed. ... The very first list of "troubled housing authorities" was compiled in 1979. And that was no coincidence.

Among other things, the amendment turned rent into a virtual income tax for tenants of public housing—rent would henceforth be a percentage of household income, rather than a function of family size. For public housing tenants, every new dollar of income would now be taxed not only by the IRS, but by their government landlord as well. Not surprisingly, public housing quickly became more attractive to those with no income than it was to the working poor. "More and more people showed up claiming zero income," Gentry recalls. "The population began getting more and more poor, so rent receipts plummeted and the need for operating subsidy began skyrocketing."

The slide into ever-deeper poverty grew steeper and slipperier in the 1980s, when the newly elected Reagan administration made its own contribution—in some ways the deadliest—to public housing's four-decade March of Folly. In the first great exertion of Reaganomics, the Omnibus Budget Reconciliation Act of 1981, Congress raised the monthly rent to 30 percent of tenants' income, up from 25 percent, and eliminated the maximum rent altogether. Imagining that this would bring a windfall of new revenue to public housing authorities, the act therefore slowed the growth of operating subsidies in proportion.

But no new revenue ensued. The higher rents only exacerbated the penalty for working, of course. For a typical mother in public housing, the consequence of leaving welfare and going to work at the minimum wage would have been an immediate rise in payments to the IRS and to her public landlord, and a prompt zeroing-out of her welfare and Medicaid. In all, this amounted to an effective "tax" of 120 percent.

But that wasn't the end of the 1981 reform. To ensure that public housing served the "truly needy," OBRA also created three "priority categories" for public housing tenants: the homeless, those paying more than 50 percent of their income for rent, and those living in substandard conditions. The effect was a virtual guarantee that tenants of public housing would henceforth be drawn from the most profoundly troubled hinterlands of American poverty.

However charitable this approach may have been in concept, in practice it upended the sound principle of mixed tenancy that any housing complex requires to keep order. It also put an end, once and for all, to the slowly eroding tenant-screening policies with which public housing had been created and, for most of its history, preserved.

The federal preferences had the effect of opening the doors of public housing to hundreds of very young single mothers who had never lived independently. Meanwhile, working poor families—many of whom had spent years on waiting lists—were passed over for apartments that instead went to first-time applicants in the priority categories. Those who were already in public housing made a dash for the exits. "It didn't take long for them to figure out," Gentry explains, "that if they were going to be charged this level of rents, they probably didn't need to be living in public housing, next door to teenage mothers or other families with severe social problems. So you had a huge out-migration of working families."

Thus did hard-strapped public housing authorities increasingly find themselves trapped in a dead-end (and often factually flawed) debate over "who is most deserving?" and "whom should society care for first?" From the perspective of responsible housing management, the questions are not simply irrelevant but destructive: The concentration of *any* narrow group of profoundly needy people into already densely packed apartments—and then walling them off, literally or figuratively, from the wider community—is simply asking for disaster. Yet for nearly thirty years, more and more housing authorities, prodded by Congress, did precisely that, and got what they asked for.

❑

Until the final months of the twentieth century, it was possible to visit just one public housing project and see the whole panorama of economic mismanagement, bad architecture, skewed tenant selection, slovenly maintenance, and pestilential social consequences encapsulated in one miserable package. Chicago's notorious Robert Taylor Homes, which has finally begun a long-deserved demolition, was for nearly four decades the world's largest public housing project. It sprawls across two miles, with more than 4,300 units in twenty-eight nearly identical sixteen-story concrete slabs.

The sheer, malevolent, brooding massiveness of the place would have embarrassed Mussolini. Yet there it was, gnawing away at one of America's most vulnerable neighborhoods, on Chicago's depressed South Side. Even though construction of these high-density projects ended in the 1970s, more than twenty years later, one out of every seventeen public housing units nationwide is still in a mammoth high-rise like these. And in big cities, where such projects were concentrated, the ratio is much higher than that—as is the incidence of federal receiverships, serial management "restructuring," and finally, at long last, gradual demolitions and redesign. In the worst cases, as at Robert Taylor, the high-rises are lined up like tombstones, barricading huge sections of the city from any hope of redevelopment or community control. The consequences are visible in the eerie wasteland of vacant and abandoned property that grew up around Robert Taylor Homes and other dense Chicago projects of its generation.

One illustrative consequence: In the 1990 Census, eleven of the country's fifteen poorest Census tracts contained a project owned and operated by the Chicago Housing Authority. Of the Authority's 67,000 tenants, 95 percent were African American and the median income was just $5,000 a year. At Robert Taylor, the census at its peak was 20,000, of which adult men made up only a tiny percentage. The impression that Chicago had rounded up the poorest and most vulnerable black families and corralled them in a subsidized Devil's Island was, if not strictly accurate, practically irresistible.

Congress's 1981 "priority categories," with their deliberate concentration of problem families into public housing, systematically destroyed the sense of common responsibility on which all communities, at all income levels, depend. Yet long before the new "priorities," another equally well-intentioned rule on tenant selection had been working more subtly, and for a much longer time, to prevent public housing from becoming a real community or taking part in the community around it. HUD's "Tenant Selection and Assignment Plan," which dates to the 1960s, had by the 1980s become yet another federal prohibition against selecting tenants for public housing who might actually appreciate and participate in the neighborhood where they were going to live.

The plan started life as a worthwhile outgrowth of the 1964 Civil Rights Act—a necessary ban on assigning public housing tenants to segregated, race-specific projects. Before the Civil Rights Act, most public housing was classified by race, and African-American applicants could safely assume that they would all be sent to the same projects, in predominantly African-American neighborhoods. The act, and the ensuing assignment plan, rightly destroyed that system.

But with typical federal overreaction, the assignment plan then went much further. The plan forbids public housing authorities from even allowing *tenants* to select where they would like to live—apparently out of a fear that too many would self-segregate. (This rule was finally eased in the 1998 Public Housing Reform Act, though a year later HUD had still not approved any alternative assignment schemes.) The result was that, by federal edict, no poor family seeking to live in public housing could request a specific location. If they needed and wanted public housing, then they could say farewell to any tie with a particular community—where relatives live, where children go to school, where church or job or social connections attract them. It would be hard to conceive a more ingenious way to ensure that tenants will, on average, have little stake or interest in the neighborhoods where they end up living.

The combined effect of these blind assignments and the 1981 selection "priorities" was a sort of poverty gulag: people thrown together at random from disparate backgrounds and localities, with nothing in common except extreme poverty and desperation. (Yet unlike any real gulag, the whole diabolical system grew out of profoundly philanthropic sentiments, with the highest aspirations, in what may have been the most generously-minded era of American government. It's important, if ironic, to remember the excellent intentions from which all this mismanagement flowed.)

As the concentration of poverty deepened, and more and more inexperienced, dysfunctional, and sometimes criminal tenants entered the public housing rolls, tenant organizations became less and less effective at representing the needs and values of more responsible, lawabiding residents. Many tenant councils gradually evolved into advocacy organizations for the most disruptive (whom they also recognized as the most desperate). And in some cases petty criminals, con artists, and gangs took effective control of the councils. The executive director of the Philadelphia Housing Authority wrote in 1992 that tenant leaders in his city "really ran the show in the developments and kept the peace. In return, they expected certain perks, jobs for relatives and friends, transfers to better developments, trips to conferences, etc."

In an environment of organized criminals and delinquents, and a disorganized or neutralized adult community, it was not hard to guess whose rules would predominate. The most committed and responsible tenants—the people who, in most other neighborhoods, would organize crime-watch groups and help keep troublesome youth in line—soon learned that hassling armed teenagers was dangerous to their health, and that no legal authority was likely to back them up. Legal authority, in fact, was on the side of protecting the "tenancy rights" of the most disruptive.

One unsavory little exchange in the mid-1980s, though it didn't involve public housing, perfectly illustrated the philosophical conundrum that both government housing and homeless programs faced in those bewildering years. After visiting an especially Dickensian New York City welfare hotel in 1984, Mayor Ed Koch was asked by reporters how he could have allowed conditions for poor tenants to sink to such a level. He answered with a trademark sneer: "Why are you asking *me?* I didn't piss in the hallway."

The hotel owner, who arguably bore at least as much responsibility for the building's deplorable condition as the mayor did, later answered Koch's rhetorical question: "Why are we asking him? He may not have pissed in the hallway, but he found everyone in New York City who *would* piss in the hallway, and he put them in my hotel." (The city's contract with the hotel made it nearly impossible for the owner to evict those who vandalized or misused the property.) The city and the hotelier have since parted ways.

In Miami–Dade County, Florida, as in cities and counties all over the country, this debate over who would house disruptive tenants was replayed in courtrooms week after week, as beleaguered housing authorities brought eviction proceedings against the families of vandals, gang members, and drug merchants, often to no avail. "Where will they go if you turn them away?" misguidedly compassionate judges typically asked. In one especially contentious eviction proceeding in Miami-Dade, a judge in 1992 put exactly that question to then–Housing Director Earl Phillips.

"Your Honor," Phillips answered, biting back his anger, "our mission is not to harbor those who are so destructive that no rational landlord would rent to them. Our mission is to provide housing for hundreds of poor families who, at this moment, can't leave their apartments without fear for their safety. Our mission is to maintain decent housing where windows aren't routinely broken and freshly painted walls aren't instantly covered with graffiti. We are asking you to allow us to discharge that mission."

It was a cry for help, but one that all too often just floated off into the ether. "I don't remember for sure," Phillips said later, recalling his reply to the judge, "but I think I lost that case."

❏

It is becoming more and more reasonable, as the 1990s draw to a close, to declare these dark ages of mismanaged public housing effectively finished. After forty years of folly, one makes such a statement only cautiously. But it seems more and more to be demonstrable fact. Quite beyond the Clinton administration's determination to demolish 100,000 of the worst units, and the careful replacement of those units with better-configured developments, the really significant change in public housing has been in the gradually vanishing government monopoly over its ownership and management.

Suddenly, a government bureaucracy, with its reams of federal mandates and local political accommodations, isn't the only entity that can own and operate a public housing unit. Not only can community organizations, other nonprofits, or even private developers take a role in public housing, but the residents can own it, too. Suddenly, it is possible for a public housing resident to have a stake—literally as well as figuratively—in the future of the neighborhood where she lives.

One small example is on the Lower East Side of Bridgeport, Connecticut, in the quiet single-family community of Pembroke Green (where, unlike the great public housing "greens" of the past, there is actual *green* on the premises). In March 1999 the *New York Times* spoke to Carolyn Bellamy, who was then moving with her three sons from a dilapidated North End public housing project into a new Pembroke Green duplex, situated on part of what had been the thirty-seven-acre public housing behemoth known as Father Panik Village.

Bellamy told the *Times* not only that she will pay less to own her new home than she used to spend on rent, but that she will be *collecting* rent from the family in the other half of the duplex. Thanks to a mortgage subsidized by the Federal Home Loan Bank, she owns the

Father Panik Village, a Bridgeport, Connecticut, public housing project, in 1970. (Carl T. Gossett/NYT Pictures)

Father Panik Village in 1999, renamed Pembroke Green, with smaller structures in a more open configuration. (Carl T. Gossett/NYT Pictures)

whole building. The family next door, whose income is a good deal lower than Bellamy's, will have its rent subsidized by HUD, just as in any public housing complex.

In other words, Carolyn Bellamy, former public housing tenant, is now a public housing landlord.

She is not, of course, the sort of public housing tenant for whom judges and tenant councils have been so concerned in the past—the "where-will-they-live-if-not-here" tenants whose behavior made them suitable for no other dwelling. Bellamy works steadily, pays her rent on time, and wants to plant roots in a community she regards as home. At $35,000 a year she earns less than Bridgeport's median income, and too little to qualify for conventional home ownership. But she is now one of many working adults who are turning the redesigned Father Panik complex into a mix of moderate-, low-, and very-low-income families, where role models for children are plentiful and the landlord is not an agency, but a human being, a neighbor with a huge stake in keeping up the property.

"The entire notion of public housing changes with this program," Colin Vice, deputy director of Bridgeport's housing authority, told the *Times*. Change is hardly the word.

❑

In many ways, the showcase of Hope VI and the entire public housing revolution is Atlanta's Centennial Place, successor to the locally infamous Techwood Village apartments, the mother of all housing projects.

Franklin D. Roosevelt personally dedicated Techwood in 1936, as America's first public housing and a cornerstone of the New Deal. The adjoining Clark Howell Homes came four years later, a combined development of nearly 1,100 apartments on a massive fifty-seven-acre parcel that abuts the campus of Georgia Tech. It was, for a time, one of the more famous buildings in America, a symbol of hope that later claimed a spot on the National Register of Historic Places.

But sixty years after it was built, by the standards of most big-city public housing complexes, Techwood was no longer especially remarkable. Its mass and macabre ugliness, its compact destitution (some 600 families were living on less than $5,000 a year, and nearly all the rest still fell below the poverty line), and the pervasiveness of teenage single mothers with children, all would have folded nicely into Cabrini-Green or Robert Taylor Homes or Bridgeport's Father Panik Village.

Techwood returned to the national spotlight in the 1990s not because of its historic pedigree or its latter-day misery, but because it was in the way of a gigantic media event. When Atlanta hosted the 1996 Olympic Games, the Techwood/Clark Howell complex would be a crumbling monstrosity smack in between the planned Olympic dormitories and the competition fields. For hundreds of millions of viewers worldwide, tuned in to watch the Games live from Atlanta, the hulking Techwood would be an unavoidable TV icon, impossible to ignore or to forget.

When the city won the Olympic competition, it set out to reform its Housing Authority and clean up Techwood and a few other public housing eyesores before the media trucks started rolling in. But the city soon discovered what Jane Byrne and many public housing directors had learned years before: It wasn't so easy to just "clean up" a federal housing project. Getting the money for a significant transformation would be slow and difficult enough. But the nearly unthinkable challenge would be changing the federal rules under which the housing had gone to hell in the first place.

Evicting large numbers of disruptive tenants, tearing down unworkably dense apartment clusters, mixing incomes, and building defensible spaces—all these were the sensible necessities that any responsible landlord would have considered Job One. Under normal federal practice, though, these things were all officially unchangeable. So in the early 1990s, Atlanta asked HUD for money to renovate some units and bring in additional public services to try to make the complex at least presentable in time for the Games.

But then something nearly unprecedented happened. Going over the city's proposed Band-Aid for Techwood, both the city and HUD came to the same realization: This was likely to be a colossal waste of millions of federal dollars, just as other public housing fix-ups had been. Cisneros and the rest of the Clinton administration, like Atlanta's new housing management, had finally gotten the lesson of decades of paste-and-paint fiascoes in public housing. Truly saving Techwood would first mean destroying it. The lesson of Pruitt-Igoe had finally come to Washington. It had taken a mere twenty years to get there.

In 1994, Atlanta shredded its proposal and started over. In the process, America's first public housing development became America's first genuine public housing rescue. Instead of just buying a load of new cabinets and drywall, the Authority used its $42 million federal grant to leverage another $40-plus million in private investment for a complete overhaul. In 1995 Atlanta began systematically demolishing Techwood Village and Clark Howell Homes, and replacing them with a mix of sizes, densities, and incomes that more resembles a real neighborhood. The result became a model for what would happen at Cabrini-Green, Robert Taylor, Blackwell, and dozens of other projects.

The new Centennial Place contains nearly the same number of units as the two predecessor projects (900, compared to a former peak of 1,100), but they are less concentrated, with a three-tier mix of rent levels, including 40 percent of the apartments at unsubsidized market rates. But far more significant is that Centennial Place is no longer just a "housing project"—a mere agglomeration of apartments block after block—but also offers a new elementary school, a state-of-the-art YMCA, a high-tech public library, child-care facilities, and a host of employment and social services to help residents solve problems and raise their families. It has gone from being a project to being a community, part of a larger social whole.

Like other Hope VI sites, Atlanta has given rent vouchers to the people displaced from Techwood and Clark Howell, and most have found housing elsewhere. Some, it seems, do not do well with vouchers, and in some cities the private market can't or won't accommodate the poorest families. A mixed-income vision of public housing therefore doesn't eliminate the need to develop other kinds of affordable apartments for poor families—a need that constitutes unfinished business all over the country.

But neither do those apartments belong in a 1,100-unit stalag. They didn't represent decent housing for the poor in 1995, and they haven't for decades. Cramming desperate families into a dangerous, unmaintainable ruin is no favor to them, and it is an insuperable obstacle to any other improvement to the Atlanta community. Just how much of an obstacle is now apparent with any visit to the newly constituted Centennial Place.

The streets around the complex are now busy with pedestrians. Centennial Place residents mix with others in the YMCA and the library. Centennial Place and other parents volunteer in the school, and students walk safely to and from extracurricular activities. The project wasn't done in time for the Olympics (the millions of viewers never got to see what may have been the Games' final victory). But it has sparked a national awakening far more significant than any briefly televised image could have accomplished.

Presumably, Centennial Place will weather the decades better than its predecessor, both because it is more responsibly designed and built and because it has ceased to be an island apart from the wider community. But the most important change about Centennial Place is not that it's nicer, or more durable, or more rational. It's that it's no longer a monolith, immovable and impenetrable. It is now several kinds of housing woven together, with different kinds of financing and different systems of mission and regulation. If things don't work well in the future of Centennial Place or the other Hope VI projects, their failure will spell much less of a disaster than did Techwood's. This or that piece of the new project can always be realigned; rules are more pliable now, and no one part of the project has to bear all the obligations of all the other parts. Some of the management of the new Hope VI housing is in the hands of community organizations, some in private hands, and some is by housing authorities. All of it is changeable.

Deregulation, versatility, and diversification are at the core of the federal government's long-delayed success with public housing, and those may be the same elements that are working—much more tentatively, to be sure—to save public education. Compared to the scattered islands of public housing, the nearly ubiquitous failure of inner-city public schools will be a much harder obstacle to move, but just might be movable by the same kinds of levers.

Chapter 9

THE SCHOOLHOUSE DOOR OPENS (A CRACK)

IN HIS best-selling book *There Are No Children Here,* about two boys growing up in public housing, *Wall Street Journal* reporter Alex Kotlowitz gave this description of Henry Suder Elementary School, adjacent to the boys' housing project:

> The parking lot behind the school had been the site of numerous gang battles. When the powerful sounds of .357 Magnums and sawed-off shotguns echoed off the school walls, the streetwise students slid off their chairs and huddled under their desks. ... [The boys' fourth-grade teacher], along with other teachers, placed the back of her chair against a pillar so that there would be a solid object between herself and the window.

Kotlowitz is at pains to point out that, by the standards of Chicago public education in 1988–89, when most of the events in the book take place, Henry Suder *was one of the better schools.* Despite the gunplay just beyond its walls, Suder was run by an excellent principal, its halls were orderly and clean, and although students' reading and math scores were well below average, they at least showed improvement for each year a student was enrolled.

In other words, there was *some* benefit to attending Henry Suder Elementary School, despite the risk to life and limb. Elsewhere in the Chicago public school system, that benefit was scarce. Students in many public schools were merely dodging bullets and serving time; their main achievement from years of schooling—if they were lucky— would be to graduate or drop out more or less uninjured.

Children who were fortunate enough to attend the better-performing Suder Elementary School soon learned that their luck would promptly run out the day they graduated. If they made it that far, they would next be bundled off, like it or not, to the notorious Richard T. Crane High School, "one of the city's worst," according to Kotlowitz, where eleven security guards barely maintained a daily cease-fire, and seniors had recently scored in the eighteenth percentile nationwide on reading tests.

Kotlowitz tells the story of one eighth-grade boy at Suder who deliberately filled in random answers on a reading test, in hopes of failing and being held back from a high school where he literally feared for his life. No good. Even random answers were sufficient to get a student passed on to Crane High without a second thought. There was, of course, no choice about which high school the terrified boy would have to attend.

By the end of the twentieth century, some dozen years after the events in Kotlowitz's story, these facts no longer shock most Americans. The degradation of urban public schools is now such a commonplace that hardly anyone bothers to describe it any more. The assumption that inner-city classrooms will be time-wasting death traps is by now so general that one midwestern city official (speaking off the record) said he believes it would take at least a full generation for middle-class parents to regain confidence in his city's schools—even if those schools magically became excellent tomorrow and stayed that way.

This no doubt explains the sudden free-fall in national opinion polls about the future of public education. In a 1974 Gallup poll asking respondents to grade their local public schools, 18 percent gave theirs an "A." One decade later, the figure had plunged to 8 percent. Perhaps more telling, in 1997, Gallup reported that 44 percent of Americans favored allowing students to attend a private school at "public expense." Fifty-two percent were opposed. Supporters of traditional public education were quick to hail that finding as proof that a majority still opposes school voucher schemes. Fair enough—except that only three years earlier, a mere 24 percent had approved of the idea, and 72 percent had been opposed. In just three years' time, government control of the schools had lost nearly *a third* of its public support. There is nothing on the horizon to halt or even slow that trend.

Among minority respondents, despair over public schools is profound and deepening. In the 1997 poll, 72 percent of African Americans favored private-school vouchers. Three years earlier, it had been only 45 percent. Another 1997 poll, by the Joint Center for Political and Economic Studies, an African-American think tank in Washington, found a somewhat lower percentage of black support for vouchers—57 percent rather than 72. But that lower figure still constituted an eleven-point increase in just twelve months. Among Hispanics, the Joint Center reported, support for vouchers ran to 65 percent.

We hold no special brief for vouchers. Nor is the purpose of this discussion to advance one school-choice model over another. The fiscal economics of a citywide voucher system—or even an open system for all residents of inner cities—would be fantastically complex, and are still untested (though some tests of partial, selective systems are now under way in Cleveland and Milwaukee and, more recently, in Florida). Charter schools, a slightly less controversial idea, are also relatively new, and the experiments thus far are intriguing but inconclusive.

The point is that Americans—especially minorities and residents of inner cities—have stopped thinking of public schools as merely another policy problem to be tinkered with. The most striking quality of American public debate on education today is that hardly anyone (with the discordant exception of teachers' and principals' unions) is prepared to discuss modest solutions any more. More and more often, urban communities feel it necessary to take matters into their own hands and create the kind of schools that government has refused or failed to provide for them. The immune system of the urban public school monopoly is breaking down.

If the frightened eighth grader in Kotlowitz's story had attended Lazear Elementary School in Oakland, California, he would have been scarcely better off than in inner-city Chicago: The Oakland public school system sent Lazear graduates to a middle school plagued by guns and gang warfare, a place not all that much better than Chicago's Crane High. What makes the Oakland story different is that some parents there eventually had enough, and they fought back. In 1992, they approached the respected principal at Lazear and started planning a charter school of their own. The Pacific Research Institute, a policy think tank across the bay in San Francisco, helped them find professional help with accounting, law, curriculum development, and navigating the charter-approval system. Despite the predictable opposition of education unions and their flag bearers on the school board, the parents got their school, with the principal they had chosen.

On the surface, this sounds like something radical and destabilizing: a gang of ordinary parents—virtually all of them members of minority groups—storming the Bastille of public education and toppling its oligarchs. But in fact, this story is radical only in the inner city. Elsewhere, wealthier families, most of them white, have been doing almost exactly the same thing for decades. Instead of waging a messy war against intransigent urban school boards, they have simply stepped over the border into suburbia and carved out thousands of tiny new school districts that they alone control. Same end, different tactic.

Compared to the behemoth of most big-city school systems, suburban districts tend to be small, well-run, quality-conscious, and promptly responsive to the least stirring among their constituents. In suburbia, where some metropolitan areas feature scores, sometimes hundreds, of micro-districts, American public education is *already* decentralized and customer-driven. Poorer residents, concentrated in big-city school monopolies, simply missed the train.

It is dangerously easy, and often wrong, to cast teachers and their unions solely as the demons of this story. Education unions have, it's true, put up the fiercest and most skillful defense against school choice in inner cities. But their members are hardly unanimous on the point. The nation's first charter school, City Academy in St. Paul, Minnesota, was the creation of teachers, not primarily of parents. They were frustrated by the public schools' inability to retrieve kids who had failed or dropped out, and convinced that they could do better. One of the more famous of the 1990s charter schools, Boston's City on a Hill, was likewise a result of teacher frustration. "I was banging my head against the wall," one of the two teacher/founders recalled later. "The time had come to try something different. The charter law gave us the freedom to start from scratch."

City on a Hill opened in a neighborhood YMCA in 1995, with just 65 students in grades nine and ten, 70 percent of them minorities. It expanded gradually to grades seven through twelve, with 225 students by the end of the decade. The program is what you might expect from a school organized by crusading teachers: rigorous, rich, and creative. It boasts a solid core curriculum of basics, an emphasis on civic education, and partnerships with nationally known cultural institutions, including the Boston Ballet, the Huntington Theater, and the Boston Symphony Orchestra. The students are predominantly lower-income, and overwhelmingly minority.

And where did these teachers first conceive of such an idea? Both had previously taught in Chelsea, one of the more entrepreneurial of the 130 small suburban districts around Boston.

❑

There is, on the other hand, nothing automatically magical about small districts or suburban schools. Many residents of older, "inner ring" suburbs now complain that even their relatively small public school systems have become hidebound and bureaucratic, and have stopped responding creatively to new problems and changing (often lower-income) populations. As the disastrous urban school-decentralization experiments of the 1960s and '70s proved, small potentates do not necessarily run better schools than large potentates. The key to running an effective public education system is not changing the size or shape of the monopoly, but ending—or at least profoundly challenging—the monopoly.

For a lesson in what happens when giant systems feel unthreatened by market forces, consider the Big Three automakers in the 1970s and early '80s. Many of their products—especially those for the lower end of the market—ranged from the shoddy to the downright lethal. Their attitude toward the great lumpen mass of their customer base was something between indifference and open contempt. Sound familiar?

Who, then, saved the Big Three (and by extension, their customers)? Not Ralph Nader. Not Lee Iacocca, or some other inside reformer. Japan saved them. When Americans found an alternative to American-made cars, they bolted straight to the Japanese competitors. Then ensued one of the shortest learning cycles in industrial history: Shocked and traumatized, Detroit suddenly rediscovered quality engineering and customer service, roared back like a challenger instead of a retired champion, and now less than twenty years later finds itself in the midst of a historic boom. Its monopoly is gone, but its customer satisfaction has skyrocketed.

Why would that same dynamic not work for public education? Already, even before we can conclude much about student achievement under charter schools, we are starting to learn the effect they have on teachers. Preliminary research is finding that, although they earn about the same amount as teachers in conventional public schools, charter school teachers work longer hours, perform a wider range of duties, and enjoy far more autonomy than their counterparts in the conventional system.

Harvard education economist Caroline Hoxby offers this explanation: "If my class were to go from 75 students to 20, I could obviously spend much more time with each student. But if there was no incentive for me to give each student more attention, I might decide, 'Well, I'm just going to have an easier life.'" That is a brief but crystal-clear explanation for why increased spending on public schools produces no clear pattern of increased performance. Resources are important, but without an incentive to perform, all big organizations become sluggish.

Here we start to understand why some teachers may not see the school-choice issue the same way their unions do. "Longer hours" and "expanding duties" are fighting words to most labor leaders (and anyone who remembers sweatshops will agree that this is often a good thing). But something remarkable happens when you offer a dedicated teacher what former Education Secretary Lamar Alexander called the "old-fashioned horse-trade" of a charter school: more autonomy for the teacher in exchange for harder work and accountability for results. Many teachers, including loyal union members, will take that deal in a heartbeat.

The effects of competition go far beyond motivating teachers (many of whom are plenty well motivated already). The deepest effect of opening a market to competition is that it engages the energies of people and institutions outside the monopoly—people who previously used their gifts elsewhere. At the same time, competition motivates consumers to trade their rage for something positive—a different model, a different setting, a different provider—and to keep changing until they're satisfied. And finally, of course, it offers extinction to anyone unwilling to compete.

The best argument against school choice is one that attacks this last claim. Under school choice, opponents fear, poor-performing schools will never in fact reach extinction. They will perform the indispensable but grim task of warehousing the poorest-performing children—or at least, those whose parents are too inattentive to seek other alternatives. That is a realistic concern. But there are two persuasive answers to it.

First, thus far, charter schools are at least as likely to target "difficult" students as "easy" ones. Charter schools like St. Paul's City Academy have sprung up specifically to serve students who were falling through the traditional system's cracks. Some, like Detroit's Sierra Leone Educational Outreach Academy, are specifically for students who would otherwise have been in conventional special-ed programs. A great many, like the Raul Yzaguirre School of Success in Houston, have a student body of nearly 100 percent minority kids from tough neighborhoods. So far, we are not seeing a movement dominated by elite "MENSA schools" that so many critics feared. And even if success in the charter-school movement eventually brings out more profit-motivated operators chasing after the brighter students, there are also thousands of nonprofit youth- and community-development organizations who would deliberately seek out a tougher clientele.

Second, the "warehousing" system that critics fear is already a reality in most inner cities. Economists call this effect "sorting"—that is, students end up being "sorted" into schools that more or less suit their abilities and socioeconomic circumstances. As Caroline Hoxby describes it:

> People tend to tremendously underestimate the degree to which students are already sorted out in American schools. Take two different places: One that has many school districts—like Boston, with 130 school districts in the metropolitan area—and at the other extreme Miami, with

just one school district for the whole metropolitan county. You might think the kids were much more sorted out in Boston, where parents can "shop" among districts, than in Miami. But they're actually very well sorted out in both areas. Parents sort their kids out, period.

In the current system, however, the parents who are least likely to "sort their kids out" are the ones without the wherewithal to move near a better school. Families fed up with their public school, unless they are financially better off, are stuck in the warehouses next to the few who are content to remain there. In that system, there is no reason to hope that the "warehouse" will ever get any better. In a charter system, at least, there is always the hope that someone—community leaders, pastors, nonprofit organizations, *some*one—will help parents wake up to the availability of alternatives. And there is even some evidence that independent schools will actually "sort" themselves to recruit and serve the very kids who today are merely warehoused.

❑

In any case, it is becoming increasingly naive to discuss the status quo in public education as if rejiggering some budgets and tucking up a few curriculum plans are going to save it. The meltdown in public support for today's inner-city schools (and in some respects, for government schools in general) is too profound to be swept away with small reforms and some happy talk. Something fundamental will have to be done. Insisting on preserving the government monopoly intact is lately having only one effect: enlarging and radicalizing the opposition.

Suddenly, longtime friends of the inner city, including heads of minority groups, community advocates, and many loyal Democrats, are starting to talk about wholesale privatization, including universal vouchers, as an answer to America's discontent with public education. Journalist Charles Wheelan, a Democrat and a public-school parent in Chicago, wrote in a 1999 op-ed column in the *New York Times:*

Vouchers will bolster urban tax bases by stemming the flight of middle-class parents who move out of the city because they do not trust urban public schools and cannot afford private ones. Vouchers are pro-city, which is something that we Democrats are supposed to care about.

Without taking a position on vouchers per se, it is clear that the status quo is transparently anti-city. You will not read this as an official position of many city governments, but it is an opinion widely held in city halls all over the country. Most of the people we've talked to in policy positions share the opinion of a Cleveland official speaking off-the-record: "Unless we turn the schools in this city around—and do it convincingly, and soon—we will continue to lose our tax base and our ability to govern this city." This is not a small-stakes game.

Cleveland, it should be noted, already has a small experiment with school vouchers, though the results are still uncertain and the total number of students with vouchers is tiny compared to the size of the public school system. But Mayor Michael White in effect staked his reputation on reforming that system, and to that end has persuaded the state to give him control of it. His challenge, if Cleveland is to retain the middle-class families who pay the majority of local taxes, will be to run a system that offers enough choice so that residents of the city won't feel forced to choose between failing schools or a continued exodus to the suburbs.

❑

The still-unfolding alternative of the charter school—publicly funded and accountable, but independently run—owes its popularity to something more than the mere fact that it is, for now, a less radical idea than vouchers. Charter schools, many of them organized by parents, teachers, and other grassroots types, have suddenly created a point of entry for organized community influence in the way children are educated. Their appeal is not just that they are competitive and entrepreneurial, but that they are very often community-based.

The whole charter-school movement, in fact, seems strikingly familiar to a story we have heard before. Look at the elements: A community institution falls apart, residents grow first despondent then angry, and governments are unable or unwilling to provide a solution (in fact they are in some ways part of the problem). Eventually, through a combination of desperation and moxy, the residents take charge of their fate, wresting control of at least some small piece of the problem, and building something better. They get financial and professional help from civic and philanthropic groups. Some of the more enlightened government agencies help them with money and technical support, but otherwise stay mostly out of their way. And in a few years, a whole new system of community control and accountability starts to take shape.

That is the story of community development, which we summarized in Chapter 2. And sure enough, community development corporations and the charter school movement have quickly found their common ground. All over the country, CDCs are starting or joining charter schools—which they obviously regard as a crucial building-block in their general drive to save their neighborhoods.

The fit between CDCs and charter schools is based on more than just the fact that both are neighborhood institutions accountable to resident stakeholders. Charter schools also need something that CDCs are demonstrably excellent at providing (and governments, by and large, are not): sound, inexpensive buildings, newly built or renovated to community specifications.

The question of buildings is crucial to understanding the value of charter schools, and the economics that make them so attractive. What makes charter schools such a bargain for most school districts is that, although they get *tuition* payments from the public school system—the day-to-day cost of educating an average student—they typically don't get money for buildings or other capital expenditures. When opponents of school choice argue that vouchers and charters "drain" money from public education, this is a point they conveniently omit. In most states, every student attending a charter school is freeing up space, *at no capital cost,* for the usually overcrowded public school system. Want smaller class sizes in jam-packed inner-city schools? This is one way to get it. Even when school systems are not overcrowded, relieving the government of its building costs and obligations provides substantial relief to the school board.

So where *do* charter schools get the money for buildings? In most states, the government gets involved only to make sure that the proposed building meets regulatory standards. How it's financed and built is the charter holder's problem. Paul Carney, reviewing this problem for the Local Initiatives Support Corporation in 1999, summarized the situation this way:

> Because of the structure and limited amount of their public funding, the biggest problem confronting charter schools at this point in their evolution is obtaining and paying for permanent facilities. Some of the schools are able to acquire donated buildings or space in buildings, such as churches, lofts, warehouses, abandoned parochial schools, etc., and a few states allow or require charter schools to take over existing schools. However, most schools are forced to enter into a short-term lease for an "as-is" facility, and to pay a relatively high rent that reflects the landlord's requirement of a risk premium to lease any space at all to the school. ...
>
> Although most educators would rather focus entirely on their instructional program and not be in the property management business, being a tenant has risks. Renting a facility increases the school's instability, because the school might not have its lease renewed, might face a steep increase in rent and operating fees, or might have to pay passed-through property taxes. In addition, the building and fire codes for a school are strict, and as a tenant, the school is usually responsible for paying for any required renovations. It is in the school's best long-term interest to try to secure a permanent facility, and that is the biggest challenge for most charter school founders.

And so, enter the community development corporation, or some other neighborhood-based institution. Filling the capital gap is a service that development organizations have experience performing, as is renovating or building local institutions. The partnership is a natural one, and not surprisingly, it's turning up more and more often on the spreading landscape of charter schools.

But the courtship between the charter school movement and community organizations may have consequences far beyond the creation of a few new institutions. Take the case of Chicago's North River Commission, a nearly forty-year-old community organization on the city's northwest side. NRC didn't open a charter school, didn't build a school building, and in fact never turned one shovel of dirt for a new educational institution. Yet it caused something of a minor earthquake in the Chicago school system, simply by threatening to apply for a school charter. "This community was losing 1,500 kids a year," recalls NRC executive director Joel Bookman, "from families moving to the suburbs as soon as their kids reached high-school age. You keep that up, eventually you lose your community. We weren't going to have that. If we had to create our own school, then so be it. But when the school system realized we weren't kidding, we ended up with an even better deal."

The "better deal" was the new 800-student Northside College Preparatory Academy, a $37 million public magnet school. "This is part of our overall strategy to develop higher quality high schools," said Tim Martin, the school system's chief operating officer. It was a remarkable coincidence, to put it mildly, that the system's "overall strategy" was to begin on Kedzie Avenue—on the very site that NRC had proposed for its charter institution.

But NRC wasn't complaining: The organization played a central role in designing the new school's curriculum, student-selection criteria, even its architectural design. Not only had the Chicago public schools responded positively to the neighborhood's competitive challenge, but the school board was apparently embracing the message of competition citywide: Magnet schools like the one on Kedzie, said Martin, "will force some of the principals [in other schools] to do better, to find new and improved ways to teach their kids. ... You push the next group of kids, force a little bit of competition out there. You have teachers wanting to do better."

For now, NRC's charter application is on the shelf, while the community waits to see what the new magnet school will accomplish. Meanwhile, the organization is mobilizing support and training for volunteer school councils at the area's five other high schools—"to make sure," in Bookman's words, "that they won't simply lose out to the new high school, and just get worse, but will take up the challenge to compete."

From the perspective of community development groups, education is the next frontier. For decades, they had found themselves hamstrung by the impenetrable wall around their neighborhood public schools. They could fix housing, revive shopping areas, raise the level of public services, even help reduce crime. But the schools—probably the biggest factor in families' decision about whether to remain or flee—

were simply beyond the reach of the organized community. Many critics of community development correctly pointed out that, even when CDCs visibly transformed their communities into more livable, attractive places, the middle class sometimes kept moving out. Look down the block at the neighborhood school, and the reason isn't hard to figure out.

Charter schools are slowly providing an answer to that problem. Why slowly? Because in most places, charters are few, student enrollment is limited, and the application process for charters is tortuous. But more and more, schools are showing up for the first time on the radar of community development, and the process is almost certain to accelerate.

So it was that in 1998, a coalition of church groups in Youngstown, Ohio—a group that had already built and renovated housing through its affiliated CDC—opened a new charter school in what had been an abandoned public school building. The Greater Youngstown Coalition of Christians simply wanted a better school to serve the local kids, and hoped to hold on to neighbors who might otherwise have moved to a place with better schools. But in the process, the group also rescued a derelict school building, a structure that would otherwise have been simply an eyesore (or worse) as the years went by. The school system, meanwhile, would have had to pay to maintain the building—just to keep it from becoming a hazard—or else would have had to pay to demolish it. Instead, the Coalition bought the building, relieved the school system of unwanted real estate, and made a productive community asset out of it.

❑

All these stories are recent, most are very small-scale, and none is certain of success. The point is not that community-based schooling is the proven answer to the collapse of public confidence in government education. Like CDCs, charter schools will have to prove themselves, and that will take time. In fact, an important (if cautionary) similarity between school-choice reforms and community development corporations is that neither one works quickly, or necessarily produces exactly the right result first time out of the box.

Many CDCs can tell depressing stories about cost overruns, design flaws, ill-considered compromises, and management headaches on their first project or two. Some—including several of the oldest and best—had to weather serious crises of confidence among their neighborhood constituents when an early project didn't live up to expectations. Anyone who has started a business or two, made mistakes, lost some customers, and bounced back smarter and stronger will recognize this story. That is how start-up ideas (the good ones, anyway) take shape in free markets.

Urban public schools have rarely had to become acquainted with market forces, so their worst mistakes have tended to linger indefinitely. The assumption that a school may get worse but rarely better, and that tomorrow's results will be no better than today's, is an understandable but deadly cynicism. It gives reformers little latitude for trial and error. Worse, in the world of American public policy, attention spans are short, and judgments hasty. The more intense the publicity, the shorter is the time public opinion will wait before making up its collective mind and moving on. It's small wonder, then, that so many in the school-choice movement feel compelled to produce fantastic successes in their first few years.

So far, not surprisingly, the results have been mixed and hard to interpret. To begin with, the few charter schools in operation are dissimilar (as you'd expect) and therefore don't add up to a neat scientific experiment. If three schools fail and three succeed, and all six are fundamentally different from one another, what did the "test" prove?

Voucher experiments like those in Cleveland and Milwaukee are likewise dissimilar and small. Thus far, the evaluations of both those programs have mostly been exercises in dueling data. One study finds no effect on student achievement (which by itself would not be shocking after so brief an experiment), then another takes issue with the first study and finds significant improvement. This will almost certainly go on for a few more years. And then, if the initial data are disappointing, independent schools will need time to adapt and try again. Conventional schools have enjoyed that opportunity for a few centuries; surely independent schools ought to get at least a decade or two.

This is where the school story diverges disturbingly from that of community development. The latter was born largely in obscurity, grew by fits and starts, went mostly unnoticed, and became a minor media darling only after it had learned hard lessons and racked up a critical mass of impressive results. Will charter schools, or vouchers, or other reforms get the same break?

This is not an argument for leniency, only for patience—and for the kind of open-minded experimentation so alien to most government-run systems. Ultimately, school-choice plans must be accountable, just as CDCs must be, to all three of their constituents: their immediate customers, their neighborhood or wider community, and the government systems that help them with money, technical support, and licenses to operate. But it is disingenuous to reckon that accountability in the first two or five years of operation. Remember the initial reputation of Japanese cars? It takes a while to engineer a complex new product to top performance.

❏

To be fair, public schools themselves have had bad breaks in the realm of public policy and lawmaking, where they have routinely been called upon to take on all of society's unsolved problems and serially fix them. Americans asked the schools to forge our democracy in the late eighteenth and early nineteenth centuries. In the late nineteenth and early twentieth centuries we asked them to assimilate the torrent of immigrants pouring into U.S. factories and farms. In the mid-twentieth century we asked them to win the Cold War by creating young American scientists, engineers, and mathematicians. In the 1960s and '70s, we asked public schools to cure the poisonous legacy of racial discrimination. Today, they are supposed to supply our antidote to drugs and gang violence (even as they battle those same scourges in their corridors) with a mélange of in-school social programs, anticrime initiatives, and after-school services that once were the domain of families, churches, and neighbors.

So we are a country that asks too much of its schools. Even acknowledging that, it is surely reasonable to ask whether there are ways of getting more from public school systems than we now get. The system on which all these demands are placed—including the perfectly reasonable ones of maintaining order and teaching the three R's—has largely been designed and built on the model of the early twentieth-century factory: top-down, hierarchical, mechanistic, overbureaucratized, and cumbersome or impossible to change. That model won't budge unless exposed to market pressures from customers or competitors.

Fortunately, the customers are already at the gates. And the smarter urban politicians are responding. In what at first seemed an almost death-defying crusade against the failure of Chicago's schools, Mayor Richard M. Daley took personal responsibility for the public school system, arguing, in effect, that someone needed to be accountable for it—someone whom voters could easily fire if they were unhappy. Other mayors, including Michael White of Cleveland and Dennis Archer of Detroit, have since followed suit.

This seems to be much more than the usual political grandstanding, for two reasons: First, some of these mayors (perhaps not Daley, but certainly White and Archer) occupy vulnerable political posts. Their willingness to be held accountable for public schools really could be a life-or-death matter for them at the polls. Second, all of these mayors have made a public connection between the future of their schools and the future of their city, a political equation that opens the agenda to unprecedented measures and profound change.

If it's true, then, that the status quo in public education is effectively over, or soon will be, the consequences for inner cities can't help but be life-altering. The greatest of the "grim immovables" may actually be moving at this moment. Where it will end up—in crippling culture wars, a limbo of inconclusive evaluations, or in a constellation of new, accountable, competitive institutions, both public and private—could ultimately determine whether inner-city neighborhoods go up or down in the early decades of the new century.

Chapter 10

SLIPPING THE WELFARE KNOT

I F SCHOOL choice, in Charles Wheelan's phrase, is clearly "pro-city," can the same be said of welfare reform? Here, the answer is not quite as clear.

At the end of the 1990s, with welfare rolls plummeting across the country, a higher and higher percentage of the U.S. welfare population is now concentrated in cities, where people are leaving welfare more slowly (albeit still in record numbers). The effect, at least for a time, has been to make welfare appear to be even more of an urban problem than it was before—surely not a good sign for cities, even if the general trends are encouraging.

There are at least a few lessons from the last half of the twentieth century suggesting that a welfare overhaul is in fact indispensable for creating healthier cities—and inner cities in particular. The current version of welfare reform may, in time, prove to be misguided—although experience so far hasn't supported the earliest and harshest criticisms of it. Further reform will probably be necessary to make sure that people find jobs and don't fall into destitution.

All the same, preserving the old system was surely untenable—both politically and morally. That is true in general, and it's especially true in inner cities.

Welfare as we used to know it—like much of the public housing and public school systems—bore all the hallmarks of those other "grim immovables": federally imposed rules indifferent to local markets; special, stigmatizing status for a narrow class of poor people (in this case single minority women with children); giant entrenched bureaucracies bulwarked by fiercely ideological defenders; and an incentive structure that, at least for some beneficiaries, made it much harder (or scarier) to leave the program than to stay in it for life.

Most of all, in many of the poorest inner-city neighborhoods, welfare spread its roots so deeply into the local way of life that it became self-reinforcing and concentrating. Locked into an income stream that will never rise, families have tended to concentrate in areas where the fixed costs (mainly rents) are lowest. Those tend to be the same areas where employment is rare, crime and drug use are widespread, and schools abysmal. In short, the worst of the inner cities.

In *The Truly Disadvantaged*, William Julius Wilson describes this "concentration effect" in detail—not as the by-product of welfare alone, certainly, but as the combined effect of intergenerational poverty and joblessness, the flight of working-class whites and blacks, a lack of self-supporting role models, and failed schools. "In such neighborhoods," Wilson writes, "teachers become frustrated and do not teach, and children do not learn. A vicious cycle is perpetuated through the family, through the community, and through the schools."

It's important to acknowledge that Wilson's point is about chronic unemployment, not about welfare per se. But his critical insight—relevant to our broader discussion—is that the dysfunction in areas of concentrated poverty is not individual, but communal: The social *structure* is rigged for failure, and people are trapped in it. "People experience a social isolation," he writes, "that excludes them from the job network system." This isolation—and the attendant feelings of exclusion, hopelessness, and victimhood—keep many residents from developing any form of work ethic.

Through the narrow windows of the typical urban welfare compound, the normal life of working communities—daily routine, regular attendance at work and organized activities, self-discipline—appears alien, pointless, and even vaguely hostile. The result is a community that's far less likely to take action to improve its circumstances: to mobilize against crime, say, or demand better services from City Hall—or for that matter, even to vote.

Traditional welfare has buttressed this isolation and communal lethargy by providing a guaranteed "support" with utterly no expectation that recipients will earn an income or otherwise provide for themselves any time soon. In areas where the advantages of work are invisible (because no one is working), that guarantee makes for a powerful social narcotic.

Yet however much the sense of community may be anesthetized, individuals in even the poorest neighborhoods can show surprising resourcefulness and entrepreneurship—within the perverse incentives of the welfare and poverty systems they are forced to navigate. One example: In New York City, poor families learned in the 1980s that they could move to the front of the long queue for government housing vouchers if they became "homeless." They would have to move out of their (often overcrowded) apartment; present themselves at a tiny, remote office of the city's homeless shelter system; pass an eligibility review that mainly required saying the right things to a series of interviewers; and then wait in shelters, sometimes up to two years, for a rent voucher to materialize. Until recently, this process worked quite well: The families got their vouchers, much faster than they would have if they had simply stayed home and waited their turn on the normal list. (In 1997, the city finally persuaded a state court to permit a more exacting eligibility review.)

Despite the enormous complexity and inconvenience of this process, many thousands of families navigated it ingeniously for more than fifteen years. The problem was not a lack of individual resourcefulness and persistence. The problem was that people were using their resourcefulness and persistence *within the suffocating confines of the public-aid system* (and in the process proving themselves far more clever than their bureaucratic controllers), rather than in the ordinary marketplace occupied by most of society.

Another example, perhaps more obvious, is the drug trade. Here, highly entrepreneurial young people endure a dangerous apprenticeship (often costing them jail time, if not their lives) for the potentially high returns that flow from manufacturing, distributing, and retailing drugs. There is a highly refined, if ghastly, risk-return calculation to this career choice. It is not for the lazy or the feckless. But unlike other work, it can be carried out completely within the confines of the welfare system (which supplies the customers' purchase-money as well as part of the dealer's own family income).

These examples suggest that, given an offer of indefinite financial support, and walled off from the normal inducements to work, save, and advance, people will take the handout. They will find other outlets for their energy and ambition, and even achieve a kind of career advancement in the process. But they won't leap spontaneously to the conclusion that finding a job, enduring the perils of the labor market, and suffering the unpleasantness of most entry-level jobs are preferable to a free monthly check.

To be sure, even in its most generous days, the greater portion of the welfare system has always been exactly what most Americans wanted it to be: a temporary safety net to protect people from economic downturns, upheavals in the job market, family breakups, or other interruptions in a person's working life. The vast majority of welfare recipients spend only a few years on welfare, have average-sized families, and soon end up back at work or married to someone who is working.

The problem with welfare does not spring from the way *most* people used the system. The problem was the effect of that system on specific, vulnerable communities: those already-poor areas, usually in inner cities, that were simultaneously being abandoned by working-class families, small employers, home owners, and other sources of economic opportunity and stability. Combine those hardships with a system that promised unlimited "maintenance"—a frayed security blanket that would vanish if the recipient took a job—and you have the makings of a dependent subculture.

Those who used welfare as a temporary safe harbor tended, like most poor people, to come from families or communities where people work, and support themselves, and hope for advancement, either for themselves or for their children. That is, they came from the great majority of ordinary families and communities. Only when those normalizing influences are absent—especially in neighborhoods characterized by racial segregation and widespread, long-term joblessness—does welfare become something it was never meant to be: a way of life.

When that happens, more than just economic well-being suffers. To borrow once again from William Julius Wilson, the effect of intense, long-term dependency is a breakdown in "social organization"—the ways in which neighborhoods enforce norms of behavior, shared responsibility, and shared expectations. Absent those organizing forces, neighborhoods cannot recover, but can only spiral downward.

❏

Curing welfare won't, by itself, end the isolation and restore "social organization" to the poorest inner-city areas. That will take many kinds of effort, including those we discuss in other sections of this book. But for inner cities to regain a place in the normal economy—including access to ordinary jobs, opportunity, and mobility for their residents—it is essential to break open the cocoon of indefinite income "maintenance" and "support" that was the psychological foundation of old-fashioned welfare.

That much, at least, was accomplished in the watershed federal welfare reform of 1996. The act put an end to the ironclad "entitlement" to welfare, and turned over most policy decisions—including the ability to tailor welfare programs to local market conditions—to states and localities. It imposed work requirements and a five-year lifetime time limit on nearly all recipients. Mix in a fantastically strong economy, heating up just as the new law was taking effect, and the result was a nosedive in welfare rolls, even in the cities where unemployment and dependency rates have been persistently highest.

By July 1999, welfare recipiency in the United States was cut nearly in half nationwide. According to an Urban Institute study that same year, fewer than a third of those who left the rolls to take jobs later returned to welfare; 60 percent of the remainder were working (and some, no doubt, had left welfare by what used to be the most common route: getting married).

The act was hardly a masterpiece of policymaking. Its intellectual underpinnings were almost nil, and the congressional wrangling that produced it was a classic example of the rancor and ideological cant that dominated 1990s American politics. Even so, a once-impregnable wall was breached: For the first time in more than thirty years, American poverty policy now presumes and requires that people will support themselves by working.

The dangers of this are obvious: Come the next recession (or certainly the one after that), we will learn whether the time limits imposed in 1996 are too short to protect people through all the years in which the economy won't be able to employ everyone. Over a longer span, we may learn whether children suffer neglect when their single mothers are required to work, or whether they benefit (as earlier generations of poor children did) from parents' example of industry and responsibility.

There could be many reasons why the answers to some of these questions are discouraging. There will probably be some chastening lessons along the way. The law will almost certainly need to be fine-tuned, preferably when the political atmosphere of shrillness and hysteria has mellowed a bit.

In the meantime, though, the authors of the haphazard 1996 reform got a colossally lucky break in the late 1990s, a stroke of pure serendipity that may be the best thing to happen to welfare reform. To win governors' support, lawmakers guaranteed the states a fixed allocation of welfare money for five years after the new law was signed, regardless of the size of their caseloads. So when caseloads fell through the floor in the full-employment labor market, states ended up with a financial windfall of extra antipoverty money. Most used it to experiment on employment and training services, tuition supports, child care programs, and other ways of helping the people who face the longest odds of success in the job market.

Those experiments may go a long way toward helping a future Congress think through the issues left unresolved in the slapdash 1996 reform. What does it really take—beyond mere coercion—to get people with few skills and no work experience into lasting jobs? When they are working, what is society's role in making sure their children are properly looked after? (Society will certainly pay, and pay dearly, if the children are brought up poorly; compared to the later costs of criminality, ill health, and illiteracy, responsible child care and after-school programs are almost certainly a bargain.)

Most of all, is the five-year time limit realistic? It's one thing to say that welfare must not be treated as a lifetime guarantee, but quite another to cut off a family's food abruptly at midnight on the last day of the sixtieth month. There are surely less draconian ways of discouraging dependency.

Still, coercion apparently plays a necessary and beneficial role, as the late-'90s labor market helped to demonstrate. In the past, welfare caseloads showed a stubborn indifference to unemployment rates. For decades, distinguished statisticians wasted miles of computer tape trying to find an economic relationship between changes in the labor market and changes in welfare recipiency. Even when they managed to tease out some contorted pattern in past fluctuations, the pattern routinely failed to predict the *next* change, whether up or down. There simply was no discernible relationship between the number of available jobs and the number of people applying for welfare.

Yet suddenly, in the late 1990s, an upturn in employment coincided with an immediate and radical plunge in welfare rates. Why? The answer will take a few years, and a few more miles of computer tape, to establish for certain. But one hypothesis seems highly likely: In the late 1990s, the option of *not* working began to disappear.

That's sound strategy in a strong market. But will things seem dramatically bleaker in a weak one? Rather than grapple with the complexities of that question, Congress and the White House simply tabled it. Sooner or later, it will be back to haunt them.

A late 1999 editorial in the *Washington Post* summed up that prospect with a justly skeptical view of the specifics of the 1996 law:

> The old welfare system perpetuated dependency; it has few defenders. The new, in which Federal responsibility for child welfare has been greatly reduced, seems to us to have swung too far the other way, and to have done so unnecessarily. In tougher times, when jobs for moms are scarcer and the states are facing budget problems of their own, who will support the considerable number of children at the bottom of the economic heap? That's the unanswered question.

Well, it's one of the unanswered questions. There are others, some of them a good deal more positive, that will also be answered in the first decade or two of revamped welfare. For instance:

What will be the effect on young people in communities where, beginning in the late '90s, there were suddenly many more adults at work than there had ever been before? When more young people in poor neighborhoods presume that their school days will end in employment rather than welfare eligibility, how will that affect their attitude toward school, job training, and career planning? When more heads of poor families see a prospect for actually increasing their incomes instead of just "maintaining" them, what will be the effect on their decisions about where to live, how to organize their lives, and what to hope for?

These essentially psychological questions will exert a profound, but gradual, influence on the changing life of poor, inner-city neighborhoods. The answers will certainly be more positive if Washington continues to allow states to spend their former welfare dollars on employment services, training, and education programs, rather than indulging in the false thrift of pure spending cuts. The intelligent foundation of welfare reform was never primarily budget savings. The point was to change the incentive structure, and to rebuild an ethic of opportunity in poor communities.

Wisconsin, which is among the national leaders in accomplishing those ends, provides an important lesson in what it takes to make welfare reform work. From a caseload of 100,000 families a decade ago, Wisconsin's welfare program today serves just 7,700. In 1999, Wisconsin was among the top five states in the rate of employment among welfare recipients. But to accomplish that, the state took two remarkable steps that other states are now beginning to emulate: First, Wisconsin privatized its welfare system, removing it from an ossified bureaucracy steeped in the federal dictates of the past and subjecting it to performance-based contracting and competition.

Second, it proceeded to spend *more* money per welfare recipient than it had spent in the past. Now, though, the money is going for job-placement services, employment counseling, community-service jobs, and child care. Wisconsin even offers child care, subsidized health care, and wage supplements to people who are *not* on welfare, just to help them stay off.

"I've told Congress, and I've told taxpayers, you can't do this cheaply," four-term Republican Governor Tommy Thompson said to the *New York Times*. "You have to spend more in the beginning to save on the back end."

Congress is not yet listening carefully. Well before the first five years of reform were over, lawmakers were already searching for ways to renege on their promise to keep states' welfare budgets level. Were it not for the resistance of Republican governors—who insist on treating a promise from the federal government as if it were a real promise—Republicans in Congress would no doubt have reallocated a good portion of the money in the third year.

That would be pure folly, and it would justify the howls of liberal protest that greeted the 1996 reform law. If Congress means to reform welfare simply by pulling in the safety net and walking away, it will do incalculable harm both to poor families and to all other taxpayers, who will someday have to deal with the consequences of poor child health, delinquency, and mounting anger—quite apart from the further destruction these things will deal to inner cities. If, on the other hand, Washington takes Governor Thompson's advice and actually creates an employment-centered alternative to welfare, the benefits for poor communities may far exceed what anyone has yet dared to calculate.

Governors, on the other hand, need to use all the rights Congress has given them, something many (including Thompson) have been reluctant to do. The 1996 welfare reform lets states waive the eligibility time limits for up to 20 percent of their caseload. That is an implicit acknowledgement that many people simply aren't capable of working—including many who don't meet the federal government's strict definitions of disability. For example: A forty-four-year-old illiterate mother of eleven in Governor Thompson's state, a Hispanic woman who speaks no English and must care for an epileptic husband and a schizophrenic son, is not going to be self-supporting in the two years Wisconsin lets her stay on welfare. She's not disabled, but she isn't anywhere near work-ready. Cutting off her benefits—which the state is preparing to do as this is being written—is simply wrong. Worse, it's entirely optional on the state's part. Congress explicitly allowed the 20 percent exception to cover cases like this woman's.

Yet the exceptions, and any other fine-tuning the nascent reform requires, at least remain open to debate and further action. What's no longer open to debate, it seems, is a life voluntarily spent off work—a life in which, in the poorest communities, not a single person gets up in the morning for a job, and people of all ages simply hang around, bored and unchallenged.

In that sense, ending welfare "as we knew it" is, at least in principle, profoundly "pro-city." As we knew it, the welfare entitlement made possible the concentration not just of poverty, but of purposelessness. All the other forces we have described here—public housing, miserable schools, segregationist zoning and highway programs, and so on—created a concentration of need and frustration. To that, welfare added idleness. The result was whole neighborhoods in which the ordinary life of work and reward, opportunity and discipline, the mixing of classes and races in shared tasks—all the daily struggles and social norms that other people take for granted—were alien, irrelevant, even vaguely suspect. Work was "out there."

The exodus from welfare rolls in recent years shows that work can be brought home, and has been, even in the poorest places. It effectively proves that great numbers of people who could have been working were not working, through strong labor markets and weak ones, year after dismal year. That is no longer an option. At the end of the 1990s, thanks to a robust job market, most people in even the poorest neighborhoods were following the daily pattern of bundling children off to school, working, returning from work, and contemplating an income that, however meager, could actually *go up* someday—something welfare almost never did.

It would help profoundly if people could get the education and training they need to make that happen. It would help if jobs with advancement potential were more plentiful. Getting people back to work is an enormous achievement, but it isn't the whole battle. Welfare reform isn't right yet, and thus isn't finished. But even if it amounts to small progress, it is progress all the same.

And in the poorest, most isolated communities of the inner city, no other progress would ever have been possible without that. What had been just another grim, immovable barrier to healthy life in the inner city has fallen. Without it, much more is now possible.

Chapter 11

THE "THIRD WAY" IN CITY HALL

WHEN HE became leader of what he christened the "New Labor" Party, British Prime Minister Tony Blair caught voters'
imagination by proclaiming a "Third Way" between orthodox Tory-
ism and welfare-state socialism. Blair's Third Way fused the core ideals
of both camps—"rights and responsibilities; the promotion of enterprise and the attack on poverty and discrimination"—in a practical
drive to build markets and government systems from which everyone
would benefit. (A few years earlier, Bill Clinton's handlers were describing a similar idea with the cumbersome term "triangulation," but
it was no match for the hip mysticism of the Blair coinage.)

Yet by the time Blair and Clinton had stumbled across their respective versions of the Road Not Taken, several American big-city mayors
had long since taken it. As with most innovations in Western government, it was local politicians who first staked out the Third Way in
practice. And to this day, the best examples of it are in no capitol—
state, federal, or royal—but in American city halls.

Cleveland's George Voinovich and New York's Ed Koch were among
the pioneers—early 1980s mayors who regularly perplexed their political parties and irritated the ideologues of both the traditional Left and
Right. Their practical (if, in Koch's case, flamboyant) program involved
decentralizing control over public services, tending to the quality of

everyday life, channeling investment (not just government grants) into the central city and poor neighborhoods, and generally appealing to the common sense of a broad political center.

Not surprisingly, these mayors governed cities that, at least at the time, were deeply troubled. They did not have the luxury of ideological purity (at least not if they wanted to be remembered as anything but hacks). Their cities were nosediving into oblivion, and they each ran a serious chance of presiding over catastrophes set in motion by their predecessors. Soon, Philadelphia's Ed Rendell, Chicago's Richard M. Daley, Detroit's Dennis Archer, and Washington's Anthony Williams were in the same boat. And all of them, it turns out, are proving to be quintessential Third Way mayors.

The approach proved so popular that it is no longer necessary for an urban politician to face disaster before setting out along the Third Way. Rudolph Giuliani, for instance, came into office when New York City was in one of its periodic spells of ill humor, but was certainly no longer facing bankruptcy (nor even a fate New Yorkers would consider much worse: irrelevance). Yet even without the threat of imminent catastrophe, Giuliani managed to arm-twist city government into tackling problems that real people of both political parties actually care about, but that lesser politicians had considered ideologically doubtful (or worse, simply beneath notice). The Giuliani agenda equally benefited Wall Street brokerage firms and Chinatown restaurateurs, poor and middle-class African-American and Latino families from Harlem to Queens, and both the tourists and the maids at the Waldorf-Astoria.

Giuliani took credit—much of it well deserved—for curbing public intoxication and the city's once-ubiquitous panhandling, slashing petty crime and vandalism, enforcing long-ignored traffic and public safety laws, and waging war on the state's and city's uncompetitive taxes (on this last item, he was thwarted by bad relations with a powerful state government unsympathetic to New York City). He has faced down public employee unions and their advocates, turning over many of the city's calcified social programs to more effective nonprofit organizations. And although he doesn't share Koch's passion for neighborhood redevelopment, Giuliani's issues, more often than not, are the neighborhoods' issues.

At this point, the roster of mayors who have planted their flags along the Third Way is constantly growing: Stephen Goldsmith of Indianapolis, John Norquist of Milwaukee, Susan Golding of San Diego, and Thomas Menino of Boston are examples. Extend the list to less famous names, and it would go on for pages. Goldsmith, in fact, was among the first people to identify this cluster of new-style urban politicians, in his 1997 book, *The Twenty-First Century City:*

A new breed of mayors now occupies city halls across America. With a deep understanding of the need for smaller government, and determined to attain a better life for citizens in tough urban neighborhoods, these new mayors have blurred the lines between Republican and Democrat, conservative and liberal. They do not want bigger checks from Washington; they want the freedom to solve their cities' problems in their own way. In many respects, they have more in common with each other than they do with some of their respective parties' national leadership.

Inc. magazine in 1999 declared inner cities "America's best-kept secret" and devoted most of an issue to profiles of fast-growing companies in inner city locations. (Inc. Magazine ©1999)

Illustrating Goldsmith's point perfectly, here is Democrat John Norquist looking back on the national response to the 1992 Rodney King riots in Los Angeles:

> The United States Conference of Mayors Advisory Board held a meeting three thousand miles away, at its Washington, D.C., headquarters, located a convenient few blocks from the White House. The topic: how to capitalize on the riot and convince the Federal government to establish an urban agenda. ... Excitement ran through the room. For the mayors, it was a like a chance to sit on Santa Claus's lap and ask for Federal presents. ...
>
> My turn came. I agreed that we had the Federal government's attention, but I wasn't happy with how we got it. And I suspected it wouldn't last long. As soon as CNN stopped covering the riot, ... only two groups of people would remember what happened in any meaningful way.
>
> The first group would comprise the people in the neighborhood who had lived through a nightmare and would pay its price for a long time to come. The other group would consist of bankers, insurance companies, and investors from around the world, who would be reluctant to put their money where it seemed likely to burn. Not only would these people long remember to keep their money out of South Central Los Angeles, but to the extent that they looked at the riot as a problem shared by all large U.S. cities—which is precisely how we mayors were asking everyone to view it—they would withhold money from all our cities. ...
>
> You can't build a city on fear, and you can't build a city on pity. ... You can build a city on its natural advantages: its efficient proximity and density, its processes and markets, and its extraordinary capacity to promote the success of its citizens.

This little reflection, early in Norquist's 1998 book *The Wealth of Cities: Revitalizing the Centers of American Life*, exactly pinpoints the difference between new mayors and old. The old-style mayor sought help fixing his or her city; the new style seeks investment in its strengths. The old-style mayor viewed the cities' ills as part of their natural condition, an inherited suffering that other people in other places had a duty to relieve, probably in perpetuity. The new mayor asks just two things of outsiders: First, cease to do harm—stop subsidizing sprawl; stop forcing people into destructive housing and failed schools; and second, take a

fresh look at cities whenever you seek investment opportunity, employees, a convenient business location, and an attractive place to live. Beyond that, in the new mayor's view, the cities' problems are for the cities
themselves (with reasonable state and federal help) to solve: conquer
crime, encourage investment in housing and business, improve schools,
and free residents to plan for and improve their own neighborhoods.

The appeal of this message has been vastly greater than the prevailing
ideologues seem to grasp. Early in 1999, for example, Daley coasted to
reelection in Chicago with not just the support of his father's loyal
white-ethnic base, but a huge slice of the African-American vote. He
had come to office in 1989 in an election that the *New York Times* described as "the most racially polarized vote in the city's history," but a
decade later, he carried the endorsement of the city's largest African-
American daily newspaper and several black politicians who had vilified
him ten years before. When Rendell reached the end of Philadelphia's
eight-year term limit, the election to succeed him saw two candidates—
a black Democrat and a white Republican—battle each other over who
would be most likely to preserve the Rendell tradition.

This is profoundly healthy for urban America, and for American
politics in general, but it is especially urgent good news for the cities'
poorest enclaves. Consider Detroit, whose festering political resentments and entrenched machine politics under Coleman Young had
made it seem almost irredeemable to the rest of the country. Today,
Mayor Dennis Archer (leveraging a boom in the U.S. auto industry)
has compiled a surprisingly plausible vision of new development at
the city's core, and has presided over an astonishing multiyear rise in
the property values of its deeply troubled neighborhoods. A 1999 description of Archer's strategy in the *Washington Post* could have been
written by Goldsmith or Norquist:

> The Detroit Democrat is doing it with a formula not unlike that used
> by Republican New York Mayor Rudolph W. Giuliani and a few others:
> Crack down on street crime—particularly drugs, burglaries, carjack-
> ings, and prostitution—to make the city more welcoming. Tear down
> abandoned buildings, and speed up the approval process for developers
> interested in the city.
>
> Then, aggressively lobby businesses to come to the city, taking ad-
> vantage of the current economic boom and a rising desire among some

business leaders to return to the cities. Finally, keep in touch with residents by holding frequent town hall meetings and other gatherings that Archer calls "Mayor's Nights In."

[Washington Mayor Anthony] Williams has watched, learned, and copied.

This is important for inner-city neighborhoods because everything that is now working in their favor—grassroots planning and development, reductions in crime, decentralization and competition in city services, and elimination of the "grim immovables"—demands vigorous, enterprising leadership from City Hall. The old brand of urban politics—pitting races and classes against one another, insisting on central control of everything, trading union endorsements for labor contracts that virtually guarantee poor service—smothered poor neighborhoods for decades. A return to that style of leadership would stop the current rebound in its tracks.

So far, fortunately, traffic on the urban Third Way is moving forward, and the pace is quickening.

CONCLUSION

Seizing the Moment

A RE AMERICA'S inner cities on the way back? And if they are, can they complete the journey? The case for answering Yes to the first question is powerful, if still circumstantial. But answering Yes to the second question, at this point, would be no better than a hunch—though surely a plausible one, under the right circumstances. Nothing in this book conclusively refutes the experts' official despair, bolstered as it is by decades of dismal (if dated) statistics. Most of the smart choices and favorable market forces that are bringing cities back to health today could easily be reversed tomorrow, with a combination of carelessness, bad luck, and bungled politics.

Yet the evidence we've offered, however much episodic and evolving, nonetheless makes clear that *something is happening* in formerly bleak neighborhoods all over the country, something unforeseen and, at least in recent decades, unprecedented. Empty-nesters taking up residence in once-hopeless downtowns; merchants, police, and nonprofit groups restoring order and vitality to neighborhood markets, communities retaking control of derelict housing, parks, and even schools; capital flowing into inner-city markets at unheard-of rates.

Individually small and uneven, when these changes are seen together, they add up to something coherent and phenomenal.

They are not ordinarily seen that way. And statistics, particularly those in the glacial progression of U.S. Censuses, will not tell their consolidated story for years. It is possible, therefore, that whatever is happening will go unnoticed and uncredited for so long that it simply dies of neglect and brute fatalism. It's encouraging, certainly, that so much has happened without official ballyhoo. (And some things, it must be said, have happened precisely *because* there was no official ballyhoo.) But to make of all these positive stirrings a force that is great enough to reverse urban decline nationwide will take concerted effort, investment, and a willingness to change national attitudes and policy.

All of that, in turn, demands the thing that the United States seems most to be lacking as the twentieth century closes: confidence that an urban rebound is achievable and worth the effort.

At the risk of stating the obvious, these accomplishments are already the result of people *doing* things differently, struggling—against long odds and learned discouragement—to build a new version of poor and working-class urban neighborhoods. If this point ought to be obvious, it's nonetheless overlooked a surprising amount of the time. Fatalism has become so deep-rooted in urban politics and scholarship that many people tend to regard every change in cities as if (appearances notwithstanding) it were yet another sign of inexorable decline, as sure as the laws of falling bodies. Every so often, forced to confront a clear reversal in the fortunes of some supposedly lost neighborhood or city, some expert will politely concede that, well, after all, *some* bounce was inevitable after so great a plunge—but a bounce shouldn't be mistaken for levitation. In other words, for areas that are hitting bottom, a little rebound, especially in a favorable national economy, is hardly remarkable.

That might sound reasonable, if you buy the premise that cities are fundamentally in free fall. Yet even then, there's a curious problem with the "natural bounce" theory: Not all once-falling cities are rebounding alike. In fact, in any given place, there seems to be an uncanny coincidence between the amount of "bounce" and the deliberate effort and ingenuity of local action. New York, Boston, Chicago, Houston, Cleveland, Oakland, all tell stories of intentional effort, intelligent public policy, and a stubborn confidence that inherited conditions and traditional methods can be changed dramatically and for the better. A buoyant national economy has obviously accelerated the accomplishments (and the local confidence) beyond anything that would have been possible in harder times. But the variations from place to place tell a story of local investment and ingenuity that is too particular to be merely the fallout from a national boom.

The confluence of innovation and effort in these places may sometimes be serendipitous, but there is an underlying logic to it. The various undertakings—even when they are the work of isolated players not intentionally working together—share a coherent rationale that links all four of the forces we have described: neighborhood-based development, private capital, public order, and deregulated or decentralized service systems. It is the rationale of the market, combined with the homespun values of mutual responsibility and local self-determination. By directing capital, profit incentives, and more-effective social organization and services into neglected places, government and civic and community organizations can create an inviting environment for investors to develop local assets. By taking responsibility for their environment, education, and quality of life, communities and individuals can shape that development and profit from it, both in economic and social terms.

❑

This talk of markets, investment, and incentives sounds suspiciously like the political cant that periodically volleys over the aisles on Capitol Hill. But in fact, at the level where the actual work is taking place, philosophical disputes tend to be more rhetorical than practical, if they arise at all. The most successful urban reforms are the common invention of both Left and Right, Republicans and Democrats, big government and tiny neighborhoods, grassroots volunteers and corporate CEOs. The reconstruction of cities may be among the first truly postideological issues of the twenty-first century.

The renaissance in urban law enforcement, for example, is the brainchild of streetwise urban cops and woolly university professors, tough law-and-order types working in some of America's more historically

liberal cities like Boston and New York. The issue simply doesn't move
the ideological needle very much. A hunger for order is at least as
keenly felt in poor, minority neighborhoods as in wealthier ones, probably more. Poor households are more often the victims of crime, and
they can't afford the gated communities and private security contracts
to which better-off families retreat when government fails them.

Even school reform, doubtless the most politicized of the issues
we've raised, gets its partisan gelignite more from the mutual dependence of Democrats and teachers' unions than from deep-running ideological disagreements in American society. Parents tend to set aside
their philosophy texts when their children's education is at stake. No
urban politician, Democrat or Republican, will long thrive on the
message "I bravely preserved the status quo." Significantly, even the
most far-reaching experiments, those involving private-school vouchers, have started in two traditionally Democratic cities with big minority populations: Milwaukee and Cleveland.

Public housing reform was ignited, it's true, during the earliest exertions of the conservative 104th Congress, elected in 1994. But there,
Congress supplied only one crucial half of the equation that is saving
public housing: It issued a death threat to the worst public housing authorities, and seemed eager to roll out the guillotines. A real solution
emerged only when then-Secretary of HUD Henry Cisneros, surveying his limited options, discovered the wisdom of working affirma-
tively with Congress on a complete transformation of the public housing system. From that point on, it became impossible to identify
which parts of the reform were "conservative" and which parts "liberal." At this point, everyone takes credit for it, and much of that
credit is deserved on all sides.

Grassroots revitalization, embodied in the nationwide community
development industry, has long since shed its 1960s trappings. Born in
the aftermath of the War on Poverty and still led, in some places, by
former disciples of antipoverty firebrand Saul Alinsky, community development corporations today are more conversant with computer
spreadsheet programs than with any of the sacred texts of the once-
radical Left. They continue to work with poor and unemployed
neighbors, demand fair lending and equitable public services, and otherwise press business and government in their neighborhoods' interest.

But the levers they seek to pull are nowadays more likely those of the market than of power politics or official charity. Like any urban industry, they have interests in public infrastructure, planning, and zoning; in effective safety and social-welfare policies; in the effective supervision and discipline of young people; and in creating a favorable climate for investment. Left or Right scarcely enters into it.

More specifically, Left and Right have spent the past four decades proving they had little to offer. For much of that time, for example, the traditional Left has treated social problems as the ill effects of cruel market forces, and sought to thwart the laws of economics by government fiat. The result has been a harvest of failure and public discontent that discredited not only liberal methods but, by overextension, liberal goals. The Right, meanwhile, has stubbornly regarded those same social problems as the fruit of government meddling in an otherwise benign market—a bountiful if unseen hand that always does much better for everyone when left entirely alone. That attitude, lately in the ascendancy, has certainly helped dismantle some of the more hamhanded government attempts at social engineering. But it meanwhile inspired a cynicism about all forms of public remedy, even as the public was learning with dismay how harsh the effects of unguided private forces can be.

This cynicism (or, in its kinder-gentler manifestations, a shrugging fatalism) has been evident nowhere more than in the inner cities, and in most federal policy toward cities. If the "free market" has given up on old urban centers, the argument goes, then what can anyone do— short of some hopeless neosocialist folly—to save them?

Whatever market has dropped the hammer on cities, it is certainly not the fabled "free" one, but a market systematically manipulated by both Right and Left in ways that have undermined cities and destroyed their neighborhoods. Those effects weren't intentional—at least not usually—but they weren't "free" forces of some unseen hand, either. They were regulated, subsidized, built, and otherwise willed into being by Congress and state legislatures, often acting in concert. Government (at every level) manipulated inner cities into some of their deepest trouble, and government can help get them out of it.

In other areas, public "interference" in free markets has given birth to some of the triumphs of American civilization. Federal investment and intervention in the marketplace tied the country together with highways, airports, and bridges; propelled military and basic research; invented the secondary mortgage market; made modern communications a nearly universal resource; and most recently incubated the Internet. The right-wing melodrama, pitting virtuous markets against evil governments, is just as nonsensical as the reverse casting by the Left. (Each side has occasionally tied the other to the train tracks, but that's hardly the central theme of American history.)

So removing the worst of the perverse antiurban incentives—like federally-funded beltways that skirt cities altogether and encourage sprawl—and injecting positive incentives that actually help cities, would be a perfectly appropriate role for government. And some such incentives are in fact *already working* in embryonic form. This combination—respecting market dynamics while injecting strategic incentives—is precisely what government is learning to do in other areas of public policy from clean air to health care. It would apply just as well to cities, but thus far only a few national leaders have even noticed the potential.

One reason is that, although the forces we have discussed form a coherent set of ideas, they are not yet being applied in an especially coherent way at the front lines. For all their logical connection, they have mostly arisen helter-skelter and separately—as independent breakthroughs in one or another area of public life, or as reactions against the miserable detritus of some failed program or other. The fresh, clear-headed architects of successful anticrime policies have not, in the main, come around to connecting their ideas with expanding credit and reviving retail markets, with school reform, or with the work of neighborhood development groups. The school-reform advocates thus far have won the attention only of a few of the more visionary mayors and urbanist think tanks. Their issues are still debated mostly where educators dissect student achievement scores, not where states and localities set urban development priorities.

In fact, the very idea of an "urban agenda" has lost its currency—another casualty of America's habitual despair over cities. Outside the dusty corridors of HUD and the lecture halls of graduate public policy schools, the phrase scarcely has a meaning. Or more precisely, its meaning is more and more taken to be something dreadful, like the massive utopianisms of the past: An "urban policy"—here one can detect the muttered prayer "God save us"—is what we had under Urban Renewal, the War on Poverty, and Model Cities. Spare us any more of that, if you please.

True enough, the lore of "urbanism" still provides something of a reveille for the Old Left, whose ranks may be depleted and disorderly, but are by no means gone. In some circles, "urban" and "inner-city" programs remain code phrases for statist social engineering and racial or class warfare. Those who continue to regard cities as charity cases can't help confusing "urban" policy with income redistribution. Anyone with a taste for race warfare might regard largely minority "inner cities" as their natural battlefield. These old reverberations make it hard to talk about "urban" and "inner-city" affairs without the risk of being classed with some leftover extreme from an earlier decade. Yet fringe groups didn't ingeniously co-opt this vocabulary; it was surrendered to them by a larger political culture that simply lost interest in the things these words properly stand for—meanwhile shifting its attention (like much of its wealth and population) outside the city limits.

As a result, most self-respecting urbanists have lately shaken off the "urban policy" mantle altogether, in favor of the more visionary (and vastly more complicated) study of "metropolitan" or "regional" issues, like city-suburban annexations, consolidated taxing and service districts, and "smart-growth" ideas to limit sprawl—none of which has yet picked up much political traction. But at least, unlike "urban" affairs, their new subject hauls no baggage from the past. Curing sprawl, for instance, would unquestionably have massive benefits for inner cities and suburbs alike. But that cure, if there is one, remains pure theory nearly everywhere (even in trail-blazing Atlanta, where some of the toughest growth-management policies have generally been trampled by undeterred development).

Metropolitanism may be "pro-city" in its effects, but it is a far cry from a here-and-now urban agenda. Its strength is its deliberately suburban and rural appeal, and its ability to enlist environmentalists, commuters, and people concerned with the ex-urban quality of life. Those are powerful and important constituencies, but they have little near-term stake in what happens to Cabrini-Green, or West Oakland storefronts, or Milwaukee welfare recipients.

The United States consequently lacks a coherent, modern urban agenda—one that addresses the whole range of urban issues that we have discussed here, and in which public and private forces are prepared to invest heavily and in concert. It has a few useful and effective urban programs, though those, like the four themes we have raised, tend to operate in isolation and relative obscurity.

Yet what if by "urban agenda" we came to mean a systematic, concerted application of the four elements we have outlined—letting neighborhood groups set and manage their own priorities; enforcing order and safety in public places; freeing market forces to rebuild what was abandoned or destroyed; and deregulating the critical public systems of education, housing, and social welfare?

We would then be talking about something vastly different from the messianic programs of the past, something pragmatically nonideological around which a significant constituency (including the regionalists) could rally. And best of all, these four forces, thus far disconnected and haphazard, could finally make up a single blueprint for healthier neighborhoods and more prosperous cities.

❑

That would mean spending money, of course. But it doesn't—and shouldn't—mean more prescriptive, bureaucratic programs in which the federal government picks target areas, approves projects, develops government-owned buildings, and so on. For an example of a wholly different approach, consider the Low-Income Housing Tax Credit, a small, investor-driven program in which the sole federal role is to grant tax credits to private companies that invest in low-cost housing. The program lets CDCs and other developers pick sites and design projects, and submit those projects to a state-level competition. The "prize" in this competition is a federal tax credit that, over time, lets the private investors recoup their outlay in those projects, provided they keep the housing affordable to lower-income tenants for at least fifteen years.

If the project makes money—collects its low rents on time, keeps tenants who don't destroy the building, and manages its costs prudently—the investors will turn a competitive profit. If it loses money, however, the government will not protect them. Their profit, if any, comes both from complying with the affordability rules *and* from running the building responsibly. Fail on either front, and the investors are on their own.

The beauty of the Tax Credit program, therefore (apart from an admirable administrative simplicity), is that it relies on investors' self-interest to keep the projects affordable and well run. Even though nonprofit organizations like CDCs often develop and manage the projects, they do so in behalf of a limited partnership of private investors. If the CDC or other developer mismanages one project, it will be unlikely to find investors for a second one. The government doesn't have to enforce this kind of quality control (something it has repeatedly proven unable to do); the market will.

If the building deteriorates so that tenants stop paying rent or refuse to move in, if apartments sit vacant for months between tenants, or if the rents are set too high or too low, the federal government doesn't lose money, the investors do. That is a powerful incentive for performance. Compare it to the old Public Housing or Section 8 program, in which the federal government simply paid the rent up front (often in fantastically high amounts), and then prayed that the landlord would operate a quality building. In a Tax Credit project, the landlord—and his or her financial backers—collect their federal subsidy only over time and through tax relief, provided that their buildings stay affordable and meet quality standards. The result is a more than seven-to-one return on public investment—that is, roughly $7 billion worth of affordable housing for every $1 billion spent by Washington.

The Housing Tax Credit is a good, capsule example of how market forces can be harnessed to the broad challenge of urban recovery. It doesn't simply pour money into an area of need, it creates an opportunity and then gives private actors a carefully calibrated incentive to pursue that opportunity *with their own money.* It even goes a necessary step further: By allowing developers to "syndicate" the Tax Credit among corporate investors, it encourages a business relationship between nonprofit organizations, who often scout out and design the best projects, and the private investors, who pay a fee to have the investment thus packaged for them. It is not the government that subsidizes the nonprofits in this case (at least not directly); it is the private investors, who then have a built-in stake in working with the nonprofit to ensure a successful project—and more projects after that.

Now, why does this apply only to housing? Why wouldn't there be similar tax credits for inner-city commercial developments? The question perfectly illustrates the federal government's narrowly compartmentalized approach to cities and their neighborhoods. Housing advocates and federal housing officials designed and piloted this idea, so it has stayed in the realm of housing, seemingly forever. But it could just as easily apply to Main Street commercial strips, welfare-to-work and job-training programs, child care, park development, even education. Pennsylvania has taken a very simple but intriguing step in this direction, with a state tax credit for companies that make donations to nonprofit organizations. The program isn't targeted to cities, or much else, nor does it enlist the self-interest of the companies in seeing that the donations are well used. But it has nonetheless sparked a rise in support for CDCs. With a little focus, it could do much more.

Let's look, then, at each of the four forces we have discussed thus far, and imagine what public and private actors could do with them—if they wanted to embrace a true urban agenda driven by market insights and community values rather than Washington diktat.

Grassroots Development

In April 1994 syndicated columnist Neal Peirce argued succinctly that the community development industry was now ready for billions in new investment from foundations, corporations, and government:

> Would [a significant expansion in the number of CDCs] cost a lot more money? Yes. But we know we now have a multi-partner formula to construct housing that works, to increase shopping centers and other commercial developments, to build strong community in troubled neighborhoods.
>
> Conceptually and practically this is the polar opposite of the '60s and 70s formula of throwing billions of federal public housing money into neighborhoods devoid of strong grassroots organization.... This new formula is the compellingly obvious way to go.

In other words, a vast new system of local grassroots organizations is ready for major investment. It has been tested by years of lean support and proven itself against exacting performance standards. The investment ought to be made—not just because it's right, but because it is a sound bet on hugely significant returns.

But CDCs need to do more as well. For instance, although a large fraction of these groups sprang from African-American churches, in many neighborhoods CDCs and faith-based institutions are not working together. The separation reveals a lingering system of turf boundaries and subtle distrusts at the neighborhood level that ought to be broken down. Even in well-organized Boston, for example, the CDCs have not fashioned a relationship with the churches of the fabled Ten Point Coalition, which were so effective in reducing gang violence. Given the intimate connection between crime fighting and other forms of neighborhood revitalization, that should have been a natural partnership. But it hasn't happened.

In general, foundations need to find more collaborations between groups doing highly related work in the same neighborhoods, and support them. In a similar vein, more churches should be exposed to the opportunities *for them* in becoming involved in community development. For every church or group of churches that has organized, many more have not. As a result, many cities still lack the kind of credible, broad-based neighborhood coalitions and voluntary institutions that can carry on a long, sustained effort. Because these paths to success are becoming more and more visible, it ought to be possible to recruit many more religious organizations to grassroots development.

For the federal government, if the goal is to stimulate neighborhood-based residential development, one simple, obvious step would be to expand the Low-Income Housing Tax Credit. The demand for it, among CDCs and for-profit developers alike, is vastly greater than the amount Congress has set aside (hence the state-level "competitions," in which many worthwhile projects are turned away once a state's last dollar of tax credit has been allocated). The Tax Credit's effect on inner-city redevelopment is significant, but that's not the only reason to expand it. Another reason is the desperate shortage of affordable rental housing in the United States.

The long boom of the 1990s has been very good for the housing industry and for American home owners. According to the Joint Center for Housing Studies at Harvard, more than two-thirds of American households now own homes, the highest rate ever, and 5.4 million new home owners were added in just the last four years of the 1990s. It doesn't hurt that the United States subsidizes home ownership lavishly through virtually unlimited income tax deductions for mortgage interest and local real estate taxes. But few of these benefits go to low-income home owners, because many do not itemize.

But this same strong market and the relative paucity of housing subsidies for the needy is punishing those at the low end. The Joint Center points out in its latest report that

- nearly 6 million very-low-income renter households either pay more than half of their income in rent or live in structurally inadequate housing;
- the number of affordable rental units has steadily eroded for twenty years;
- of the 14.4 million very-low-income renter households, half live in center cities;
- two-thirds of the 2.5 million structurally inadequate units located in cities are renter occupied;

... and so on. In view of this, a massive new effort to provide decent housing to low-income families would have the double benefit of continuing the urban revival and extending housing opportunity to millions of Americans whose housing choices are few, often inadequate, and dwindling. And as we have seen, strengthening inner-city residential markets is an economic development strategy all by itself.

In the past, the argument against this would have been that federal housing programs were a disaster and enlarging them would be throwing good money after bad, creating more slums into the bargain. Nothing of the kind can be said of the Housing Tax Credit. Yet its success has not been rewarded with expansion. It remained in 2000 exactly the size it was when it was introduced in 1987. It creates about 100,000 apartments annually at a cost of about $4 billion in "tax expenditure"—meaning revenue lost to the federal government. In contrast, the cost to the federal treasury of tax benefits that go overwhelmingly to middle- and upper-income home owners is nearly $60 billion a year. Some balancing of these subsidies is long overdue—and dare we say, the right thing to do.

Quite apart from the effects or size of the Housing Tax Credit is the question of its fundamental principle—the idea of tax credits as an instrument of urban policy. As we argued earlier, the structure of the Tax Credit, and the way it engages investor interest in a public benefit, ought to be a model for other branches of urban policy. But it hasn't happened. Surely, for starters, expanding the tax-credit idea to commercial development should be all but obvious. Yet the idea has taken hold in just a few state capitals, and has arisen in only the most attenuated forms in Washington.

The Clinton administration's Empowerment Zone program, it's true, sought to combine industrial, retail, and residential development incentives with employment, training, and other human services. The concept resembles, in some ways, the integrated approach we envision here: CDCs have a role; the program seeks to stimulate markets rather than replace private investment; it encourages deregulation and private initiative. In practice, however, the Empowerment Zone program has been more prescriptive than its inventors intended; in some places, its load of special-purpose grants have led to massive patronage or to squabbling among competing service programs. Meanwhile, years pass in which little is accomplished. In many cases, powerful politicians have wrested control over the federal funds, and businesses have been recruited more or less in proportion to their political connections rather than just their economic potential.

The beauty of the Housing Tax Credit is that it pays for performance, mostly after-the-fact, rather than for promises and political fealty. Business tax credits could do much the same thing (in fact, former congressman and HUD Secretary Jack Kemp had something much like this in mind when he proposed the prototype Enterprise Zones). But they need to be freed from the political snares into which some Empowerment Zones have stumbled.

One lesson of the Empowerment Zone experience—in fact, of most government efforts in behalf of cities in the last twenty years—is that inner-city neighborhoods generally make the best use of public and private dollars when they are organized around some form of enterprising, locally-based development corporation. Within manageable boundaries defined by local residents and businesses, rather than by government fiat, community development groups typically respond with agility to changing local opportunities that are different from block to block, and that are mostly invisible from Washington.

If Congress wanted to stimulate the creation of new CDCs—which number in the thousands but still haven't reached their full potential—it could do so simply enough, by a strategic increment in the Community Development Block Grant, which is a prime source of CDCs' core administrative budgets. But it might also use the leverage of the national intermediary organizations we described in Part 2, in which government is a minority partner alongside large corporate and philanthropic players. Not only do the intermediaries amass private dollars to support CDCs, they help private investors find opportunities to invest wisely in community development projects. Intermediaries like LISC and the Enterprise Foundation routinely point interested lenders to redevelopment projects that meet their commitments under the Community Reinvestment Act. And they syndicate the Housing Tax Credit to investors in qualified projects.

Yet for all the difference they have made, the community development intermediaries still reach a minority of all poor urban areas. They have the potential to do much more. Neal Peirce again:

> The fiscal intermediaries—The Local Initiatives Support Corporation and The Enterprise Foundation—have made dramatic advances in securing investment dollars. But either they should be quadrupled or quintupled in size, or a whole new set of intermediaries should be created, to get up to the scale we need to rebuild decaying communities rapidly and well.

In late 1999, former Treasury Secretary Robert Rubin—arguably one of the world's most respected public figures, and someone with rather special access to capital markets—assumed the chairmanship of the LISC Board of Directors. Perhaps he can help engineer the needed scale-up. But the success of the community development intermediaries raises another question: Why haven't other, analogous institutions been created to speed the creation of high-quality job training programs, child-care facilities, neighborhood health centers, and other community assets? These other categories of community building lack that kind of infrastructure, which could mobilize capital on a national scale, circulate technology, and precipitate the broad private sector involvement now evident in the community development field.

Not only have the community-development intermediaries played prominent roles in shaping public policy at the national level—helping, for instance, to design the Housing Tax Credit—but, as we described in Part 2, they took the lead in "cleaning up" the CDC movement by bringing private-sector discipline and performance standards into cities where community development had been highly political.

Why foundations and other backers of the community development field have not sought to replicate this success in other fields is a mystery. The American system of local job-training programs operated by the public sector and nonprofit organizations, for instance, is largely a disgrace—resembling today what the community development system looked like twenty years ago. There is a sprinkling of exemplary local programs in a desert of waste and ineffectuality. Across broad swaths of the urban landscape, local employment and training systems are operated as political fiefdoms or social-service programs. There are no organized mechanisms for large-scale private capital or employer involvement, or for elevating and spreading the best approaches, or for driving out the purely political operations. This is a particular opportunity because most economists seem to believe that the relatively tight labor market of the late 1990s will persist for at least a few more years. If the right bridges to private-sector employment are built, many who are now left out can enter the mainstream.

But even though Congress could obviously do more—and get more results—by simply spending more money, that is not the main point here. The point is to learn from the successful programs already in place (which is far from all of them), and direct official attention and priority to those. The Block Grant and the Housing Tax Credit are at the top of that list.

❑

Crime

This is an area in which the federal government can make only a marginal difference, but governments at all other levels have vast room for learning, experimentation, and change. In their 1996 book *Fixing Bro-ken Windows,* George Kelling and coauthor Catherine M. Coles frame the possibilities in terms much like those we have applied to other areas of urban recovery:

> Short of imprisoning a whole generation of youth, can policies be developed and implemented that offer hope for the immediate present, while not ignoring long-range requirements? The answer is an unequivocal Yes. And while imperfect and inchoate in its present form, the outline for such policies and practices exists in virtually every city in the United States, in the shape of a new paradigm of crime-control already manifest in our communities.
>
> ... [It is a] community-based paradigm of crime prevention and control that is revolutionizing criminal justice. The foundation of this new movement is a partnership between private and public forces. Its most significant aspects are, first, the definition of crime prevention and control in new and broader terms, and second, the location of a significant source of authority for criminal justice processes in the community and delineation of a crucial role for citizens. ... Citizen or neighborhood-based groups are a key element in this paradigm.

Among the features of the new "definition of crime prevention and control," in Kelling and Coles's summary of it, is directing the attention of police officers not only at crimes, but at fear—not just at punishing misbehavior, but at maintaining order and restoring the *expectation* of order. Disruptive and threatening elements of the community, even when not in the act of committing crimes, need to feel the attention of police—just as they feel the attention of the better community organizations. Pursuing minor crimes and enforcing rules against non-violent offenses not only tightens criminals' sense of limits, it increases the interaction between the police and the community. It raises residents' expectations about how well all rules will be enforced, and it encourages cooperation between law-abiding residents and the police. Most of all, it encourages neighbors themselves to take action against crime, much as the congregation at Saint Sabina's did in Chicago.

This last element, trust and partnership between police and residents, is crucial, as the New York City experience has shown. In New

York, despite stunning reforms in police practice—and subsequent results that more than justify the effort—police/community relations remain tense and distrustful in places. That has not prevented remarkable collaborations from forming in areas where CDCs and other local groups could help build trust and widen channels of communication. But it has stymied some of the best efforts of police in less well-organized neighborhoods. (Some recent polling, significantly, has found that many African-American New Yorkers aren't all that hostile to police, despite the drumbeat of criticism from some black leaders. Progress against crime, apparently, has won friends for the Police Department even in the face of serious police missteps.)

Ironically, 1999—hardly the best year for police-community relations in New York—saw the beginning of an intriguing new experiment in combining the effects of community policing with those of neighborhood-based development. Toward the end of 1998, Mayor Rudolph Giuliani announced "Safe at Home," an $88 million program directed at two reviving but still troubled neighborhoods: Crotona Park East in the Bronx, and Bedford-Stuyvesant in Brooklyn. The CDCs representing those communities are to get city subsidies to fix every derelict building and reuse every vacant lot. The police are to bring a significantly enhanced street presence. And the residents will oversee the strategy through new broad-based community coordinating councils. This is the "Broken Windows" principle carried out to its logical conclusion. Though the work has barely begun as this book goes to print, it bears watching as a field test of what good policing and effective community development can do in tandem.

Kelling and Coles' second crucial ingredient, devolving more control of law enforcement to local precincts, is also another way of building better police-community collaboration. Giving precincts wide latitude to scope out sources of crime and fear, and to devise effective responses, is one way of opening the police-station door to the people who understand the community best: residents and leaders. The essential corollary, of course, is that precincts must be held accountable for results, measured not just in apprehension of serious criminals, but in the orderliness of the streets, the contentment of residents, and ultimately in lower rates of crime.

States and localities, then, could hardly do better than to continue learning from and emulating the growing number of cities that have applied these principles to excellent effect. But the federal government (which is never going to stay out of the crime-control arena, and probably ought to remain a partner) can do more, if it chooses, to encourage "Broken Windows" policing. Helping cities pay for more police officers, as the Clinton administration has done, can't hurt, though Washington is unlikely to spend the fortune it would take to make a major difference in the size of the uniformed workforce.

So besides helping to pay for officers, Washington could help cities institute the whole spectrum of management and technical changes that new policing methods demand. This could be—really ought to be—the common work of the Justice Department and HUD, whose anticrime and community development programs, respectively, have a nearly equal stake in success.

❑

Capital and Commerce

There is some reason to hope that the 1999 congressional assault on the Community Reinvestment Act will be the last major assassination attempt for a while. Simply leaving the act alone to do its job (or, in the ideal case, undoing some of the minor damage that took place in 1999) would by itself represent a significant federal reinforcement of the credit revolution now under way. But Washington isn't the only, or even the main, player with a stake in urban recovery. The return of capital and credit to inner cities has mostly occurred despite, rather than because of, the policies of those cities themselves.

It's possible that capital will continue to find its own way to urban markets with no help from government. Success feeds on itself, and if the coming years are successful for today's inner-city retail pioneers, then the momentum will surely continue. So far, the early signs are good. For instance, the Pathmark superstore in Harlem that we described in Chapter 6 is doing a land-office business since it opened in mid-1999.

But very serious barriers continue to block a full return of the private market to inner cities. Many of them have been pointed out in the research conducted by Michael Porter's Initiative for a Competitive Inner City. For starters, few American cities have a real economic development strategy. They have partial strategies, like restoring their downtowns; or recycling their formerly industrial waterfronts for residential and recreational use; or rebuilding neighborhood commercial corridors; and some of these are working very well. But in the main, city governments are performing two rather limited functions: processing proposed real estate transactions brought to them by private developers, and administering a hodgepodge of economic development programs funded (and largely designed) by state and federal governments.

One ICIC study found, for example, that Boston receives more than $100 million a year in federal support for "economic development." Not bad—except that the money is scattered among more than 100 different federal, state, local, and nonprofit agencies. In the job training area alone, forty-four nonprofits, thirty-five for-profits, twenty-five academic programs, and two trade unions hand out the money. Piecing these shards of funding into a strategy is well-nigh impossible. Yet Boston is among the country's better performers in guiding its own economic development; the picture in other cities is even more chaotic.

A second problem with today's public support for urban businesses is that it is virtually all in the form of debt. Access to low-cost debt is important, but equity is even more important, and inner-city businesses are starved for it. Some private venture capital funds that focus on inner-city companies are beginning to appear, but Porter believes the federal government should cut—or even zero out—capital gains taxes in high-poverty areas to spur more investment.

Finally, too many business-assistance programs are strictly limited to the most "needy"—marginal or tiny businesses struggling to stay alive. Praiseworthy as that might seem, Anne Habiby of ICIC argues that mid-size businesses that are already succeeding (meaning, say, businesses with $1 million to $30 million in annual revenues) would make better use of government help. The reason is that those businesses have already passed some market test of viability, and usually have great potential to grow, thus generating the jobs, income, and wealth that these communities desperately need.

One of the great contributions ICIC has already made is to point out that there are far more of these companies than most people realize. A city that was really intent on expanding its investment and job base would concentrate a good part of its effort on helping those businesses grow. But cities also need better information—on what businesses are out there and how they're doing, on the consumption patterns of inner-city residents, on how to align the city's economic advantages with the wider regional economy. If city halls remain solely occupied with real-estate transactions and administering largely ineffectual programs, it will be difficult to achieve a strategic vision.

But the private sector has much to answer for as well. Even such an apostle of the free market as Michael Porter admits that the market, supposedly so omniscient, is still missing much of the inner-city opportunity. Poor data is part of it. But so is racial bias and the perceptual legacy of the long urban decline. ICIC's research and the promotional efforts of *Inc.* magazine and others will help. But the private sector also needs to be challenged—at times even confronted—for its tardy response to the inner-city opportunity. Jesse Jackson has a point when he asks why American companies pour money overseas while overlooking comparable opportunities in their own central cities— places without a language barrier, political disruptions, unstable currencies, and the other imponderables that come with Third World investment. Even when they are comfortably ensconced in suburbs, businesses have a material stake (even if an unacknowledged one) in the vitality of their nearby cities, and in the role those cities play in the national economic and political life.

❑

Deregulating and Removing the Roadblocks to Recovery

Here our recommendations grow more tentative. The policy lights are mostly yellow, not green. The first hard choices in public housing and welfare have been made—impregnable federal mandates and inflexible rules have been undone. What should come to replace them, however, is still unclear. At this stage, employment, training, and education programs for former welfare recipients are doing reasonably well (at least in places), their shortcomings partly hidden by a labor market groaning for entry-level employees. Plenty of research on how to improve them is under way in all the best universities and think tanks. But they have been fueled, in their early years, with left-over money that originally supported families directly—money freed up by a strong economy in which hundreds of thousands of former recipients were finally working.

In a few years, assuming some slowdown in the economy, those dollars will again be needed for basic support of unemployed families. And unskilled workers will find less-patient employers, offering fewer training opportunities. Already, welfare rolls have come more and more to contain people whose physical, psychological, or learning-related problems make them unlikely to benefit from standard employment and training programs. What happens to them when time limits on their welfare benefits expire—and what happens to all marginally employed people in a recession—will be the real test of welfare reform. At this stage, it seems likely that some softening of the time limits, and some adjustments for the least job-ready, will be necessary before long.

Likewise, the families displaced from public housing may not all be easily relocated to less-concentrated housing elsewhere. Are rent vouchers a sufficient guarantee that families won't go homeless? Studies are still inconclusive, and experience may suggest changes in the amount or structure of the subsidy. But the deconcentration of poverty and social problems in public housing is now firmly under way. It is urgent that the task be completed effectively and not allowed to lapse, like so many federal reforms before it, into lethargy and lip service.

Sooner or later, if the reengineering of public housing is carried out effectively, it will be nearly impossible to avoid the question of why the United States continues to need federally chartered Public Housing Authorities *at all*. These New Deal institutions, which started with so much promise but in most cities are now moribund, seem to have outlived their useful life by a matter of decades. When urban housing markets can now tap an army of competent nonprofit development, management, and human-service organizations (as today's HUD reforms are proving), why do they need free-standing agencies cloned by the federal government, invisibly controlling giant chunks of their neighborhoods?

The principle of local self-determination—and certainly that of flexible response to changing markets and changing human needs—suggests that public housing ought to be accountable to locally elected officials, just as other city services are. Mayors ought to take responsibility for the condition of housing in their cities, including (in fact, *especially*) the publicly owned and subsidized housing. Just as they are increasingly taking charge of their school systems—in the face of enormous risk but also of irresistible public pressure—they should have both the means and the responsibility for ensuring that housing serves their constituents and enriches, not poisons, their cities' neighborhoods.

School reform, the most fragile of the nascent deregulations, is the domain of states and localities, and it's unlikely to benefit much from federal interference. Research, experimentation, and a lively discussion about what works best are among the few things that can be asked of the federal government on this issue, and those are, to a considerable extent, under way. Because progress on this issue has been so slow, it might be reasonable to ask presidents and members of Congress to use the bully pulpit of national leadership more effectively to accelerate the pace and creativity of change in education. Yet we raise that prospect with natural trepidation: At least among presidential candidates, and often among those seeking House and Senate seats, it has seemed hard to resist the temptation to pander either to teachers' unions or to extremist enemies of public schooling. Leadership in those veins would be substantially worse than silence. In any case, in the realm of practical governance, state legislatures and city halls, facing mounting pressure from parents, will have little choice but to continue their experimentation and expand what works.

To reengineer all these broken systems—schools, public housing, welfare—the exact next steps may not all be clear, and all sorts of technical issues still have to be ironed out. But that obvious fact shouldn't obscure the fundamental, and genuinely historic, step that this country has taken on all three fronts: Stepping into the twenty-first century, there no longer remains any significant debate about whether these ossified systems ought to be preserved in their old form. That discussion is concluded, to the enormous benefit of troubled cities and neighborhoods. The ironclad, formula-driven welfare entitlement, for example, will not be resuscitated, whatever comes along to replace it. Public housing could, it's true, be abandoned in midreform, to fall back into decay and misrule. But if that happens, the political price could be high. The broad, postideological coalition that prompted the 1990s reforms has not disbanded, and it could re-form if this round of effort proves inadequate.

For schools, the next steps are the least clear, but the forces for change are in some ways the most visible and powerful. School reform is largely the crusade of legions of ordinary people—parents, teachers, principals—who outnumber politicians and union officials many thousandfold. And they are roilingly angry, a phenomenon that has been known to topple empires. The obsolescent, bureaucracy-choked system of American public education is done for, and with it will fall the last great barrier to livable, competitive inner-city neighborhoods. The question is only whether that system will be thoroughly reengineered by wise public leaders, as mayors like Chicago's Richard M. Daley and Cleveland's Michael White seem to hope, or whether it will be exposed to the scorched earth of a parent revolution.

But the principle of "deregulation" in the sense that we have used the word—that is, getting the federal government out of the way of inner-city recovery—clearly has strong applications beyond the boundaries of schools, welfare, and public housing. The federal government continues, for example, to spend a disproportionate share of its transportation budget on the construction and repair of beltways and other interstate highways that feed and enlarge suburbs at the expense of public transit systems that feed central cities. (A "free market" choice, we presume.) Some advocates of "limited government" argue that it's not Washington's business to subsidize the commuting choices of city dwellers. Yet they seem to have no problem subsidizing the commuting desires of suburbanites and families eyeing the newest ex-urban subdivisions. As the Brookings Institution's preeminent regionalist (née urbanist), Bruce Katz, puts it:

> While market forces and individual preferences have contributed to urban decline and suburban growth, government subsidies and policies have reinforced these tendencies. ... Major federal and state spending

programs, tax incentives, and regulations have also worked to the disadvantage of cities, facilitating the migration of people and jobs to the outer metropolitan fringe and reinforcing the concentration of poverty in the older core.

If Congress sees no advantage in helping cities recover, that is a sad negligence in our view. But there is utterly no advantage (other than an apparent political one) in paying the cost of urban depopulation and exurban sprawl. That course eventually harms rural communities as well as central cities, and damages the environment. To get the federal government truly out of the way of urban recovery, retreating from decades of massive sprawl subsidies would be an invaluable next step.

This resembles, in some ways, the thesis of the "smart growth" or "regionalism" movement, which has built a passionate following among thoughtful planners and academics. But one tenet of "smart growth"— that metropolitan governments might be persuaded to pool their resources and authority (and even merge) in the interest of halting sprawl—still strikes us as fanciful. Cheap energy, the American tradition of letting developers' ambitions dictate the patterns of settlement, and the balkanization of local political jurisdictions are all good insurance against any proximate change in how metropolitan areas are planned, developed, and governed. Short of environmental calamity or an enormous new energy crisis, much sprawl will continue. But as we have seen, cities have assets of their own to compete with suburban regions, even if those continue to expand. What they can't do is overcome mountains of public giveaways to their competitors. Even if some state and local governments seem hooked on indiscriminate suburbanization, the federal government doesn't need to pay for it, and certainly doesn't need to retard the recovery of central cities in the process.

Yet that is precisely what's happening. Besides Congress's taste for centrifugal highways, Katz readily ticks off several other federal policies that gnaw away at cities' competitive opportunities: Uncapped tax deductions for homeownership, for example, favor people who are in high tax brackets, and thus give a richer break to buyers of large lots and houses (nearly always in suburbs). And a clutch of environmental policies make the cleanup and redevelopment of old urban industrial areas prohibitively expensive—especially those that expose new owners to a nearly endless risk of lawsuits over pollution by past owners. These and other policies evidence a continuing antiurban bias, long overdue for extinction. "Deregulating" the cities has to include an end to policies that hold cities back by keeping them uncompetitive. It is past time to level the playing field.

Putting It Together

The remarkable fact, at the turn of the twentieth century, is that the forces that can transform and rebuild inner cities are *already under way.* They do not, in the main, need to be dreamt up, nor is it necessary to posit some utopian society or seismic political shift to envision how it might all come to fruition. Consequently, none of the suggestions thus far seem particularly radical or idealistic, in the more fanciful sense of the word. But put them together, and the consequences can be explosive.

We are talking, in short, about making more deliberate and coherent use of the positive trends already in motion. This is where we most deeply part company with the learned community of "regionalists," many of whose goals we share. David Rusk, for example, in his 1999 book, *Inside Game/Outside Game: Winning Strategies for Saving Urban America,* makes the appealing if ambitious argument that

> State legislatures must [adopt] regional revenue or tax base sharing to reduce fiscal disparity, regional housing policies to ensure that all new developments have their fair share of low- and moderate-income housing to disperse concentrations of poverty, and regional land use planning and growth management to control urban sprawl.

(The quote is from former HUD Secretary Henry Cisneros's warm endorsement of the book.) We'd be thrilled to see any of that happen.

Meanwhile, however, our sights are decidedly more near-term, and are rooted in the achievable politics of today. That is possible not because we have dreamed up something remarkable, but because the work *already in progress* in today's inner cities is in fact vastly more remarkable than the distant-horizon reformers seem to realize. If legislatures can be persuaded to redraw their state's entire structure of local governments in the way Rusk counsels, more power to them. The consequences for inner cities would surely be excellent. But in the meantime, we see no need to wait for that.

Instead, to the extent we would alter the recovery now under way, we would urge the emerging generation of mayors and pragmatic state leaders to start treating these four threads of reform as *interwoven parts of a much-larger fabric*. As Rudolph Giuliani has done in the Bronx and Brooklyn, it's time to view community policing and community development as related components of a *single* assault on neighborhood disorder. As HUD and local housing authorities are doing in reengineered public housing complexes, it's time to pursue property development, social services, and welfare reform as a *single,* multifaceted drive toward economic opportunity and integration for poor neighborhoods. Connecting community-based development, the maintenance of public order, private lending and investment, and a thorough rethinking of public systems of education, housing, and welfare would bring about at least as profound a change in the fortunes of inner cities as creating regional taxing authorities or metropolitan governments. But it would be fantastically easier, because huge parts of the work are already in progress.

Direct these various energies toward their logical goal—the restoration of long-abandoned and mismanaged neighborhoods—and it will be possible to build livable, civil, tranquil communities in the roughest places of the inner city. They may not become as wealthy, as chic, or as densely populated as they were in their heyday. But so what? It is sufficient that neighborhoods be orderly, pleasant, and convenient to live in, and appealing to new residents when old ones leave. To be sure, life in most city neighborhoods would be better if the regionalists get their way. But in *this* world, there is no need to postpone or despair of building healthy inner-city communities just because cities and suburbs can't sort out more rational boundaries, or learn to share their revenues and authorities. The South Bronx, for example, made the whole transition from war zone to strong community without a single border moving even one inch.

❑

The greatest threat to a rebound in American inner cities is not in the design of any particular policy or institution, or in the political fortunes of any party or faction. Like most great political challenges, reviving inner cities will depend mostly on a reservoir of public will and confidence. And in that arena—perhaps in that arena *alone*—American cities remain in crisis.

Two generations, at least, have grown up with the supposition that cities are finished, and that public policy toward cities is a time-tested waste. Radicals of the Left and Right have done wonders to confirm this view, as have decades of whinging mayors bent on making charity cases of America's great urban centers. Even if the worst of these influences is over (especially judging from the enterprising buoyancy of the recent crop of mayors) the residue is knee-deep, and its effects are everywhere in public debate.

The 2000 Census, which is still in progress as this book goes to press, could either reverse or deepen the national despondency—even presuming that it captures all the early signs of the recovery now under way. By the time the new data gain wide circulation, in late 2001 or 2002, casual observers may be expecting to see giant strides befitting a decade of national prosperity and smart policy. In fact, the data will present only the first few years of measurable turnaround—mostly ending in 1999. Those have been remarkable years, but they will surely continue to show some of the vast aftereffects of the long urban decline. If an impatient public wrongly takes this evidence as a small return on giant opportunity (much here will depend on the interpretation of an academic establishment already in need of antidepressants), then the fatalism could well be engraved in the national consciousness for another ten years. That much moroseness could destroy anything.

That is just one example, though a potent one, of how a deeply ingrained national habit of gloom threatens cities more than any swing in policy or demographics. For most Americans, the urban glass remains half (or two-thirds) empty. Overcoming that level of skepticism will take a cumulative mass of physical and economic achievement that can't have been racked up in just the past five or ten years or, in some cases, even in the next ten. The political challenge for cities and their supporters—and specifically for the next president and Congress—is to draw the national imagination toward the astonishing accomplishments already under way, the pace of those accomplishments, the intelligence that has led to them, and the mounting opportunity they will create as they continue to pile up.

This isn't so far-fetched. Precisely that kind of leadership has happened before. After the 1950s, when many Americans had grown fearful over their prospects for winning the technology race, and by implication the Cold War, a massive investment in science education and the vision of a New Frontier revived the national confidence and determination to succeed. There followed a revivifying conquest of space and a technological explosion in the United States that continues to the present. In the 1980s, when national confidence in American industry and public management had hit bottom, a president with a genius for upbeat politics (and a bracing jolt of corporate restructuring) gave the country the confidence to weather a crushing recession and launch a decade of unprecedented growth.

The point is not that either of these struggles was won simply by politicians rousing the country with a little locker-room oratory (or for that matter, that they were won by politicians at all). The point is that both episodes combined slow, persistent, intelligent, often complicated policy on many fronts with the kind of leadership that could sustain a national optimism *long enough* to bring the hard work to fulfillment. That sort of leadership—together with a good deal more of the persistence, intelligence, and so on—is what cities most need if they are to finish the rebound they have started.

The blueprint is in hand. The ideological battles have mostly sputtered to a close. The signs of new vitality are everywhere to be seen. And the bad days—barring a tragic reversal of wisdom or will—appear to be over. If Americans—and most of all, urban residents themselves—have the stomach to finish the job, American inner cities in the next few years can demonstrate the same resilience for which the rest of the American economy—in fact, American society in general—is the envy of the world.

NOTES ON SOURCES

Most of the published work referred to in this book is listed in the "Selected Bibliography." Particular references to other material—mostly articles and interviews—are described more fully here, according to the chapter in which the reference appears.

Chapter 2

Page

37 Kasarda, John D., Stephen J. Appold, Stuart H. Sweeney, and Elaine Sieff. "Central-City and Suburban Migration Patterns: Is a Turnaround on the Horizon?" *Housing Policy Debate* 8, no. 2 (1997): 354–358.

Farley, Reynolds, and William H. Frey. "Changes in the Segregation of Whites and Blacks During the 1980s: Small Steps Toward a More Integrated Society." *American Sociological Review* 59: 23–45.

41 Massey, Douglas S., and Nancy A. Denton. *American Apartheid: Segregation and the Making of the Underclass.* Cambridge: Harvard University Press, 1994.

Jargowski, Paul A., and Mary Jo Bane. "Neighborhood Poverty: Basic Questions." In *Inner-City Poverty in the United States,* ed. Lawrence E. Lynn Jr. and Michael G. H. McGeary. Washington, D.C.: National Academy Press, 1991.

42 Thomas Bier. *Housing Supply and Demand: Cleveland Metropolitan Area, 1950–2005.* Cleveland: Cleveland State University Press, 1988.

Orfield, Myron. "Metropolitan Regions Facing Their Futures Together Have Less Racial and Economic Segregation." *GRIPP News & Notes,* Grass Roots Innovative Policy Program 1, no. 1, spring 1999.

43 Downs, Anthony. "The Challenge of Our Declining Big Cities." *Housing Policy Debate* 8, no. 2 (1997): 362–364.

44 Nowak, Jeremy. "Neighborhood Initiative and the Regional Economy." *Economic Development Quarterly* 11, no. 1 (February 1997): 3–10.

Chapter 3

58 Interview with Don Mullane, 1998.

59 Porter, Michael. "New Strategies for Inner-City Economic Development." *Economic Development Quarterly* 11, no. 1 (February 1997): 11–27.

Schwartz, Alex, with Bill Traylor and Michael Bornheimer. *At the Crossroads: The Economic Impact of New York City's Housing Investments on the City and Its Neighborhoods.* New York: Local Initiatives Support Corporation, 1997.

El Nasser, Haya. "Snubbing the Suburbs: Middle-Class Blacks Opt to Stay in the Cities." *USA Today,* International ed. (October 20, 1997): 1-A.

Part Two

Passim: Interviews with each of the CDCs representatives named.

63   Broder, David. "Look What Happened to the Neighborhood." *Washington Post* (April 23, 1997): A–21.

Von Hoffman, Alexander. "Good News!" *Atlantic Monthly* (January 1997): 31–35.

64   *Boston Globe.* Editorial, "The Business of Fighting Poverty." (March 30, 1998): A–10.

Stodghill, Ron, II. "Bringing Back Hope to the 'Hood." *Business Week* (August 19, 1996): 18.

Chapter 4

98   Radin, Charles A. "A Neighborhood Reborn." *Boston Globe Magazine* (November 15, 1998): 12.

Chapter 5

Passim: Interviews with Anita Miller and Sandra Rosenblith.

115   Gelfand, Mark I. *A Nation of Cities.* New York: Oxford University Press, 1975.

124   Labaton, Stephen, "Close, but No Banking Cigar." *New York Times* (October 22, 1999): C–1.

Chapter 6

128   Goozner, Merrill. "The Porter Prescription." *American Prospect* (May-June, 1998): 56–64.

132   Pristin, Terry. "On 125th Street, a Plan for Shopping Center and 10-Screen Multiplex." *New York Times* (April 15, 1999): B–9.

133   Elias, Jaan. "Supermarkets in Inner Cities." Harvard Business School, Case Study N1-796-145.

Gosselin, Peter G. "Return to Investment. *Boston Globe* (December 15, 1996): A–1.

Edelson, Sharon. "Re-storing Downtown USA." *WWD* 15, vol. 174: 68.

138   Jacobs, Andrew. "Vibrant Area of Newark Suffers with Success." *New York Times* (March 10, 2000): A–1.

Chapter 7

152 Butterfield, Fox. "Reason for Dramatic Drop in Crime Puzzles the Experts." *New York Times* (March 29, 1998): 16.

155 Kelling, George, and James Q. Wilson. "Broken Windows." *Atlantic Monthly* (March 1982): 29–38.

160 McDonald, Heather. "How to Fight and Win." *Wall Street Journal* (July 20, 1999): A–20.

162 Winship, Christopher, and Jenny Berrien. "Boston Cops and Black Churches." *Public Interest* (summer 1999): 52–68.

163 Winship, Christopher, and Orlando Patterson. "Boston's Police Solution." *New York Times* (March 3, 1999): A–17.

172 Phuong Le. "This is Smart Policing: Community Partnership Revitalizes International District." *Seattle Post-Intelligencer* (November 23, 1999): 1-A.

Chapter 8

Passim: Interview with Richard Gentry.

190 Husock, Howard. "Public Housing as a 'Poorhouse,'" *Public Interest* (Fall 1997): 73–85.

196 Von Hoffman, Alexander. "High Ambitions: The Past and Future of American Low-Income Housing Policy." In *New Directions in Urban Public Housing,* ed. David P. Varady, Wolfgang F. E. Preiser, and Francis P. Russell. New Brunswick: Center for Urban Policy Research, Rutgers—The State University of New Jersey, 1998, pp. 3–22.

Chapter 9

Passim: Interview with Caroline Hoxby.

217 Wheelan, Charles. "Turning the Tables on School Choice." *New York Times* (May 25, 1999): A–27.

219 Carney, Paul. "Charter Schools and CDCs." Internal memorandum, the Local Initiatives Support Corporation, September 9, 1998.

Chapter 10

231 *Washington Post.* Editorial, "Welfare Happy Talk" (August 25, 1999): A–16.

Chapter 11

240 Cottman, Michael H. "Seeing Detroit as a Role Model." *Washington Post* (August 30, 1999): B–1.

Conclusion

250 Peirce, Neal. "Powerful New Allies for the Poorest Neighborhoods," *Times-Picayune* (April 4, 1994): B–5.
252 Staff of the Joint Center for Housing Studies of Harvard University. *The State of the Nation's Housing: 1999.* Cambridge: Joint Center for Housing Studies, 1999.
262 Katz, Bruce, "Beyond City Limits: A New Metropolitan Agenda." In *Setting National Priorities: The 2000 Election and Beyond,* ed. Henry J. Aaron and Robert D. Reischauer. Washington: Brookings Institution Press, 1999.

SELECTED BIBLIOGRAPHY

Beauregard, Robert. *Voices of Decline: The Postwar Fate of U.S. Cities.* Oxford: Blackwell Publishers, 1988.

Bissinger, Buzz. *A Prayer for the City.* New York: Random House, 1997.

Bratton, William. *Turnaround: How America's Top Cop Reversed the Crime Epidemic.* New York: Random House, 1998.

Cisneros, Henry, ed. *Interwoven Destinies: Cities and the Nation.* New York: W. W. Norton and Co., 1993.

Ferguson, Ronald, and William Dickens, eds. *Urban Problems and Community Development.* Washington, D.C.: Brookings Institution, 1999.

Goldsmith, Stephen. *The Twenty-First Century City: Resurrecting Urban America.* Washington, D.C.: Regnery Publishing, 1997.

Halpern, Robert. *Rebuilding the Inner City.* New York: Columbia University Press, 1995.

Jackson, Kenneth. *Crabgrass Frontier: The Suburbanization of the United States.* Cambridge: Oxford University Press, 1985.

Jacobs, Jane. *The Death and Life of Great American Cities.* New York: Vintage, 1961.

Jargowsky, Paul A. *Poverty and Place: Ghettos, Barrios, and the American City.* New York: Russell Sage Foundation, 1996.

Kelling, George L., and Catherine M. Coles. *Fixing Broken Windows: Restoring Order and Reducing Crime in Our Communities.* New York: Touchstone, 1997.

Kennedy, Randall. *Race, Crime and the Law.* New York: Pantheon Books, 1997.

Kotlowitz, Alex. *There Are No Children Here: The Story of Two Boys Growing Up in the Other America.* New York: Anchor Books/Doubleday, 1992.

Lehmann, Nicholas. *The Promised Land: The Great Black Migration and How it Changed America.* New York: Vintage, 1992.

Local Initiatives Support Corporation. "Building Community: A Report on Social Community Development Initiatives." New York: LISC, 1993.

Marciniak, Ed. *Reclaiming the Inner City: Chicago's Near North Revitalization Confronts Cabrini-Green.* Washington, D.C.: National Center for Urban Ethnic Affairs, 1986.

Moe, Richard, and Carter Wilkie. *Changing Places: Rebuilding Community in the Age of Sprawl.* New York: Henry Holt, 1997.

Muller, Thomas. *Immigrants and the American City.* New York: New York University Press, 1994.

Norquist, John. *The Wealth of Cities: Revitalizing the Centers of American Life.* Reading, Mass.: Addison-Wesley, 1998.

Orfield, Myron. *Metropolitics.* Washington, D.C.: Brookings Institution, 1997.

Orlebecke, Charles. *New Life at Ground Zero: New York, Home Ownership, and the Future of American Cities.* Albany, N.Y.: Rockef er Institute Press, 1997.

Peirce, Neal R., Curtis W. Johnson, and John W. all. *Citistates: How Urban America Can Prosper in a Competitive World.* Washi ,ton: Seven Locks Press, 1983.

Peirce, Neal R., and Carol F. Steinbach. *Enterpr ig Communities: Community Based Development in America.* Washington: Cou l for Community Based Development, 1990.

Porter, Michael E. "The Competitive Advanta of the Inner City." In *Harvard Business Review* (May-June 1995): 55–71.

———. "New Strategies for Inner-City Ec omic Development." In *Economic Development Quarterly* 11, 1 (February 199 : 11–27.

Rusk, David. *Cities Without Suburbs.* Was agton, D.C.: Woodrow Wilson Center Press, 1995.

———. *Inside Game/Outside Game: Winning Strategies for Saving Urban America.* Washington, D.C.: Brookings Institution, 1999.

Siegel, Fred. *The Future Once Happened Here.* New York: Free Press, 1997.

Silverman, Eli. *NYPD Battles Crime: Innovative Strategies in Policing.* Boston: Northeastern University Press, 1999.

Skogan, Wesley G. *Disorder and Decline: Crime and the Spiral of Decay in American Neighborhoods.* Berkeley: University of California Press, 1992.

Varady, David P., Wolfgang F. E. Preiser, and Francis P. Russell. *New Directions in Urban Public Housing.* Newark: CUPR Press, Center for Urban Policy Research, Rutgers University, 1998.

Wilson, William Julius. *The Truly Disadvantaged: The Inner City, the Underclass, and Public Policy.* Chicago: University of Chicago Press, 1990.

———. *When Work Disappears: The World of the New Urban Poor.* New York: Random House, 1997.

Winnick, Louis, *New People in Old Neighborhoods: The Role of New Immigrants in Rejuvenating New York's Communities.* New York: Russell Sage Foundation, 1990.

INDEX